Animals and Animal Dreams

The Cat, The Dog and The Horse

by

Regina Abt - Baechi

Living Human Heritage Publications, Zurich

Studies from the

Research and Training Centre
for Depth Psychology
According to C. G. Jung and Marie-Louise von Franz

Animals and Animal Dreams

The Cat, The Dog and The Horse

by
Regina Abt - Baechi

Living Human Heritage Publications, Zurich
2011

First edition 2011
Living Human Heritage Publications
Münsterhof 16, 8001 Zurich, Switzerland
info@livinghumanheritage.org
www.livinghumanheritage.org

ISBN-10 3-9522608-9-4
ISBN-13 978-3-9522608-9-0
EAN 9783952260890

LAYOUT: Pınar Tuncer and Theodor Abt

PRINTING AND BINDING:
MAS MATBAACILIK A.Ş.
Hamidiye Mahallesi Soğuksu Caddesi
No:3 34408 Kağıthane, İstanbul / Türkiye
T. +90 212 294 10 00 (pbx) F. +90 212 294 90 80
info@masmat.com.tr

Contents

Acknowledgements 7

Introduction 11

Part I: The Cat 15

Part II: The Dog 73

Part III: The Horse 147

Part IV: Appendix 213

1. Bibliography 215

2. List of Pictures 218

3. List of Dreams 221

4. Index 223

Acknowledgements

This book has evolved from a lecture about animal dreams at the C. G. Jung Institute in Küsnacht in the early 90s and later at the Research- and Training Centre for Depth Psychology according to C. G. Jung and Marie-Louise von Franz. I am grateful to Susanne Doebel, who first decided to translate this lecture into English, and thus motivated me to go on with the interpretation of animal dreams. I am also indebted to Barbara Hannah for her lectures on animals, which first galvanised me into action on the subject of animal dreams. This led me to write an article on the topic, and I was pleased when it was accepted by the board of *Psychological Perspectives*. I would like to thank David Roscoe for his work with the translation and proof-reading, Erik Hornung for his valuable articles about animals in Ancient Egypt, Sabine Mayer-Patzel for her help with text editing, and all the analysands, students and friends who contributed to this work with their dreams. My most heartfelt thanks go to Marie-Louise von Franz, who, up to her death in 1998, encouraged me to continue with the absorbing and complex but ultimately rewarding topic of archetypal dreams. My memories of her teachings and her writings have been a constant factor in my understanding of the psychology of C. G. Jung and its application in dream interpretation. Finally I wish to thank my husband Theo, who supported me with his boundless enthusiasm and belief in the significance of such a work. He was also involved in the editing and layout of this book. I am, of course, deeply grateful to my animals, who allowed me a glimpse into their secret world, which is also our own.

Oetwil am See, Summer 2011

«The animal embodies something that is at first manifested as the animal instinct in man, but behind which the secret of individuation, that is, the acquisition of inner wholeness, is concealed.»

(M.-L.von Franz, *Archetypal Dimensions of the Psyche,* p. 93)

Introduction

When animals appear in our dreams, we sometimes feel deeply touched, often helpless or even startled. Dreams of suffering animals rank among our most horrible nightmares – especially if they involve our own pet. Sometimes there are strange, primeval animals, which seem to come from a world long gone. They seem to belong to a past world from the history of our physical and psychological development. And yet there they are, here and now, as a part of us which seems to live alongside us, somewhere in the unknown background of our psyche, in the unconscious. In the course of the development of human consciousness we have forgotten these animal instincts, the components of our development and the basis of each individual life. If they did not now become apparent in various ways, for example, in our dreams, then one could simply say: let sleeping dogs lie! Why are we bothering with them this book? Hand in hand with the development of consciousness goes a loss of the ability to act 'instinctively correctly', as is a matter of course for any animal. However, as human behaviour is dictated not just by the brain, but still largely by the animal within us, this loss is becoming more and more of a problem. Today, in the world of 'cyber space', this problem has grown more urgent than ever before because the instincts, our animal sides, being cut off from the conscious world, can no longer fulfil their function in the overall structure of the personality and the collective. In many respects we have lost touch with our instincts or – and this is the reverse side of the coin – we are completely at their mercy.

If we are dealing with animals here, then this time it is not out of zoological, but out of psychological interest. As creatures of instinct, these animals embody a part of our own unconscious psyche. If we dream about them, then they represent something which leads a secret independent existence in our soul, usually without us being aware of it. If they appear in a dream, this can be interpreted as a sign that we should understand what they represent and that it could be to our advantage to get in touch in this way with the instinctual side of our nature. Our psyche is also telling us that our mental equilibrium depends on whether we are willing and able to consciously allow the animal to resume its place in the 'household' of our personality. «Separation from his instinctual nature inevitably plunges civilized man into the conflict between conscious and unconscious, spirit and nature, knowledge and faith, a split that becomes pathological the moment his consciousness is no longer able to neglect or suppress his instinctual side», says Jung.[1]

Cats, dogs and horses have been living alongside human beings for many thousands of years. Nowadays, however, with more and more people living in big cities or otherwise alienated from nature, many of them have completely lost touch with these animals. They might never have stroked a cat or played with a dog or ever sat on a horse. For some of them, a cat is as alien as an Indian tiger. And yet it can happen that they dream of household pets they have never actually owned. For these people, it is almost impossible to understand pet animal motifs in their dreams.[2]

We want therefore to try to stretch the framework further and see what cat, dog and horse have always meant to humans since time began, what sort of role they have played for them in their tales, myths, images and ideas. Mythical narratives are of great value to us because they are usually of inestimable age and can be regarded as original revelations of the pre-conscious soul. They are "spontaneous statements about what is going on in the unconscious, and as such are of vital importance."[3] Animal tales from the dim and distant past thus tell us something about the processes in the deeper layers of the unconscious psyche, processes which are no different in modern man than in his archaic ancestors.

1 C. G. Jung, *Civilisation in Transition*, [*Coll. Works* 10], § 558.

2 For an overview see Barbara Hannah, *The Archetypal Symbolism of Animals.*

3 M.-L. von Franz, *Archetypal Dimension of the Psyche*, p. 111.

M.-L.von Franz tells us that archaic people such as the so-called hunters and gatherers, have a fund of animal stories that speak of the origin of the universe and the continuing flow of life, and they are nearly all animal stories. Animals in these stories are like animal-people gods, because mentally and psychically they behave just like people. «We can recognize through these figures that our mental and emotional inner processes were originally fully subordinated to our instinctive animal modes of behavior.» It is only «in the process of cultural development that more human-shaped deities gradually developed from the animal-people gods, and this reflects a development of consciousness in the course of which we have gradually become conscious of the specifically human quality of our behavior.»[4]

Today we have largely lost sight of the specifically animal aspect of the way we behave which is still a part of us. If we still tell animal stories at all, it is to small children, who really love them. They no longer have a deeper meaning for us. Animals have also been banished from religious life to a large extent. But they live on as before in dreams and dream images, as if the experiences made by humans with animals throughout the ages had become indelibly embedded in the mental background of mankind and gone on from there to unfold their mysterious secret effect on our life. Thus the animals in our dreams convey an image of mental structures and processes which still affect the psychological health of the individual and society today, without us realising their full significance.

Archaic communities respected animal gods and allocated them their definite place in their own lives and rituals. In various rituals, these gods had to be placated, so that they would help with hunting and protect the hunters from all the dangers that might occur. Archaic religions are full of such rituals. M.-L. von Franz explains that «there is nothing either mystical or transcendent or special about it; the basic religious attitude is linked with the idea of survival, and therefore to be religious is an immediate advantage for it ensures survival.» At its origin «religion is something instinctive and completely natural.»[5] So animals are at the source of religion,

4 Ibid., p. 111

5 M.-L. von Franz, *Alchemy*, p. 97.

and behind the animal instincts there is the whole phenomenon of religious insight and experience.[6] This is probably the reason why animals in dreams often touch us more than anything else. Our reaction has something to do with religion in an archaic sense, relatedness to a higher, inner authority

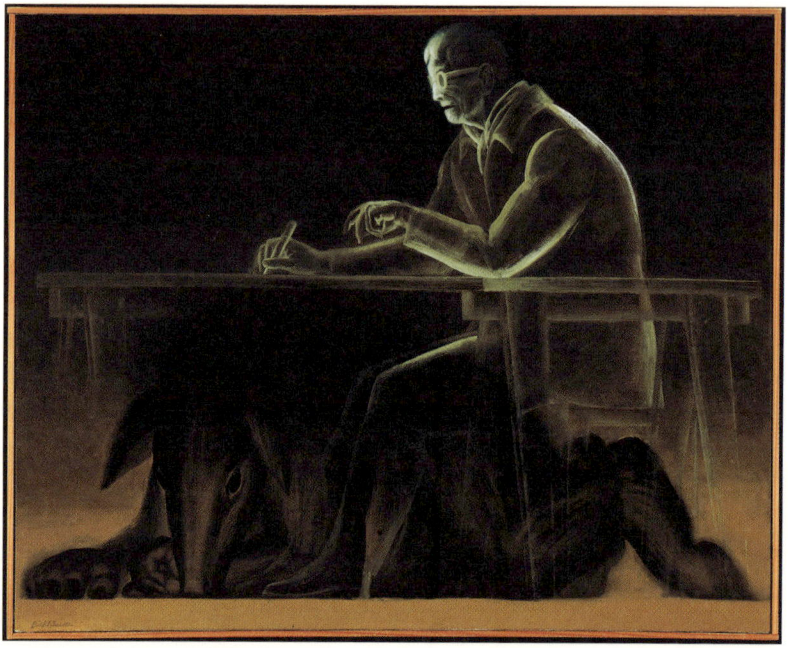

Fig. 1: *At the Studio Table*: Painting by the Swiss Artist Peter Birkhäuser (1911 – 1976). The picture shows the painter himself at his working desk. Below his table here is an animal, with the features of a dog and a boar. It is a symbol for the enigmatic wholeness of the animal kingdom that is lying in the dark, below the creativity of this artist. If it is not neglected or suppressed, it protects him and is at the same time the source of inspiration for his work. – The dream belonging with this picture was: "*I was sitting at the table concentrating on my work, and had forgotten the fact that my 'dog' was lying under it (half-dog, half-boar, very big and strong). When I got up, I kicked him. I was very sorry about that. I stroked him and apologized. He was very tame and rubbed against my legs in an affectionate way.*"[7]

6 M.-L. von Franz, *Alchemy*, p. 97.

7 E. Wertenschlag-Birkhäuser, *Windows on Eternity*, p. 104-105.

which allows us to act according to our instincts. The animal in dreams, being non-human, is the symbol for the superhuman or divine in our own psyche, as Jung puts it.

Animals in myths and legends are not always benevolent. Like nature in general, the animal world has a terrible dark side, and the side it is going to show to us depends very much on how we relate to it. If the conscious attitude towards the inner world of the animal – the unconscious – is positive, the animals in dreams may be helpful; if not, they can be frightening or aggressive. Then they sometimes mirror an instinctual drive in a state of repression, which makes them dangerous and nightmarish.

The more we know about animals and their symbolic meaning, the better we understand their appearance in dreams, the more clearly we can see the forces that influence our lives and where we underestimate, violate or fail to respect this instinctual life energy with its hidden knowledge. Jung says that the instinct is the unconscious mental functioning of man, in which there are the possibilities of extracting the gold of consciousness.[8] So when we look at dreams as an expression of this unconscious mental functioning of man in the following work, we are, so to speak gold-diggers, with the hope of now and then finding a grain of gold! Since they are domesticated animals, we will most frequently find the cat, dog and horse in dreams. They are closer to us than wild animals. When they crop up in dreams, we can better understand what is meant. As we are able to have a relationship with these animals, they embody contents of the unconscious which are relatively close to consciousness.

Once I was asked why I do not relate these interpretations more to the dreamer's personal life and problems. How could dreams be understood without taking into account the person's associations and life circumstances? One answer might be that dreams such as the following can be looked at like fairytales. We choose them because of their archetypal material. This book is not primarily about the personal analysis of the dreamers, which is not only confidential, but would also take up more space. It is essentially about an approach to the archetypal, symbolic language of the dream. With that we try to contact the deeper level of the psyche, where the healing impulses for the personal and collective life come from. What we do with

8 C. G. Jung, *Vision Seminars,* p. 1065

our interpretations is to practise deep-sea diving, so that we can get an idea of what it might look like in those murky depths. With our little personal headlamp, we swim around in the darkness of the collective unconscious and try to find some orientation. C. G. Jung was the great pioneer in this kind of the deep-sea diving. It is to him we owe valuable and proven aids and tools for navigation within the murky depths of the unconscious, where we, of course, are as blind as bats.

One of these tools is amplification, a process of enlarging a symbol by collecting comparative material. In this way, we can create an average set-up. We study mythology, legends, rituals, folktales and fairytales in order to collect the stones for a mosaic, that conveys to us a fairly clear image of the archetypal background of a symbol.

For instance, if a horse appears in a dream, it may be an important horse for the dreamer for personal reasons. At any rate, his or her ideas must be brought into the personal analysis. But it might also be a completely unknown horse, about which the only thing we know is that it is basically there to carry us. However, that is by no means all that can be said about the horse symbol. There are so-called dream encyclopaedias which promise a simple understanding of dreams, but they do so by reducing the richness of a symbol to the lowest common denominator; thus they remain on the surface, so that the unique meaning of a dream is usually missed. It is as if a prescription is applied to the dream.With amplification we search for the broader background of the symbol, which will help us to better understand the specific meaning of the dream. It will connect consciousness to the archetypal level of the psyche, where the healing impulses stem from, and widen the horizon for our understanding of dreams. In my experience, very few dreams can be adequately understood without the application of the depth psychology of C. G. Jung and the hypothesis of the collective unconscious. This work is therefore essentially based on the works of C. G. Jung and M.-L. von Franz, his most competent disciple.

I am grateful to the people who allowed me to look at a number of their dreams with archetypal material, but we must make it clear that no all-embracing interpretation of this dream material can be given. What these dreams mean for the personal life of the dreamers in detail must remain mostly a matter of the personal analytical situation.

Part I

The Cat

Fig. 2: Ancient Egyptian Cat-Goddess. Bronze, Late Period, 664-332 BC.

All cats originate from Egypt. The old Egyptians had a strong relationship with their animals, and special importance was attributed to the cat. Ancient Egypt generally provides us with rich amplification material concerning animals. It would be hard to find any other ancient civilisation that lasted over 3000 years which had the animal so deeply integrated into its highly differentiated religion and everyday life. Erik Hornung has given us a beautiful description of this relation in an essay about the *Ambiguity of Animals in Ancient Egypt.*[9]

According to Hornung, animals in Ancient Egypt might appear as an embodiment of the the Ba, which is usually translated as the soul. The word 'Ba' was even written with a hieroglyph of an animal, a stork or a ram. The Ba of a god was also depicted as an animal; the Ba of Osiris, for instance, was a falcon. Hornung explains that in divine animals, the godhead could be experienced in a concrete way. Attributes of animals, for instance their obviously superhuman capacities such as being fast, strong and gifted with senses far superior to human senses, can explain the importance of all the numina in animal form. In Ancient Egyptian religion, gods appeared in the form of animals: Anubis as a dog or jackal, Hathor as a cow, Thot as a pavian or ibis. Later they were rather depicted in a combined shape with an animal head and a human body, or a human figure with an animal attribute on top of the head. These attributes and animal heads always point to certain characteristics of a god or a goddess.

Egyptian creation myths speak about men and animals as having been created at the same time, unlike in our Christian creation myth, where man is, so to say, the ultimate and the highest product of creation, while animals rank somewhere on a lower level of the hierarchy. In Ancient Egypt, the Creator takes care of all living beings from the beginning. A hymn from the time of the New Kingdom says that He cares for the fledgling in the egg as well as for the snake, for the fish in the river, for the birds in the sky, the midges, the worms and the lice and even for the tiny mouse in her hole! After their death, animals were believed to become 'Osiris' like gods and humans, and like them they get their 'hidden

9 E. Hornung, "Die Vieldeutigkeit der Tiere im alten Aegypten", in: *Die Seele der Tiere*. Wolfenbüttel, 2001.

place' in the Beyond. This explains why some of them have been given their own sarcophagi (fig. 3). In psychological language, we can say that they do not simply disappear after death, but like gods and humans they remain eternally living archetypal constants of the soul and as such are given the respect they deserve within the psyche.

Dogs sometimes appear on funerary stelae because they belonged to the king's entourage along with the nobles, and they sometimes had individual names. This could also be the case for cows. Certain species,

Fig. 3: Cat Coffin. Ancient Egypt, Late Period, 664-332 BC.

such as dogs, images of Anubis, and cats, images of certain goddesses, once they were dead, served as mediators to the world of the gods. It seems that for that purpose, such animals were even bred, killed and buried in large cemeteries.

Animals were, of course, also hunted and killed. We may find this hard to reconcile with the otherwise so positive image of the old Egyptians' relationship to animals, but we must realise that some animals, besides being needed for sacrifice and food, were also dangerous enemies. On the level of the psyche they can be seen as an instinct that was a threat to men or to consciousness. We can recognize this fact also in modern dreams, where ferocious animals threaten the dreamer. The Pharaoh, who incorporates the collective consciousness, was obliged to fight lions and other animals of the desert just like any other enemy, in order to protect his kingdom (fig.4). This was, for instance, very much the case with the lion and the snake, animals that contain the greatest opposites of negative and positive qualities, such as representing danger and unpredictability and at the same time defender against the forces of evil. Because the Pharaoh was himself was depicted as an animal and the ruler of the animal world, he also represented a god. So when he hunted and killed animals, to protect the world of consciousness from the chaos of the unconscious, as we would put it today, he was acting according to the will of the gods. Dealing with the dangers of the chaos in Ancient Egypt was therefore not only a matter of human, but of numinous powers, as was probably the case in all ancient cultures. We will see how this is connected to the psychology of men, when it comes to the problem of evil.

In Ancient Egyptian texts, numinous animals play a great role where they are turned to for help and protection. Magical writings demonstrate how to understand the voice of the birds in the sky and the animals that creep on the ground. We know that this is a common motif in European and other fairytales all over the world and at all times. It is the age-old longing of humankind to understand and be reconnected to the voice of the instinct, a capacity lost since the time of Paradise, when no consciousness had yet split the world. The great closeness of the Egyptian to animals can also be seen in the fact that in the New Kingdom, according to the Book of the Dead, the deceased had to confess at the Divine Judgement that they had not done any harm to man or beast.

Fig. 4: Pharaoh hunting a lion. Ostraka, Third Intermediate Period, 1069-664 BC.

Erik Hornung, in summarising his essay, says that each animal in Ancient Egypt incorporates a whole world of meaning. «The animal itself is no god (only in Antiquity was it misunderstood as such), but it is image and vessel of God and is animated, is Ba of a godhead. In the service of the godhead, men and animals are partners and join in common veneration.»[10] *One could also say that by carrying out the will of God in accordance with their destiny, animals are an instrument and expression of Divine Providence.* Today we have not only to esteem and protect the animals in real life, but we have to understand them in their symbolic meaning as an image of the godhead in the human soul. We do not have them represented in the religious context of our culture, but in Ancient Egypt we have them as helpful symbols in a variety of ways. At one time, the worship of Bastet was the most important of all forms of goddess worship in ancient Egypt. Cats were very well treated. It has been verified that in the first century B.C, the intentional killing of a cat incurred the death sentence.[11] At the most

10 E. Hornung, "Die Vieldeutigkeit der Tiere im alten Aegypten", p. 50.

11 *The Oxford Encyclopedia of Ancient Egypt,* s.v. Bastet.

important place of worship, Bubastis, there is a large cemetery for cats, where hundreds of cat mummies were found (fig. 6).

Now how are cats perceived in our culture? The following sentence sums up in a perfect way the most characteristic traits of the cat: «Cats are the most infuriating, independent, graceful, aristocratic beguiling creatures on four legs. From time to time they seem to think that we deserve them.»[12]

In accordance with the ambiguity of that image, some people love cats and others definitely do not. The feelings range from adoration to open aversion. While some say that cats are faithless and cunning, others, who adore cats, think they are friendly, tender and faithful. Be that as it may, cats are as they are. There is no other pet to which this applies as much as to the cat. The cat may be friendly and affectionate one minute, but then it turns on its heels and walks away. If we do not detect its change of mood from the movements of its tail, eyes and ears, we may well feel those sharp claws sinking into our flesh. But we have only ourselves to blame, because we are not familiar enough with the ambiguous nature of the cat.

The cat is the only pet that has become domesticated of its own free will. Even today, after 5000 years of domestication, it still stays with us because it chooses to. Cats love warmth, cleanliness, cosiness and comforts, but they can also survive under extremely severe conditions. The cat has lived and survived for thousands of years in the vicinity of mankind and with the support of man without losing its wild side and its need for freedom and independence. The modern tendency to keep cats locked up in apartments must thus actually be considered a form of cruelty.

We as human beings can only stand back and admire this *independence* although it is sometimes hard to accept. The cat could never be said to suffer from an inferiority complex. Dogs that have been maltreated often look downtrodden. Cats, however, just turn their backs and go their separate ways. Women who are too dependent or insecure, who suffer from a lack of self esteem, may dream about cats. This might remind them that they themselves are also independent female personalities.

There is a joke about the meeting of a cat and a dog which neatly mirrors the difference between the two:

12 P. Ingoldsby, *The Peculiar Sensation of being Irish.*

The dog says: «Oh these people – they give me food, they give me water, they provide a wonderful comfortable basket for the night – they must be gods!»

The cat says: «These people – they give me food, they give me water, they provide this comfortable, warm basket to sleep in – I must be a goddess!»

The bewildering *opposites of the intimate and the wild* in the cat have challenged mankind throughout the ages. Though the cat has, as it were, made a deal with human beings and offered its services as a hunter

Fig. 5: The Cat that Walked by Himself (R. Kipling).

of mice, only one half of it has become a useful animal. The other half has always remained true to its wayward, secretive, wild nature. There is a saying: «Never pay a cat, otherwise it won't catch any mice!» Whatever it does, it is only of its own free will. Its nocturnal side, with its strange glowing eyes, sometimes seems ominous to us. The cat can see in the dark and thus in folklore has the quality of a seer, which means it is connected with foresight and insight. Its eyes exert a magic fascination, which explains the popular witch or vampire projection.

We can say that it is the cat's very special nature that provokes very special positive and negative projections. In popular belief there is a wide range of responses to the cat, from reverence to strategies for self-protection and many kinds of precautionary measures. In Egypt though, where the cat was worshipped in the form of the cat goddess Bastet, she was particularly worshipped in her *joyful and sensual aspects.*

The cult of Bastet had developed in the lower classes of society over a period of several hundred years. As described by Herodot, in Bubastis there were orgiastic ceremonies where dance, music, flutes, wine and uninhibited women played an important role. On some amulets, Bastet is shown together with a naked dwarf. This is Bes, the god of music, dance and joy. Whenever this cheerful, lofty aspect appears in our lives and relationships, we experience more comfort, real quality of life and wealth. Bastet was responsible for the sunny side of the outer life and bestowed wealth, power, honor, health, long life and so on. A cat stretching languorously in the sunlight is the image of pure and tremendous physical well-being, and arouses envy in those of us suffering from the stress of modern civilization. A house is blessed, when there are cats living in it, popular belief tells us in Switzerland. And young women who like cats and look after them will have a happy marriage. On the other hand, men who do not like cats, will not find a wife or else will find an evil one!

In ancient Egypt, the Sungod Re is depicted as a tomcat, fighting the great snake Apophis with a knife. Apophis is an image of the chaos and the devouring darkness of the night (fig. 7). How

Fig. 6: Cat Mummies: Ancient Egypt, Late Period, 664-332 BC.

close this imagery is to contemporary psychic life can be seen in the following dream of a teacher of art, a 41-year-old woman during a period of depression.

Nr. 1: Dream of the cat fighting the shadows with knives:

I carry one of my cats on my arms, close to my heart. It is the white cat with black spots. That she is with me has a calming effect on me, but at the same time I am the one carrying her through all the dangers. We come to a river. The water is so high, that even the footpath alongside the river is covered. I fear for my cat and choose a detour, but this only gets us into other troubles. My cat has sharp knives with her, like a sculptor's knives, to protect us against dark shadows.... Finally the dangers are over, but one of the cat's paws is nearly cut off, probably by one of the knives. I go to the vet immediately.

Here the cat is not a tomcat, like in the mythology of Ancient Egypt, but one of the dreamer's real female cats. In reality this animal had undergone a lot of suffering, quite similar to the dreamer herself in her life. The knives of the cat in the dream are powerful weapons against the darkness of depression. So this cat symbolizes a psychological capacity of the dreamer to fight negative thoughts and inferiority feelings, dark shadows of destructive fantasies about her life and destiny that are threatening to overwhelm her in her daily life. But despite being a fighter armed with knives, this cat has to be protected and carried close to the heart. It has to be carefully looked after, with deep feeling. The dream seems to suggest a conscious and active attitude of eros towards this important psychic helper. The dreamer loved her cats, but she was often not able to protect her inner cat, her independent feminine self against what attacked her in the form not only of unfathomable shadowy intuitions and preconceptions, but also as distrust and rejection from her fellow men and her pupils. Consequently she often found herself close to a torrential river, which here might be understood as the threatening overflow of unconscious emotion. Time and again she was in danger to be swept away by despair about the difficulties in her life and relationships. According to the dream she consciously has to avoid this danger. Strangely enough her cat overcomes the shadows but is finally wounded by her own knives, so that a vet has to be called in. The

Fig. 7: The tomcat with its knowledge of the darkness of the night is a symbol for the Sungod Re. He is able to slay the dangerous serpent Apophis, the enemy of the Sungod. Ancient Egypt, 20th Dynasty, 1188-1075, Tomb of Onuris-cha.

sharp knives, although needed by the cat against the dark shadows, may perhaps sometimes add a sharpness and abrasiveness to the dreamer's whole attitude and behavior that could injure the friendly and tender side of her own female cat instinct. Vets or doctors in dreams often mean that the problem in a personal setting has to be analyzed.

With regards to our topic we wish to emphasize the amazing fact that not only in Ancient Egypt, but also in a modern woman's dream, the cat carries the projection of a *helper in the dark.*

Our next dream is that of a 50-year-old woman. She had a lively spirit and also a lively animus. She loved to argue, and her opinions about things were usually set in concrete. With her husband at the time of the following dream, she was suffering from a serious crisis in their relationship.

Nr. 2: Dream of the bird in the hair:

A bird lands on my head and gets tangled in my hair. Together with my husband, I manage to get the bird out of my hair. Now it changes into a multicolored cat. My husband takes it in his arms and I recognize that the cat has the same color as his woollen pullover.

The German phrase to 'have a bird' means to have crazy ideas, and this woman literally had 'a bird', an idea or fantasy that had come through the air, getting entangled in her hair. This means that finally there was always so much of her own unconscious in what she said that everybody felt provoked by her unequivocal statements, including, of course, her husband. If such a bird can become a cat, the aspect of well-being, of eros and sensuality comes into a relationship. And this relates to her husband's pullover, which conjures up images of warmth, comfort, leisure time and relaxation. A bird transforming into a cat is not something that she herself can arrange. It is a miraculous process, something happening independently. Maybe it resulted from her genuine love for her husband.

Bastet had a close connection to the sun. On their forehead, some statues of cats wear the scarab, the Egyptian symbol for the rejuvenated Sungod Re. Furthermore, being associated to the *great mother goddess* Hathor, she was also connected to the night world and to the moon. This side corresponds to the nocturnal side of our real cats: the cat can see in the night and find its ways that are dark and unknown to us. Our own nocturnal side is the unconscious, where things cannot be seen or at least only in the shadow of the dim moonlight. The moon has to do with woman's female rhythm, body, fertility, sexuality and conception. Like Freya, the Germanic goddess of love and fertility, whose carriage is drawn by two cats, Bastet is mainly a mother goddess (fig. 8). Greek mother goddesses are also accompanied by cats. Women pray to them if they want to have children and for assistance with the birth. The cat suckling and

Fig. 8: Bastet with her kittens. Ancient Egypt, Late Period or Ptolemaic Period, about 664-30 BC.

licking its little ones, and carrying them to a secure place, has been a prototype of motherhood throughout the ages. In our research about dreams of pregnant women, we also received several cat dreams.[13] In a wider sense, the cat as a mother goddess has to do with *fertility and creativity.*

In the dreams of a young woman with a negative mother complex, numerous cats were frequently in danger. She dreamt many times that her cat had run away, was lost, had been run into over by a car, or else was injured or dying. One dream went as follows:

Nr. 3: Dream of the cat Cleo and Wotan:

I find a little grey cat in a chaotic extraverted situation. I call her Cleo. I see that the fur of her stomach is slit open, as is the flesh underneath. But there is no blood running. She suffers terrible pain. I am terrified and helpless, sad. Again and again I hold her and try to sustain her. She sits on a ledge at the level of my heart.

The symbol of the cat, which unites both the joyful and dark aspects of life, is seriously damaged in this dream. Psychologically this points to a dangerous wound in the psyche of the dreamer. No blood coming out of the wound could mean that there is no healing process going on. Maybe this violent slit had already happened a long time ago, but the wound had never healed and the terrible pain had not been recognized until now. The dreamer, having a Catholic background, seemed to suffer from the damage to the image of the feminine that has so strongly influenced our Christian culture and our relationship to the feminine. It is, as Jung concluded, caused by the one-sidedness of the Christian church, which gives the highest value to the immaculate Virgin and rejects the aspects of the nature *goddess.* The dream goes on:

After that I find myself in the underground. It is like a cave and there is a meeting going on. I think it must be a sort of secret society. All the figures are shadowy, dark. ...Suddenly the door bursts open and like the wind itself, a tall figure in a large dark grey cape rushes in. He sits down opposite me. I can see his face clearly. It is shining, and has the yellowish color of honey. The skin is stretched taut over the cheekbones,

13 R. Abt, I. Bosch, V. McKrell, *Dream Child.*

he is bald and has a pointed nose. He is angry and starts speaking indignantly about the fact that the thoughts or the teachings in this underground world are not more widespread in the outside world. I have the impression he is a priest or master. The teachings he is talking about seem to be directed against the Church.

This figure seems to be an image of the Germanic god Wotan. He is often described in legends as suddenly appearing in a grey or green cape. With the wind he storms through the air, together with his furious army, destroying everything in his path. Wotan is a god of uncontrolled emotionality and rage, either a destructive or a holy rage. Indeed our dreamer suffered from terrible 'wotanic' attacks of anger, which she tried hard to suppress. In this dream, Wotan, together with all the other shadowy figures, is seeking to be heard and understood in the upper world of consciousness. This, of course, cannot only be taken as a personal problem of the dreamer. The injury to the unknown cat and the angry Wotan belong together and mirror the collective problem of the rejected dark sides of human nature and the feminine in our Christian culture. When the pagan cat goddess – which includes the dark, threatening side of the female nature – is wounded by misunderstanding and conventional morality, then there is no feminine to appease Wotan and he may enter the scene in collective outbursts of aggression, in wars, but also as a dangerous animus. Women can therefore never be too sure that only men are responsible for war and evil in the world. When I was working on the interpretation of this dream with the grey wounded cat for this book, this woman, now seven years later, had another little dream:

Nr. 4: Dream of the grey and white cat:

I hear some little noise outside my front door. I open the door. On the doorstep sits a grey cat with white paws and a white spot on her face. When I open the door, she comes in. It is a sweet little cat.

We were both happy about this dream. The redemption of the 'grey lady' seems to be going on. Already the paws and a little spot on her face have turned white! The redemption of the dark feminine is a frequent theme in fairytales, as M.-L. von Franz has worked out in the interpretation of the fairytale "The Black Woman's Castle" and it happens step by step, parallel to the humble work of cleaning and sweeping by the heroine.[14] Slowly, as she goes about her tedious work, the black lady almost imperceptibly turns white and is finally redeemed.

Cats are known to be extremely clean animals. Licking and cleaning their fur takes quite some time. We even have to accept that often they need intensive cleaning immediately after we have stroked their fur with our hands! Three little dreams from another woman very clearly explain this motif of washing and cleaning:

Nr. 5: Dream of washing and three cats:

I am at a place of learning. There we work actively on our shadow sides and we learn how to cope with them. - My whole body is washed by a woman and a man. - I am accompanied by three cats, who get along with each other in a lovely way.

These apparently unimportant little dreams belong together as one. They teach us that learning to work on and cope with the shadow sides has to do with washing. An intensive process of washing is an important part of the work in Alchemy. It belongs to the so-called nigredo phase. «The nigredo, – the blackness, the terrible depression and state of dissolution – has to be compensated by the hard work of the alchemist and that hard work consists, among other things, of constant washing; therefore even the work of washerwomen is often mentioned in the text, or constant distilling, which is also done with the object of purification.»[15] In this process, shadow problems, all the different instinctive drives that generally first appear in the form of a projection, are «the prima materia which has to be constantly washed and distilled and thus the first activity of the opus is distilling, washing and cleansing, over and over again. Here it says nine times; others say fifteen times, and some say ten years. It is really a very long process and sometimes means endlessly rehearsing the same problem in its different aspects. That is why also in alchemical texts they always allude to the fact that this process can go on for a long time and is characterized by endless repetitions- just as, unfortunately, we fall again and again into complexes

14 M.-L. von Franz, *Archetypal Dimensions of the Psyche,* p. 174 f.

15 M.-L. von Franz, *Alchemy,* p. 220.

which have not been worked out and have to be looked at time and again. But through this hard work, the matter becomes white.»[16]

The dream image is very clear about the washing, the becoming conscious and learning to cope with the shadow sides. But what have cats to do with this? The fact that cats are present in the process of shadow work might indicate that they are interested in the shadow of the feminine, the feline qualities of the feminine, so to speak. Maybe the cat's ability to see in the dark, to catch mice even at night, has to do with an instinct that pursues this hard work in the darkness of the unconscious with dogged patience, like a cat in front of a mousehole. And at the same time, these dream cats radiate something joyful. It seems that even a certain cheerfulness can come out of this work. Cats never complain. Lamenting about one's shadow as it turns up again and again, does not help and merely galvanises the animus or the anima into action. Usually one hates to stumble over one's shadow sides and all humour gets lost. The animus will kill anybody who dares to laugh or tease in such a situation! It is pointless to moan and groan, because the person ensconced in that blackness just has to bear with it, until, as the alchemists say, the whiteness appears and things get easier. Then the cats are there, content and relaxed, just being themselves, creating for the moment an atmosphere of relief and repose.

On the other hand, the appearance of the cat, being also a shadow, can be bewildering and not easy to accept initially. Just like any other unconscious shadow element, unless it is integrated into life, it might manifest itself as greed, envy, aggression etc., for women usually in team play with the animus. Only when this state of blackness has been 'washed' can the cat qualities that belong to the feminine personality become a part of conscious life. Some women submit too readily to everybody's demands and, by way of compensation, become inconsistent in their feelings. To the surprise of those around them, they all of a sudden react like a cat that unexpectedly digs her claws into our hands. 'Washing' can bring out their independent, self-confident, joyful cat side, enabling them to utilize their claws in a controlled way whenever it seems necessary.

In the next dream is of a fifty-year-old man.The main part of the dream says:

16 M.-L. von Franz, *Alchemy,* p. 221 f.

Nr. 6: Dream of the black cat and the knife:

In my house I find a black cat that is obviously not well. I discover that this cat is severely hurt. She has a long, thin knife with the whole blade embedded deep into her back, right up to the handle. She has to be taken to a vet immediately.

As this is only a small part of the whole dream. I concentrate on the main problem, namely the cat's injury and the knife. We talk about 'sharp thinking' and 'clear cut argumentation' etc. So here the knife has to do with a discriminating and penetrating thinking, a sort of logical reasoning, which severely injured the dark cat, the dreamer's unconventional, unconscious feminine side. Consequently outer life was dominated by depression. The suffering of the cat is the suffering of the feminine soul, violated by a prejudiced, self-opinionated attitude against the unconscious. Hand in hand with such an attitude, there is often a tendency to be bogged down in childhood shortcomings and family complexes, a central topic of Freudian psychology. With such an approach, there is a great temptation to pinpoint in a rational way the root of all the evil in childhood rather than to take the responsibility for one's actual life. As a consequence, the real message of the dream is often missed, because one remains on the level of what is already known and familiar. Jung, by way of contrast, learned from thousands of dreams that they never shed light on what is already known, but the deeper message of a dream is always something new, which tends to broaden and transform our conscious standpoint. The really striking and healing new aspect comes from the archetypal level of the psyche and can only be discovered by careful amplification. Here it has to do with the problem of the rejected feminine in our culture. The dreamer, as a contrast to his rational understanding, also had the strangely passive and dangerous expectation towards the unconscious, that it would some day solve all his problems. To go and see the vet would mean entering actively into the process and analysing this problem. The dream leaves it open whether the cat can be saved or not.

Now let us move on to our cat amplifications. The dark, dangerous side of the cat-headed Bastet was venerated in the figure of the fierce lion-headed goddess Sekhmet (fig. 9). Sekhmet mirrors partly the Wotanic aspect of the female. She is not only related to Bastet, but also to the great mother and goddess of love, Hathor. In one myth, Hathor is described as a lioness in the Nubian desert. The Sungod Re sent Thot, the god of wisdom, to bring her to him for protection and companionship. The story goes that on their return, Thot immersed the lioness in the cool water of the Nile in order to quell her fierceness, thus rendering her calm and joyful.[17] One legend says that Thot, with the aid of wine and the right words, managed to convince her and bring her back. Once back, she was worshipped in the form of the cat goddess Bastet.

Although Bubastis in the Nile delta was the town of her origin, Bastet was also worshipped in Memphis, south of Cairo, where she was identified with Sekhmet. How close the two goddesses Sekhmet and Bastet were in Ancient Egypt can also be seen in the fact that during the feast of Bastet, lion hunting was forbidden. Sekhmet was primarily feared for her wild and warlike qualities, but also as the hot desert wind, connected with pestilence and illness. Interestingly enough, she was also an apotropaic deity, who could be called upon for protection from illness and plague and her priests were notable physicians.[18] This is reminiscent of the commonly held European belief that some saints, such as Saint Anthony the Hermit, could, on the one hand, bring pestilence and plague, and on the other hand offer protection from them![19] It is a very pagan but psychologically true image of the basic ambivalence of all archetypal qualities that human beings would do well to respect and be conscious of. Sekhmet was also the desert sun, destroying all life. She represented the burning aspect of the sun in contrast to the warm stimulating sun of Bastet. It has been suggested that Bastet had originally been a wild lioness, whose features in the course of time had lost their ferocity and softened into those of a benevolent cat with female fertility, sexuality, and the protection of pregnant women and infants. However, it makes more sense to view her as alternately representing both aspects.[20] This is because the Sekhmet aspect of the psyche will always exist even if, as Bastet, she can periodically be brought close to consciousness, transform and become helpful. The fact that the worship of the fierce Sekhmet also brings out her healing side means that recognizing

17 *The Oxford Encyclopedia of Ancient Egypt*, Vol. II, p. 84.

18 Ibid., Vol. I, p. 90 and p. 326.

19 R. Abt, *Der Heilige und das Schwein.*

20 *The Oxford Encyclopedia of Ancient Egypt* Vol. I , p. 513.

Fig. 9: Sekhmet. Pendant. Third Intermediate Period, 1069-664 BC.

and respecting this side of the human psyche has a healing effect in the sense of connecting a part of the unconscious psyche with the conscious personality, making the latter more whole or healed.

Psychologically, Sekhmet's burning desert sun is also an image of too much daylight consciousness – a neurotic state in which we are no longer connected with our unconscious, and easily get carried away by drivenness and obsession with desire. The lion is associated with the greed of a beast of prey. A woman possessed by Sekhmet would place ambition or material values at the centre of her life and lose some of the 'Bastet-quality' we consider to be female in a positive sense. She would experience that everything living and growing around her, namely relationships or creative seeds, is drying up and the joy of life disappears.

Sekhmet is also the penetrating, attacking and burning wind of the desert. Where female emotions which have been suppressed for too long burst out, Bastet turns into the raving Sekhmet! The anima of a man can also be in a Sekhmet state. Men then suffer from Sekhmet tempers. They run around in a state of obsession, barking at their family, their employees, slamming doors and telephone receivers. Eros has disappeared into the desert and it needs wisdom and a glass of good wine to bring it back!

The fiery raving aspect of Sekhmet also breaks out when a complex is hit. Then one might dream of a fire which has broken out in the night. If one is bound up in a complex, one raves like a cat that is held against its will. It will bite and scratch in blind panic and destroy everything around it. There is no chance for access on the level of reason. Trying to convince a person in such a state that this is the wrong attitude really makes no sense. Better let that person run free! Give the god of wisdom time to help and transform him or her from Sekhmet back to Bastet!

Going back to Bastet, we recall that she is also the goddess of fertility, like all mother goddesses. In dreams of cats, we can often find that something new comes up and wants to be born, not only on a physical level through pregnancy but also on the level of the spirit. This is a dream of a 65-year-old man at the beginning of analysis:

Nr. 7: Dream of the cat and the hole in the wall:

I am with a friend, a teacher, who campaigns for the protection of nature and birds. A cat huddles up against my chest and chin. The cat asks if she can make it easier for me to carry her. I say yes and that if she lies round my neck, it will relieve my arms a bit. Later I have to pass through a hole in a wall. First I hand the cat over to a friend through the hole, then I try to pass through myself, feet first. My head nearly gets stuck.

The beginning of a new life with a deep change of attitude is often similar to being stuck in a wall. Being a scientist, this man had the problem of getting through this wall with his head. Scientific rational thinking seemed to hinder a change of outlook. But he holds on to the cat anima, even if she is not an easy burden. She even has to go ahead when he can no longer see his way. When the anima appears as a cat, she does so as an instinctual feeling that might upset a rational world-view, but being a mediator between the world of the unconscious and consciousness, she is also a guide on the path to individuation. The dream gave grounds for optimism that in future analysis his creative cat instinct would help him to seize the new impulses from the unconscious.

The fertility of the moon goddess also promotes children of the spirit. A 28-year-old man who was at that time busy with a challenging thesis had the following dream that speaks about the creative side of the cat:

Nr. 8: Dream of the cat and the distillation process:

A huge copper vessel is filled with grape grounds. This is what is left after the grapes have been pressed. It has to be distilled in a special distillation process. What is special about this process is that our cat must be present in a niche near the fire. The fire has been burning for a while under the ground. Then all at once the fire mysteriously changes. There is – as in an explosion – a dazzling flash as if lightning had struck and then all the alcohol escapes from the vessel and visibly makes its way up and then down through glass tubing until finally - through condensation and cooling – it enters a huge copper vessel as 'spirit' (liqueur). Each time the lightning strikes the copper vessel with the grape grounds, the cat is upset and quickly runs away. The next step is to calm down the cat and to place her into the niche again, which my wife manages to do. Thus, the distillation process continues to run smoothly.

In this dream, the symbol for the creative work is the image of the distillery. This is where the extraction of alcohol from the grape grounds takes place, i.e. spirit out of matter. The flash indicates a sudden flash of inspiration or intuition, coming with some cosmic power. The overwhelming and shocking character of such insights can only lead to a successful conclusion if the cat can be kept near by. The dreamer's cat is startled by the flash on each occasion, but his wife – his anima – being closely connected with the cat, brings the cat back for him. Thus, the symbol of the cat is closely connected with a spiritual process, with spiritual birth. The cat, as a motherly nurturing instinct, would in this case represent a quality that accepts this man's new ideas with female care, permitting it to grow until he finally manages to distil his experiences in a form that is understandable for everybody and which is nourishment for the spirit. He himself must attend to the process of distillation, but at the same time also rely on his cat instinct, allowing this instinct to contribute to the transformation of his inspirational ideas by containing them in a female and motherly way. The dreamer was an intuitive. If he does not manage to brood over his ideas with a great deal of emotion, time and composure, like the cat, and to connect them with his own specific experience, then nobody would be able to understand them. They would have no practical application; in other words they would remain spirits in the air. The cat is connected with an individual peculiarity that goes its own way and is always earthbound with its four paws. Thus, this man, when he was writing, could not abide by any collective rule or custom or restriction but had to concentrate on this independent creative cat-spirit in the unconscious, which helps the archetypal contents with their transformation. The cat that runs away after every explosion because of its fear of being burnt is also his feeling side. It is important that in spite of the alarming intervention of such alien creative contents from the collective unconscious, the 'cat-spirit' returns to become involved in this process again and again.

Being unconstrained and independent like a cat, a woman or a man's anima is effectively able to care for the children of the spirit. The difficulty is only that the cat as a creative principle can be so terribly unpredictable! She is therefore rarely helpful when we wish her to be so! Sometimes she is also bone idle. Just as the enlightening, growth-promoting sun aspect of Bastet is connected with the burning and drying-up quality of

Fig. 10: *The Cat*. Painting by Peter Birkhäuser.[21] "She is the 'Great Mother' who can paralyse those who desire to regress to her, but who also possesses the age-old secrets of the instincts and nature…Her negative aspect is a reflection of a negative attitude towards her. This gives her the expectant, watchful look, as if acceptance of her would reveal quite a different side. Then she could become, like the Egyptian cat goddess Bastet, a bringer of joy and vitality." [22]

21 E. Wertenschlag-Birkhäuser, *Windows on Eternity*, p. 52.

22 M.-L.von Franz, *Light from the Darkness*, p. 32.

Sekhmet, the other side of the cat's independence can be a lack of responsibility or laziness. Cats can be incredibly lazy, just sleeping all day long in a nice warm place in the house, and then they get up, turn their back on you, and just walk away.

There are many stories, some of them mentioned by Gubernatis,[22] about deceitful cats which are too lazy to catch mice themselves and who therefore invent any trick to get them. They want the mice but they do not want to do the work. Barbara Hannah writes that laziness – especially when it is combined with ambition – can easily lead to unconscious deception. Women are quite good at this. They let their men catch the mice for them, making them believe that they need their help. Whenever there is a creative problem and something has to be done, the temptation to stretch out in the sun and to have someone else do it is strong. Some people have a special ability to let others solve their problems, e.g. intuitive types where the inferior sensation function is concerned. They simply look so helpless and yet they are so subtly demanding that there is no alternative but to give them support. And then, as a reward, they look at you so sweetly! The same happens with women who make men do something for them although they would be quite capable of doing it themselves!

Whether the cat appears as a truly helpful animal or as one using tricks, seems to depend on the attitude towards life or the unconscious. The next little dream of a middle-aged woman goes as follows:

Nr. 9: Dream about Pinocchio:

I am Pinocchio, I see him standing at the edge of a fresh hole in the earth. This hole is in the middle of a square garden. In the lower right corner of the garden there is the allegedly blind cat and the allegedly lame fox. It is dark.

Later I am in the dark, together with my own two black and white cats.

In the famous children's tale of Pinocchio by Carlo Collodi, the simple-minded wooden doll with a long nose, which had been animated by a good fairy, leads an infantile and irresponsible life, with a lot of laziness and lies. Finally, having once too often paid the price for his own foolishness, he accepts responsibility for his own life and gives up his childish claims and demands. As a result, at the end of the story the fairy transforms him into a normal, beautiful, little boy. At one point in the story, the cat and the

Fig. 11: Pinocchio. In: Carlo Collodi, *The Adventures of Pinocchio.*

fox advise Pinocchio to make a hole in the earth and to place a gold coin in it, assuring him that the next morning he would find a tree with its branches laden with golden coins. Pinocchio falls for a trick of the two animals, and loses the piece of gold which he had been given by the good fairy to help his old and ailing father (fig. 11).

The dream merges into one the dreamer and the wooden doll Pinocchio. As he has much in common with Pinocchio, the dreamer risks being tricked by a supposedly blind cat and a supposedly lame fox. What does that mean? Both animals are known in folktales and mythology as trickster animals, sometimes helpful, sometimes playing tricks on people and other animals. The dream might refer to the danger of a too demanding attitude towards the unconscious and towards life, as was the case with Pinoccio. As we know from alchemy, the tree with the golden coins is a most important symbol of the goal of individuation. There is a childishness about expecting to get something for free and it will provoke the trickster in the unconscious, the one who leads us round 'by the nose', as the German expression has it, meaning 'make a fool of us'. Life will then always disappoint us, and we will tend to blame destiny for all our troubles and to enfeeble ourselves by self-pity and complaining. Pinocchio is therefore a shadow side in our own psyche, which could be tricked by laziness and blind stubbornness. These instinctual impulses (the fox and the cat) appear here at the behest of the unconscious, as it were, to make a childish consciousness finally see reason. Cat and fox are probably in the service of the good Fairy and the goal is a greater, more conscious personality, although at the moment it just looks like another blow of fate. It is the loss of the last vestige of energy, the golden coin, which in the Pinocchio story was supposed to be invested in the renewal of the old father, symbolically of the old conscious attitude.

The dream seems to shed light on the dreamer's psychic situation with her Pinocchio- shadow, which by its childish attitude might provoke her own unconscious into playing tricks on her. It can be taken as a warning. Luckily in the end she modestly stays with her own two black-and-white cats. Although the current situation is bleak, it is open to renewal. The two cats symbolize creative instincts which truly include the possibility of the union of the opposites in her life, whichever face it shows her.[23]

Cats, like the dog and the horse, are said to have healing powers. Where does this come from? Cats have eyes similar to those of a snake and are able to see in the dark. They are also brave fighters against snakes, as we have seen above. In Ancient Egypt, we have representations of the Sungod Re as a tomcat with a knife. Here the knife would symbolically point to a discriminating ability of the instinct itself, a sort of 'instinctual consciousness'. As mice catchers and snake fighters, the cat therefore became a safeguard against natural and supernatural evil, poison and illness. Cat amulets in ancient Egypt, often in the form of an eye, were considered to be guardians of people, houses, temples and the deceased. This eye also helped against blindness. 'Cat-consciousness' could mean realizing evil and going one's own way. A remedy against darkness and depression! A 50-year-old woman in a difficult marital situation had the following dream:

Nr. 10: Dream of the dictator :

I was in a dark remote world with gloomy woods, a few sinister villages and suspicious-looking people. For some reason, my friends and me were being attacked. People were shooting at us and it was clear that

23 If we examine Jung's essay "On the Psychology of the Trickster Figure", we realize that Pinocchio is also a mercurial figure, a trickster himself. See C. G. Jung, *Coll. Works* 9 I, and M.-L. von Franz, C. G. Jung, *His Myth in our Time* (chapter X: "Mercurius").

the dictator of this world did not like us. I observed that Mr. X was occasionally taking people to some caves, into which they disappeared. I supposed there might be a way of escaping from this world. As the attacks increased, I guided my people to this cave, showed them how to reach a branch and use it to pull themselves up and into the cave. Everything was a very tight squeeze and I did not know what lay ahead. I was afraid that it might be a trap.

After this the dreamer, being semi-awake in a sort of half-conscious state of mind, entered into a continuation of the dream:

I transformed into a cat and strolled through the cave. There were big stones, so that I could easily hide in order to check the corridor. In the middle it was very cramped, but then the cave opened up again – and then I was on the other side, on a sunny slope in a wood. Still in the form of a cat, I watched people coming up the slope who seemed to be interested in the cave. That was dangerous, as I did not know how they would react. Therefore I decided that all of us had to be cats to use that escape route. We managed to escape, but as the people on the other side were still surprised to see so many cats coming out of the cave, we decided to wait until night before leaving the cave. Nevertheless, later on we had to reveal our identity.

The dreamer, a thinking type, was deeply affected by the feeling of being a cat! She enjoyed the sense of balance that a cat has, always landing on her four paws wherever she falls down. Being like a cat means being supple and enjoying freedom of movement while remaining constantly alert to the surroundings. It also means being able to defend oneself despite being small. As a cat, one has to master a difficult situation in an inconspicuous but completely independent way. The cat also has the ability to relate in a warm and loving way yet without submission. Feeling like a cat may bring about an attitude that can find surprising ways out of a situation of despair or constraint. This seemed to be the main message of the dream. To reveal the real identity could mean that one sometimes can only survive a threatening live situation as a cat or by adiopting a cat-like attitude, but finally one has to be true to ones own conscious personality again. Unconscious 'cat-women' are usually rather capricious to their vicinity!

The following dream also conveys some of this healing impact of the cat. The dreamer and her husband had lost their son a few years earlier and the anniversary of his death was imminent and feared by the mother. Being away on holiday in a distant country where everything around her was new, she felt a distance from her son and somehow dissociated from her own sorrow.

Nr. 11: Dream of the wounded animal:

I arrive at our house and see an enormous animal that looks like a large dog but also a bit like a horse. The animal is trying to lie down on the kerb, where there are shrubs and an embankment. The animal is so big that there is a risk that it might roll down. To my horror, I see that the animal has had its head almost completely cut off. I have the feeling that the animal is seeking protection in the house. I want to fetch help; I call to people and go to the animal. I feel at a loss and don't know what to do. Then the animal disappears. I cry and have a recollection of strong pain… Someone speaks to me – I think it is a man's voice – and says that I absolutely have to talk to other people about it and that this pain is due to a lack of communication. As he is talking, I see little cats playing with each other. One of them is red and the other grey.

The big dog/horse so terribly injured has to do with the dreamer's life instinct having been wounded by the tragic loss of her son. Contrary to her feeling of being away from real grief, there is still that enormous suffering in the unconscious. She is horrified to see that the big animal has had its head nearly cut off. In the imagination of people, death was seen as the mower with the scythe, an image that vividly expresses what death means for the living: a violent and definitive cutting off of any relationship and love. Death has not only killed her son, but also very nearly her own instinct of survival. The head of the animal has to do with understanding and meaning. The apparent meaninglessness of the death of such a young boy is exceedingly painful and wounds the mother in her deepest life instinct. In the dream she is helpless and lonely. The situation looks desperate. But then the animal disappears and a voice tells her to communicate with other people. This makes sense, and it might appease her concerns about her travelling and her extraversion.

What follows now has to do with quite a new life impulse, that of approaching consciousness: little cats at play, the embodiment of joy of life and healing life energy. They are grey and red. The dream places stress on these colors, so it might be helpful to look at their symbolism. Grey in its positive aspect is symbolically a union of the most extreme opposites of black and white, and is associated with the mediator god Mercury. It emphasizes the reconciliation of the most extreme opposites of life and death. Red, on the other hand, we associate with the warmth of the fire and with the life substance of blood. That is its vitalizing aspect, which brings and sustains life. We can say that out of this genuinely life-threatening situation of the death of a child, out of the blackness of sorrow and grief, the spirit of the unconscious manifests itself in a new life-sustaining instinct. The wounded animal cannot be helped, it just disappears and the unthinkable can happen: The unconscious psyche brings up new life!

In various cultures, the healing quality of the cat instinct was considered to be specifically located in the cat's tail. The tail in general attracted many projections. With its tail, the cat can express all kinds of moods and can convey what it likes or dislikes. The tail has an amazing power of expression. Its upright position is an unmistakable sign of friendliness towards us and other animals. But its nervous beating can also indicate that there will be some angry reaction or attack in the very next moment. Therefore the tail in popular belief has a magical meaning, *pars pro toto*, for the whole cat personality. The tail of the white cat was said to be healing and nourishing, destroying poison and strengthening the immune system and the healing process, whereas the black cat's tail was reputed to have a poisoning effect on human beings, causing illness and blindness. It was also believed that the tail had the power to bewitch. For that reason, cats in Japan had their tails cut off. As I was told by an old woman, until not too long ago black cats used to be subjected to the same cruel custom in our country too.

Marie-Louise von Franz speaks about the cat's tail as an expression of unconscious emotions. The tail is, so to speak, 'the face behind' in contrast to the 'face at the front', the head. With the tail one can see her moods, her emotions, her love, her aggression, irritation, friendliness and also her warning just before she digs her claws into your hand. In fairytales, cutting off the cat's tail can have a positive meaning when it leads to the redemption of the enchanted cat and makes her human. In psychological terms, this would mean analysing, discriminating, differentiating and isolating the animal emotion, the autonomous mood, so that one can understand where it comes from and what it really expresses. Once turned into human form, the cat anima or the cat shadow can be integrated.[25]

A cat's tail is essential to her perfect balance. Psychologically speaking, the concentrated expression of the cat's personality, which we can see in its tail, is a representation of the balance also experienced by human beings on the level of instinct. The cat is really an enviable example of balance and seems to be in complete harmony with itself. Therefore she is also an image of the balance of conflicting tendencies, moods, tempers and desires, something we often find missing in ourselves. It is well known that the cat's fur helps against lumbago, a sudden terrible pain in the back which in German is called Hexenschuss (shot from a witch). This is a very nice symbolic image to show how the attack of a witch mood can be healed if we consider the naturally balanced cat nature within us. The witch mood usually cannot be faced because it attacks from behind, from the unconscious. But there seems to be a possibility of alleviating its destructive effect by instinctual feminine warmth without the need for discussion. It is a 'just so' reaction that does not lend itself to analysis or argument. It cannot be done deliberately. If we are lucky, it comes up as a spontaneous instinctual reaction, sometimes the only means of nipping serious conflicts in the bud.

In our Christian culture, the cat's healing powers usually led a hidden life with shamanistic personalities, often midwives, who were only grudgingly tolerated by the Church. Before Switzerland's greatest sanctuary of the Black Madonna in Einsiedeln was founded, there lived in the woods around the cell of Saint Meinrad quite a number of so-called "wood brothers and sisters". They built the first chapel, which later developed into the cloister. While the brothers gradually joined the Benedictines in the cloister, the women either stayed in their own cells around the cloister, or they stayed together in women's communities that had their own rules. They collected herbs, healed and looked after the sick, and were also associated with the great woman mystics of their time who came to visit the holy place. The Benedictines did not approve of that, and when these communities

25 M.-L. von Franz, *The Cat. A Tale of Feminine Redemption*, p. 113 f.

expanded in the 15th century, the abbot of a nearby cloister ordered that all the women be brought together in a separate place, and finally they were all united in a closed nunnery. The women resisted vehemently but were not able to preserve their previous way of life. After 1617 they had to live according to the rules of the Benedictines. In accordance with the will of the abbot of the cloister of St.Gallen, they were no longer allowed to join the Sunday processions. Later they also had to wear the black veil, and they had to call themselves 'sisters' instead of 'women'.[26] Slowly the whole range of the feminine cat side had been cut off in favor of a masculine spirituality.

The lack of respect for the healing powers of the feminine in our Christian culture leads us to the subject of witches and the witch's cat, the darkest side of the cat symbol (fig. 12). We experience the dark side of the friendly cat, for instance, when she brings in a cute little bird from the garden or when she enjoys herself endlessly with a little mouse by tossing

Fig. 12: Witch with her broom and her black cat.

26 M. R. Schmid, *Schwarz bin ich und schön*, p. 9.

it into the air, letting it run again just to have the fun of catching it. Cruelty and cold-heartedness are therefore easily projected onto the cat as they are onto certain women. I remember a very simple and motherly farmer's wife who suddenly discovered that she could help her sick cows and calves by "laying on her hands" and passing them lightly over the sick part of their bodies. Then she also did the same with human beings and found that she could help many of them as well. She was a medium and could see strange things around her and her fellow-creatures. Once she told me about these experiences: «You know, I don't speak about this to anybody. Otherwise people might think I am a witch». That was in 1980! In medieval times she probably would have been burnt at the stake.

Jung pointed out on various occasions that in medieval times, the image of the feminine in our Christian culture suffered a severe split. On the one hand, there was the adoration of the Virgin Mary in her pure, innocent aspect, and on the other hand, there was the witch-hunt. The idea of the witch went hand in hand with the suppression of the dark, earthy feminine which had still been worshipped in pre-Christian mother goddesses.[27] After the period of the troubadours and courtly love in the early Middle Ages, the high esteem attached to the feminine, and with it the individual aspect of the relation to the feminine, was suppressed by the church and sank into the unconscious. In its place, the impersonal worship of the immaculate Virgin Mary was enforced. The split-off aspects of the feminine were then especially projected onto women who behaved as individuals and not in accordance with collective rules. And along with them the cat, which belongs to the instinctual aspect of this independent feminine, became an object of hate and persecution.

With witch hunts there also started the torturing of cats. Cats were cruelly hanged, drowned and burnt alive. It was said that cats were transformed witches and in this form were causing nightly damage. In Christian times, the Nordic goddess of love, Freya, became the witch of the mountains and the cats that drew her carriage became riding witches, flying through the night. Cats also inherited the dark daemonic aspect of Hel, the Germanic goddess of the Underworld and Hecate, the Greek chthonic goddess of nocturnal hunting and magic. So when cats appear in legends they often foreshadow death. A black cat is said to bring misfortune, although paradoxically, in

27 M.-L. von Franz, *The Cat,* p. 113f.

some cultures it does the exact opposite. The pre-Christian mother goddesses mostly belong to the moon, and in this way also to the tides, growth and the weather. We therefore meet them again in legends as cat witches, who cause high tides, flashes of lightning, thunderstorms or rock falls.

According to popular belief, witches and witches' cats are responsible for illness, misfortune and death. We can understand this only if we bring the psychology of the unconscious into play. Witches and witches' cats carry the projection of the unconscious, female shadow of the woman, but also the negative anima of the man. As the witch hunts show, this led to terrible, false suspicions and the execution of innocent people and animals. Our daily lives are also full of such projections, which poison and distort individual and collective relationships. It is not others who are to blame, but the unconscious witch shadows on the internal, psychological level, our dark, nocturnal side. Viewed thus, seemingly strange and incomprehensible popular knowledge becomes meaningful.

Witches and witches' cats carry the projection of women's shadow or men's destructive anima. On an inner level it makes sense that in popular belief, illness, misfortune and death are connected to cats, because an unconscious shadow may have this kind of effect on the soul. Our mountain legends often warn against touching a cat after dawn because at night all cats are black or, in other words, all cats become witches' animals. Cats are said to sleep so much in the daytime because at night they are out and about as witches. From a psychological point of view, in day consciousness the friendly, well-adjusted aspects of the cat are alive, but at night and in the unconscious, the witch is riding on her broomstick. This means that when we are flying into dark fantasies, into the irrational, there are destructive aims, quarrelsome and revengeful thoughts, evil gossip. Witches live on carcasses. Here there is obsession and special powers to hurt others. Witches practise black magic. There are bad spirits around, dark thoughts in the sense of melancholia and apathy. In legends, cats can lead to suicide. The cat nature of women or the anima of men, when it inclines too much to the witch side, often carries something malicious that cannot be seen or identified, such as intrigues or manipulation. As long as the witch aspect is on the cat level, it can hardly be recognized by consciousness. Such a person is not conscious of what she or he is doing because the image of an animal represents an aspect that is still far removed from consciousness.

The next dream may illustrate this problem. It comes from a young woman who had had to undergo a cancer operation on her left breast two months earlier. At the time of the dream she had just finished her radiotherapy. She had received a very Catholic upbringing.

Nr. 12: Dream of the attacking black cat:

I am a guest at a garden party. There is a huge black cat running towards me. It is angry and says it will hurt me. Then it attacks me, digging its front claws into my hair. It scratches my scalp until it starts bleeding. I feel a pain on the left side of my chest where the cat is holding on with its back claws. I myself cannot tear it off and I ask someone in the party for help. Immediately after the cat has been dragged off, I throw it out of the garden. I ask the others to close all the garden-gates so that the cat cannot come in again. The garden is completely surrounded by a dense hedge and I doubt whether the cat could get through. But I am not really sure and so I am still frightened that the cat might attack again.

In dreams, if an animal attacks us in such a way, something new wants to be known. The cat is digging its claws into the hair, head and the left breast of the dreamer. The head and hair have to do with thoughts and fantasies growing out of the head. The left breast is connected to the dreamer's feminine nourishing motherly side, which had been attacked by cancer. It is also the side of the heart. If the black cat attacks these sides, something wants to come in - which the dream expresses in the symbol of the cat. The contents of the unconscious behave negatively towards us the more we try to steer clear of them. In her outer life, the dreamer had a bad or non-existent relationship with cats. She even feared them. The black cat does not come as a healer here but rather as a witch's cat. Nevertheless we cannot ignore the idea that both the illness and the healing of the dreamer are somehow connected with this cat. The dream seems to point to something about the shadow of the feminine that may relate to the Christian suppression of the dark aspects of the feminine. Whatever is not good from the Christian point of view is not allowed. This places a woman under terrible pressure always to behave in the right way. And because this is never possible and because she constantly has to neglect her real nature, including the wild and the unconventional, she will always suffer from an inferiority complex. The cat, the real independent individuality, is locked out! Of course it is angry.

And this in turn arouses fear in the dreamer. A vicious circle! If the dreamer could discover what it is that crawls into her thoughts and fantasies and attacks her female eros and feelings in such a negative way, and could see what wants to become conscious, this could have a healing effect on her. We can assume that her being involved with the black cat and thus becoming conscious of this cat-like shadow, would lead to the witch character losing its destructive side. That would mean a transformation of the cat.

The same woman had another dream later that seemed to indicate the possibility of a considerable improvement in the relationship with this part of her soul. This time it is about a white cat.

Nr. 13: Dream of the white dancing cat:

I am on a trip with a study group. On the outskirts of a town we have the opportunity to dance Sardana with the locals. For this we form different circles. At first I am with other people in a small circle, but then we join the large circle. A white cat suddenly appears. It looks different, noble, not like a normal cat; it has long, white hair and a tiger-like face. I am afraid of it. It would like to dance with us. I have the impression that it is wild and aggressive but one of the women in our group picks it up and strokes it.

Then the cat comes up to me of all people and positions itself on my right to join in the dance. Despite my fear, I hold onto its paw with my right hand. The cat does not object – on the contrary. It is very affectionate and starts to cuddle me. And then it jumps away from our circle. It would like to go down to a marshy area. I say to it: "Don't go there; if you do, your white coat will get very dirty." After dancing, we go on to the city centre. I give my analyst my arm in a familiar way and ask him whether he would like to dine with me in the 'Lucius' restaurant.

The cat in this dream has lost almost all of its witch characteristics. The dreamer no longer has to fight against it, as in the other dream, where it was overpowering and very frightening. True, it has a tiger face, and thus still retains a wild element which fills the dreamer with fear. But now it is a white cat, and approaches the dreamer affectionately. We can recognize now that the cat – the feminine side of the dreamer – which wants to come to her is connected with that playful, joie-de-vivre aspect of the cat goddess Bastet, because it dances the Spanish folk dance, the Sardana, with her and the others. Spanish folk dances are usually spirited and full of restrained eroticism and disciplined male-female oppositeness. In Spanish dance films especially, one can see that these dances are occasionally reminiscent of a ritualised battle of the sexes. The cat brings in the connecting element which could reconcile these opposites, i.e. feminine feeling. In the psyche of the dreamer a fundamental transformation can now take place. The new thing that can now come to her could perhaps be described as an instinctive ability to unite the feminine-masculine opposites, the conscious and unconscious, in an independently feminine way. The dreamer actually had a special relationship to dancing in real life, especially to folk and group dances. What the cat does above all here is to bring in the individual element, that which is totally unique. Then it runs off again, having had enough of the collective group meeting! The dreamer is afraid that it could get its white coat dirty in the swampy area, which it is obviously aiming for.

Marshlands are always to be entered cautiously. They are often dangerous. Getting bogged down – or even sinking – in marshland is one

Fig. 13: The white cat – affectionate, joyful, full of mischief and completely individual. Who knows what is going to happen next?

of the worst fantasies one can have. It means one is being hauled in by the unconscious, losing one's conscious life and sinking into chaotic, unconscious fantasies and fears. The marsh is the negative, devouring side of Mother Earth. That is where the cat wants to go, because it belongs to the world of the mother. It might even have come from there! It might also disappear back there again. It is thus still far from sure whether the dreamer can maintain the contact with the new, joie-de-vivre cat side, or whether this side does not simply disappear back into the unconscious, so that the special experience is forgotten again, and the depression gains the upper hand once more.

The other-worldly, inscrutable face of the cat, the tiger face, cannot yet be accepted by the dreamer. It still fills her with fear. For her the white coat should remain pure and white. It will be difficult for her to learn that cat reactions are not always innocent and 'good'. They may be individual, often lively, affectionate, but they are also unpredictable and occasionally cross the borderline of what family and society expect of a woman. And they are connected with the unconscious, like the cat with the marshland, i.e. outside of conscious control. Sometimes they can also suddenly appear jet-black, the embodiment of aggression, as we saw in the last dream. She is still afraid of that. But the contact to the white cat, to the joyful and lively part of their instinctive feminine psyche has been established. The cat in her soul has become a whole lot brighter and more conscious. With the analyst, her own ability to analyse, she can try to understand these unconscious processes in the 'Lucius' restaurant. The name is no coincidence. The word Lucius goes back to the Latin *lucere*, to light up. The analysing and understanding of these processes are illuminating and nourishing! The experiencing leads to understanding, without which the whole experience could disappear again.

Old legends in the Swiss mountain regions often tell about witches or witch-like cats. But in most of these legends there is no connection between the world of the witches and the world of the Christian immaculate Virgin. Some legends tell how the witch-like cat that is encountered at night simply vanishes. But when it is attacked, it shows its negative side and causes illness and death. Sometimes it transforms into a terrible monster or one cat transforms into many sinister ghost cats with fiery eyes etc. They could make the wanderer lose his way and the next morning he would find himself far away from home. Or if the cat has one of its paws cut off, the next morning the head of the local council or the master builder's wife may lie in bed with a bandaged hand. It is not surprising that these are figures who represent a leading male principle of consciousness. In a fairytale it would be the king. His wife, the representation of a collective feeling attitude is roaming around in the night as a witch. There is no union of the opposites, of the day- and the night-world.[28] The nocturnal, instinctive, unconscious feminine has no possibility of remaining connected to everyday life.

Being afraid of the witch's cat is justified when its daemonic side predominates: cruelty, petty revengefulness, sexual greed and maliciousness. The anima in our culture has gradually accumulated all these unadapted daemonic cat aspects. The cat anima influences the relations of a man in a deeply irrational way that rejects a rational approach. This may be most irritating. He never really knows what ill turn the cat will do him next. And it is not at all obvious what it should be good for. He can, for example, slide into an unconventional love story with all the ensuing problems. This whole field of relationships, much more familiar to women than to men, has something unpredictable about it which he cannot fathom and which belongs to the cat. Therefore the temptation to suppress her is great. (Fig.14) The following dream has to do with this problem.

Nr.14: Dream of the cat's condemnation:

Somewhere a medieval play is being performed. I am in a group with my professor and some students. The play is about the condemnation of a cat, involving a real execution of the cat. I am carrying the cat; it is my childhood cat Peter. To hang the cat would be a complete disaster for me, because that is what they expect from me. It is horrible. I consider running away at the very last moment and shouting to the public: His blood shall come over you! (I awake in panic, drenched in sweat)

The dreamer is the same man of the dream with the hole in the wall, which he had to pass through with the cat. The day before he had had a

28 G. Isler, "Die Ueberwindung der Hexe" (The Overcoming of the Witch) in: *Lumen Naturae*, p. 241 f., and "Der losgebundene Fuchs" (The unbound Fox), Ibid., p. 310 f.

conversation with a friend about medieval times with these terrible witch- and cat-executions and about other ‘religious nonsense.’ In this dream, he is together with his professor and other students. They belong to the dreamer’s scientific world-view. What seems to be a medieval play suddenly becomes real. Something that happened in medieval times, namely executions of witches and witch cats, is now revealed as something happening in the here and now. Because it is the dreamer’s own cat that is to be sacrificed, the dream touches his deepest feelings and emotions. Suddenly the collective problem concerns him quite personally. The scientific world-view demands the sacrifice of the cat that is so dear to him that he even places it side by side with Jesus Christ. The problem of the cat is in fact a religious problem. His own association was that he might once have heard that the

Fig. 14: The whole field of relationships has something unpredictable about it, which belongs to the cat. Therefore the temptation to suppress her is great.

blood of Jesus had come over the Jews in the last world war because they had killed Jesus. He also says that it is not yet sure whether he can rescue the cat. And his feeling tells him that if he cannot protect it, then the whole of science can go to Hell as far as he is concerned. The conflict seems to be unsolvable.

This cat is a male cat. So we cannot just say that it symbolizes his anima. In mythology, we find tomcats wherever the cat is connected to the sun, for instance in Egypt. «Also the cat that helps the hero in fairytales, as in Puss in Boots, is a male cat and has, if we want to circumscribe it, mercurial qualities. In such fairytales he is the knower of the way, the soul guide. He is associated with the sun, and, like Mercurius, is always helping with the sun, which is rather different from the she cat.»[29] So the cat of this dream has to do with the illuminating spirit of the unconscious. «His blood shall come over you» might therefore express the dreamer's deep fear that he might not be able to save the mercurial spirit of the unconscious from his own scientific rational judgment. When something has to do with the blood, it is very real and earthlike.[30] One could say that blood, having to do with the essence of life, with emotion and passion, with the chthonic, unconscious nature of men, slould 'overcome' the scientific, lofty, even idealistic, cold rationality and also the passive spectator in him and make the whole a matter of real life and suffering. This is what the dreamer shouts in his despair. The dream has an open end, and no union of the opposites between science and the unconscious psyche seems so far to be possible. The dream was a shock and it forced the man to wake up. He had in fact not yet realized that the situation was serious. The unconscious may perhaps have shocked him into realizing that his top-heavy scientific attitude was medieval and endangered his mediating cat side, the guiding spirit of the unconscious, which alone was able to bring the opposing world-views into balance.

This mediating quality of the cat is important. It comes from the extreme polarities of her character. «According to a Gnostic belief, there was a cat in the Garden of Eden, guarding the tree of life with its knowledge of good and evil. The cat was thus seen as a medium. It formed a bridge between good and evil, with knowledge of both. It acted as a mediator

29 M.-L. von Franz, *The Cat*, p. 58.

30 C.G. Jung, *Visions*, p. 235 – 241.

between them as well as between interior and exterior life, god and supernatural forces and man. Because it has access to, and is at home in, both spheres, it has much prophetic wisdom to impart and can teach us how to hold conflicting values in balance. As a symbol of consciousness, it is a psychic entity that knows the way – provided we learn to trust it, honoring, obeying and following wherever it leads.»[31]

In the case of this man, his scientific attitude seemed somehow connected to his religious education, which was in a way as rational as his science was. Religion embraced a well-defined world where good and evil had their definite place. But in the depths of his soul there was a deep religious need, a religious emotion that had no connection with this rational world-view. To fight for the cat, to save it, to carry it, could mean paying heed to unconventional, unpredictable reactions, thoughts and feelings, and thus becoming connected to the unconscious wisdom of his soul. If he could then accept the seemingly impossible insight that in fact what this meant was an experience of God, it would mean new water of life for his religious feeling.

The exclusion of the cat aspect from Christian consciousness is also at the core of the following dream of a 40-year-old man:

Nr.15: Dream of the cat as the devil:

I am in bed. I feel that there is a cat on the bed. It huddles up against me. Suddenly it transforms. It is the Devil. I am frightened, but I stand up to him and ask him what he wants. But he is gone. I can still see the hollow in the duvet. Again he comes and he stands besides me. I become scared. He is there, but I don't dare to ask any more. Eventually I start to pray. At the same time I try to switch on the light, but the lamp cord does not work. The ceiling lamp does not work either. At one point I manage to make light.

The dreamer in reality quite liked cats, and for him it was natural to have a cat on his bed. The shock was the realization that this cat was the Devil himself. His encounter with the Devil has a parallel in a legend about Saint Anthony the Hermit. The legend tells us how St. Anthony meets the

31 Ibid, p. 57.

Devil in the Egyptian desert and asks him who he is. The Devil answers that he is Satanas and would like to know why the monks are against him and the Christians curse him. St. Anthony answers that they are right to do so, because they are much afflicted by his wiles. The Devil then answers. «I don't harm them, they do it to themselves. I myself have become nothing, because Christ reigns in all countries.»[32] The Devil is here really a "poor devil", asking for understanding!

In his book *Aion*, Jung explains that in the Book of Job, the Devil was still one of the sons of God, called Satanael, and a confidant of Jahweh. He became the enemy of God, the Anti-Christ only after the beginnings of Christianity. The dogmatic figure of Christ was so ideal that a compensation of this light image had to take form, in accordance with the saying that no tree grows into the sky, unless its roots are grounded in Hell. The Devil belongs to Christ just as the shadow belongs to the light. So the gnosis of good and evil, which means development of consciousness, always also leads to conflict, in other words to crucifixion.[33] The more a one-sided attitude tends to repress the dark aspects of the instinctual psyche, the more the tension between the opposites is increased and, according to the psychic law of compensation, the more likely it is that the Devil will turn up. This problem manifests itself even in the early days of Christianity, as we can see from the legend of St. Anthony. St. Anthony the Hermit, the saint striving fervently for holiness, is also known to be tortured by whole mobs of devils and demons, often depicted as abhorrent, animal-like creatures.

Our dream takes up this old problem, as if there were not two thousand years in between. Now the Devil has to do with the whole unpredictability of the cat instinct, the mercurial spirit of the unconscious, which was locked out by the church with her rules and regulations. The dreamer, who had worked with his dreams for several years, seemed to need a greater insight into his Christian educational background in order to see the stumbling blocks for his work with the unconscious. Because who can really accept unconventional and unpredictable instinctual reactions in dreams and fantasies if there is still a low voice in the background of his Christian attitude which tells him that this is all the work of the Devil? The

32 R. Abt, *Der Heilige und das Schwein*, p. 30

33 C. G. Jung, *Aion*, [Coll. Works 9 II], § 77 f.

dreamer desperately struggles for light and finally succeeds. Bringing light into the roots of this problem seems to be crucial and requires great effort. In Alchemy, which, as C. G. Jung pointed out, describes in a symbolic way the individuation process of men, this part of the alchemical work is called illuminatio, when one experiences a feeling of comprehension, when certain problems become clear and the life feeling begins to flow again.[34]

This is a dream of a 26-year-old woman:

Nr.16: Dream of the cat in the church:

In a church. A priest I know is preaching in a very committed and lively manner. The church is crowded. Finally all of us, including myself, are singing a song like a choral piece. Later I see a large, old and very beautiful book with a very valuable cover from which the song comes and which belongs to the priest's personal collection. On the wrapper there is a ring, held by an angel. The angel has a lively, animated, warm and almost funny face. Inside the ring is the inscription 'cum gaudet'. In the background there is a beautiful landscape (Italian?). Ring and angel are framed by a structure which looks like wooden tiles, like the scales of a fish. The priest holds up another book with the drawing of a naked man with naked genitals. But the drawing is indistinct and faint. The priest is looking for another illustration, maybe of a woman? It is his intention to explain something from his sermon. Among the books I see a McKinsey sexual report, a red book for men, a blue one for women. There he could certainly find such an illustration but I don't say anything. The priest must know himself where he can find the illustrations. He must have dealt with this subject before. Later he demonstrates something else:

In the sidewall of the church there is a secret chamber that can be entered from two sides. In front of this chamber sits a cat that never leaves or enters the chamber. The priest opens the chamber. It is illuminated inside. Several women are sitting around a table. They belong to the family of the priest. First I see his mother or grandmother. His wife may also be present. It looks as if these women have always lived in this chamber, even

34 M.-L. von Franz, *Alchemy*, p. 256.

during the sermon outside. The grandmother gives a sign of rejection with her arms – to prevent the cat from coming in or to protect herself from the glances? After a while the priest locks the chamber again.

The woman's associations to this dream showed that the priest was not so bad; he wanted changes in the church. Maybe he had a liking for such valuable old books on the subject of the Italian Renaissance art or with Italy itself. For her, the Renaissance was associated with culture, human life, the joy of life, theology. The dreamer associates 'cum gaudet' with inner joy, utter ecstasy and the feeling of the mystics.

The association with the period of the Renaissance is important here. With the Renaissance the medieval unity of spiritual and worldly power started to disintegrate. There was no longer a sense of wholeness where belief was closely connected with knowledge. Observation of nature became increasingly important, with an ensuing interest in natural science. It was the rebirth of the experience of rationalism, a rebirth of antiquity. In art, the sensual aspect of the human body was emphasized (Michelangelo); pre-Christian goddesses became favorite subjects of painting and sculpture. There was a new significance attached to the human individual. The invention of central perspective in drawing mirrored this new view, in which the individual became the starting point of the observation.

The priest in the dream apparently seems to highlight the individual human being, oriented towards joy of life and sensuality. The lively, almost joyful, angel with the ring (cum gaudet) corresponds to a more worldly attitude, which obviously tends to replace medieval sombreness. But the priest is not able to find the picture of the feminine for his sermon, though the valuable old book seems to contain some of the missing Renaissance features he is looking for. In fact the church nowadays tries to bring in these worldly aspects with all sorts of extraverted activities in order to bring back people into the church. This priest is looking for an image of the feminine, probably of a naked woman in analogy to the drawing of the naked man. This is modern and a breakup of all taboos. In his drawer, there is also the Mc Kinsey report, a modern rational and statistical record of data, a catalogue of sexual behavior. The dreamer thinks that in the report he might be able to find the image of the feminine he is looking for. The priest, however, does not seem to be able to communicate such a new image of the feminine, because on the one hand he has only his book on the Renaissance attitude with its separation of the sensual and religious experience, and on the other hand a modern, rational and purely biological theory.

Despite the open-minded attitude of this rather helpless priest, the mother, grandmother and other women are meanwhile locked up in the side-chamber of the church. From time to time the door is opened but the two worlds remain separated. The women in the dream accept this separation quite passively. We also do not know why the grandmother in the dream makes this gesture of rejection of the cat. The cat would carry the meaning of becoming free from all the Christian restraints of the feminine and would represent 'going one's own way'. For women, according to this dream, the situation is still as it had been with their mothers and grandmothers when a

Fig.15. The cat instinct sits 'in between' and is a potential mediator. Carving in Winchester Cathedral, England, ca.1306.

ruling male consciousness was laying down the law about what was good and what was not. The personal problem of this dreamer mirrors the collective problem: With the disintegration of spiritual and worldly power in the Renaissance, a development set off towards the rationalism of the 19th century and up to the psychology of Sigmund Freud, who devalued the numinous world of the gods, the unconscious, in reducing it to forgotten or suppressed contents and sexuality. In trying to add the individual, the eros and the joyful aspects of life to the old dogmatic structures of Christian religious life, modern consciousness has followed Freud's theory and landed in a materialistic and clinical attitude that keeps the feminine soul still locked off in a side-chamber (fig. 15).

There, in front of the door, sits the cat, the instinctual basis of the feminine that cannot be comprehended rationally. She cannot be found in the priest's book and even less in the Mc Kinsey Report, because she is more than a naked woman. She could be a potential mediator if it were only realized. Bastet is sitting there unrecognized! She would not only contain the aspects the priest is looking for in his books, but she could also confer, what the women seem to be missing, namely an individual and instinctual feminine independence from male dominance. With her a new image of the feminine could be brought to light, which would unite the light and the dark sides of the feminine nature. It seems that the dreamer, who follows the whole occurrence somehow reserved, needs a deeper insight into these facts.

In our rural culture, *the playful, poetic aspect* of the cat, that was not contained in the church, sometimes leads a hidden life in a far off place. In legends, as mentioned before, now and then a nocturnal wanderer meets one or several cats on fences or side rails of bridges and they may even be friendly, especially when they are treated well. These suppressed aspects are not always cut off so dangerously. They may go on living somewhere even if they are not officially accepted.

A legend from central Switzerland goes as follows:

Nocturnal wanderers had several times heard the finest music coming out of an old, partly uninhabited house close to Ripshausen, not far from the river Reuss. A courageous man once looked inside through the window and there he saw a number of cats. Some were sitting on the table, playing merry dance rhythms on wind- and string instruments, while the others were dancing to this music. The loud festivities usually lasted until the morning bells rang. Then the party spread to the neighbouring houses, but especially to the nearby untilled ground down by the stock mountain, where many wild cats were to be seen.[35]

Singing, drinking and dancing have always belonged to life, even in devoutly Christian areas, and they appear in many folktales and songs, compensating for the strict rules of the Church. For the Church, dancing was usually regarded as a major sin and seen as the work of the Devil, which is why it often had to be practiced in hidden places far away from the villages. In this way, the erotic and joyful cat aspect of the feminine or the anima still had an opportunity to find expression.

Where split-off aspects of the feminine are projected onto the legendary character of the witch's cat, unification of the opposites or redemption is rarely possible. However, in fairytales, which are somehow farther away from personal experience, coming as they do from a deeper archetypal level, a connection with the world of the cat anima is sometimes described. In the fairytale "The poor young Miller and the Cat", the hero has to serve the cat anima.[36] This anima has been turned into a cat and has to stay in her castle for seven years until she can be redeemed. The miller has to chop wood and carry water and also do other work for a long time in order to help the cat princess to be redeemed. The enchanted cat anima, representing relatedness, eros and relation to the soul, wants to become human again, which would mean that the cat qualities can live in a humanized form on the conscious level. Her redemption can only be brought about by working on the concrete level that is her everyday life, without asking for a result first. The hero has to do this patient work that has no spectacular external effect: father and brother only laugh at the dumb boy when he returns home. This work has to do with the consideration of an inner reality. These are the duties that the anima imposes upon a man. It entails the sacrifice of a purely intellectual and rational attitude. And this has an effect on daily life, even if there is no spectacular success. Working on the unconscious is hard and painstakingly slow; overwhelming success is rare and can even be slightly suspect.

35 J. Müller, *Sagen aus Uri*, Band I, p. 173.

36 *The Complete Grimms's Fairytales*, No 106.

A man who is working on the redemption of the cat anima will need to find a way to express the unconscious in his life. He may, for example, include feeling in the scientific work, daring to integrate the element of relationship in technology or politics by considering dream and fantasy an essential part of his life. From here could come the integrating aspect which brings the opposites together, left and right (e. g. in politics), up and down, good and evil, masculine and feminine. In our conscious world, these opposites cannot be brought together. Only when the anima, imprisoned in a separate chamber, can be released, respected and related to, can we hope that the integration of the opposites inside and outside will become a real possibility. The cat, which is a symbol for an unconventional feeling or impulse from the unconscious, is the creative element which could initiate such a development.

A 33-year-old man who was working on such a collective problem, dreamt:

Nr.17: Dream of the cat's queen:

While in our holiday home in the mountains I see that next to it there is another house. To my great surprise I recognise that there are only cats living in it. I see them doing the housework and I am completely astonished to have such neighbours, not having known anything about them before. The house is on the north side of ours, from where the water supply comes. However, in the dream it is not as steep as in reality but flat, which reminds me of another house I know which is a real witch's house. There is a well in front of the house and a cat has just started to fetch some water. Now comes the mistress or queen of the cats. Her fur is black and white, like the fur of the other cats as far as I can see. She can speak and very kindly offers me a drink. I may choose between three drinks they have all made themselves: gin, nut liqueur and a third distillery product, probably made from apples. I choose the gin and while I am drinking it I feel like as if I have tasted the magic potion of Asterix: this gift makes me wake up totally inspired and enthusiastic.

This dream reminds us of the fairytale of the young miller and the cat, in which it says: «She took him into her cursed castle and there she had many little cats serving her: they quickly ran up and down the stairs gaily and merrily. In the evening when they sat down at the table, three of them had to make music, one played the double-bass, the second the violin and the third the trumpet, blowing out its cheeks as much as it could [...].»

The cats in this dream do not make any music but they make 'Schnapps'. As in the dream of the distillery and the cat, for this man the extraction of spirit is closely connected with his cat anima. Similar to many old mother goddesses, she is the guardian of the well of water and the origin of all creative life. In this dream, the cats are already at work before the dreamer realizes this consciously. When he goes to his lonely holiday house in order to work, creative distillery essentials are already being prepared in the unconscious and are offered to him by his cat anima. And of course this is the magic potion – the water of life!

In the Rumanian fairytale *The Cat*, interpreted by M.-L. v. Franz, there is also a positive cat anima helping the hero.[37] By the end of the fairytale, there is a wedding for the two of them, a solution representing a union of the unconscious archetypal world and human consciousness. In the individual human being, this union has to be done by carefully analysing the cat reactions or creative cat inspirations from the unconscious. In this way, our consciousness receives something which has still not been understood for what it is, namely mighty or divine powers, i.e. gods who are in possession of the magic potion! The danger is that we might believe we could do this work of transformation ourselves. Then we would be identifying unconsciously with these gods. This is the great problem of inflation, which may carry us out of reality, isolate us and make us unrelated. But when the ego can make a distinction and accept its frail human nature, it will then contribute to the badly needed total respect for these archetypal powers without becoming possessed by them.

While still thinking of the unifying quality of the cat symbol, I came upon a short dream from a 30-year-old woman which gave me quite a headache, because it brought up the difficult topic of instincts fighting each other. The dream goes as follows:

37 M.-L. von Franz, *The Cat*.

Nr. 18: Dream of the cat attacking another cat:

One of our two cats, the little one, has chased another one, maybe the neighbor's cat. It has attacked exactly as a lion would attack its prey and injured it severely. The whole of its rear side is a terrible open wound. I find it lying on the porch of the house and I am horror-stricken. I call my partner to bring it down. He does so and takes care of her. We must help it.

In this dream, as in so many dreams, one animal attacks another. Something seems to be out of balance in the unconscious set-up in such a case. There is obviously nothing unifying in this dream; in fact there seems to be a war going on within the animal realm. The little cat, a female, usually harmless and playful, becomes a ferocious beast in the dream, attacking one of its own species in a way that would be unlikely in real life. Although there is constant war in the animal world, in that killing and devouring each other is part of nature, it is not common among house cats. We can therefore assume that there is some conflict on the depth. The opposites are, so to speak, imminent in the cat side, because one part of them has gone berserk. What would these two cats represent? The wounded cat belongs to the neighbor, a middle-aged woman living on her own after various relationships had failed. The dreamer's situation would be very similar to her neighbor's, if her current relationship were to fail. In fact she was going through an insoluble conflict. Should she stay with her partner, even though she was sometimes ambivalent about her feelings, or would the relationship have to come to an end. Maybe one could say that the conflict between the cats has to do with the contradictions of two conflicting lifestyles, namely the one connecting her feminine destiny with a man, with all the constraints involved in a tightly bound relationship, or live an independent but lonely life of her own. The conflict erupts on an unconscious level, bringing irritation, depression and injury into everyday life. There is no real solution in the dream, just the need to heal the wound of the neighbor's cat, together with her partner. It is difficult to say what that would mean for the relationship of this couple, which was on shaky ground at that moment. The aggressive little cat was in reality also very closely related to the man, because his family had been the owners of her mother. So it might also be his cat anima that comes into play. It is therefore not clear if the woman's instinctive drive for independence was violated by herself or by her partner or by both. The only thing that seems to be clear is that she is appealing to him for help, so that this side may go on living. And he does respond to this appeal. Although it might look just a superficial problem of relationship, the symbol of the cat points to a deep unconscious conflict.

The next dream has to do with the absence of the cat goddess in this day and age, which brings us once more to the collective level of the feminine and the eros problem. It is the dream of a middle-aged man who worked with Marie-Louise von Franz.

Nr.19: Dream of the Bastet temple:

I am in Berlin, on the way to Zurich in Switzerland. I am together with a woman who turns out to be Marie-Louise von Franz. We are on the border of East and West, but there is no separation visible. In place of the wall there is a highway built by the Russians. This highway starts out of the ground in the middle of an area with blocks of buildings and goes right through an ancient sanctuary. This temple is marked by four pillars. The motif of the pillars is taken up in pillars made of concrete bordering on both sides of the highway that leads to the airport. This stretch of the highway is even reproduced on the Russian 1-ruble note. We now go to have a close look at the sanctuary. There are four pillars on its sides, like the four Evangelists, but they are plant-pillars. The one to the right in front is a rose pillar, the other ones are not known. The sanctuary is a temple of the goddess Bastet, and there are also two of her images placed at the edge. They probably had to be removed from the middle to the side of the temple because of the highway. One of the images shows Bastet as a cat; on the second one she is depicted as a woman in the upper part and a cat in the lower part. Marie-Louise von Franz explains the meaning of these images. – Somehow we then get to the airport. We see an aeroplane. In the aeroplane there is a young man fooling around. One minute he is in the cockpit, the next he is among the passengers. Like this he keeps the employees on the go as they hunt for him.

At the time of this dream, the separation by the wall between East and West in Europe was still a reality. For Western consciousness this separation was clearly between good and evil, between freedom in the West and repression and dictatorship in the East, but the dream sees it differently. There is also a separation, but it is a split in the sanctuary of the goddess Bastet. It is a highway, built by the Russians – at this time the dreaded enemy – that goes right through the sanctuary, leading to the airport. This highway seems to be of high value, as it is bordered by pillars, like the sanctuary, but it is also of low value, because it is even printed onto the 1-ruble note, the most common everyday currency. Highway and airport in their negative aspect have to do with today's mobility and extraverted rootlessness, which are an intrinsic part of the common lifestyle of our time. The highway splits the wholeness of the four plant pillars in the sanctuary, and they are removed to the sides, probably neglected and forgotten from then on. There are also two images of Bastet. One of them shows her as a cat in the lower part and human in the upper part, the other one just as a cat. Where dream motifs appear in pairs of two, one more human, one more animal-like, usually something is on the point of entering consciousness. But it is Marie-Louise von Franz, for the dreamer a guiding figure of psychological understanding, who brings up the whole numinosity of the image. The sacrilege of the sanctuary of the goddess is both obvious and painful. She is an image of the soul with all the cat qualities that characterize Bastet. She has to do with nature and with eros, with life quality and with relatedness. This also shows in the rose pillar, the rose being a symbol of love, as we have seen above. This feminine principle is cast aside by the spirit of our time. The dream clearly mirrors a collective situation that transcends the dreamer's personal background. This brings us to the last part of the dream, which has to do with the problem of the puer aeternus.

What follows is the scene in the aeroplane, where a youth acts the clown, a mercurial figure that fools pilot, passengers and crew. He is to be seen as an embodiment of Mercurius in his negative aspect, who turns up where modern extraverted consciousness represses the goddess of love and nature. How dangerous he can be has been elaborated by M.-L. von Franz in her commentaries to Bruno Goetz's great novel *Reich ohne Raum*.[38] There

38 B. Goetz, *Das Reich ohne Raum*, with a commentary by M.-L. von Franz.

she makes clear that 'Fo', the youth, is an embodiment of the puer aeternus, a young god of antiquity like Dionysos, Attis, Adonis, Osiris. They were sons of the great mother goddess and were all gods of salvation and venerated in mystery cult. Dionysos, though, if not respected, sent confusion and madness instead of healing, ecstasy and genuine spiritual experience. Confusion and madness is also what 'Fo' provokes in the novel. He is the opposite of Mr. von Spät, who stands for the old and crusted traditional spirit who does not want to renounce power. He would be the old king in the fairytale. There is no feminine to reconcile these two and therefore 'Fo' goes on creating mischief in the human world instead of being a salvific god, a new creative spirit. If Bastet, the goddess of relatedness, is cast aside by the rational, extraverted spirit of our time, which still thinks in terms of "good-better-and even better", "fast-faster and even faster" (the highways and the airport), and thereby represses the values of nature and the soul, then the youth, the puer aeternus, mercurius in his confusing and destructive form causes trouble. He then becomes the reason, as von Franz puts it, for a puerile immaturity, a driven infantilism, a scallywag psychology that is becoming increasingly widespread among large sections of the population and is, according to her, a great danger to our time.[39] In the dream, the Russians, who carry the projection of evil, stand for the rational power attitude of consciousness, which suppresses spiritual renewal. As long as Bastet, the cat goddess, the uniting feminine principle of eros and relatedness is too weak or is cast aside, no reconciliation of these opposites is possible. The novel ends tragically, the union of consciousness with the creative spirit of renewal only takes place in the Beyond after the catastrophe, the death of the main figure. Marie-Louise von Franz shows that this problem has not been solved in our time. The novel *Reich ohne Raum* was, according to her, a prophetic indication of what happened shortly afterwards in the Second World War, when the negative aspect of the archetype of the puer aeternus took over with dissociation, disorientation and overwhelming emotionality. The collective psychic situation does not seem to have changed since she wrote her commentary in 1962. Bastet would help to reconcile the new spirit with the old rational attitude on the inner level of the individual psyche. This could possibly be the only way to avoid further destruction.

39 Ibid., p. 178.

The dream image of this collective situation and his own role in it came as a shock to the man. He realized that the sanctuary of Bastet had to be restored at all costs! The collective problem had to become his own, because a transformation of the collective situation can only begin in the individual psyche, small as the contribution might seem to be.

Summarizing, one could say about the subject of the cat in dreams that *this female, independent, individual instinct has to do with a quality of joy in life and sensuality, with creativity as well as the nocturnal side of the soul, with being in balance, with a self-confident, feminine freedom and independence, and at the same time with relatedness without submission. The symbol of the cat is therefore potentially healing.* The *Sekhmet side of the cat*, with dangerous fiery emotions, will come up whenever the Bastet aspect has been lost or suppressed. *Laziness and a lack of responsibility* belong to the dark sides of the cat symbol, and the witch's cat can be seen as a shadow or a compensation for our Christian attitude. In fairytales we meet the *positive integrating cat anima.*

Barbara Hannah summarizes the light and the dark sides of the cat symbol as follows: «The wild hunter can help us as Ra, the tomcat, fighting the darkness and its vermin in our unconscious, or it can endanger us as Bastet [Sekhmet [40]] losing our energy in wild untamed emotions. It can bring us destruction if it is used as plots and black magic, or healing if the magic is tamed and used for a genuine, non-egotistical purpose. It can relax us and help heal our overstrained conscious attitude as the pleasant Bastet, or make us lazy and false, like the repentant cat. It can lead us away from our human relationships into a desert of purely autoerotic isolation as the Ethiopian cat. Or it can give us access to the universal knowledge and make us truly self-reliant as Puss-in-Boots. Nothing we can do for anyone is more helpful than self-reliance. It is an indispensable help to our environment if we can become responsible for ourselves and not always turn to someone else.»[41]

The cat symbol in dreams points to a feminine aspect in the psyche that wants to be respected and cared for, even if it is *wild, independent and often unpredictable*, like a real cat. Respecting the Bastet-cat instinct according to dreams seems to be of the greatest importance for the inner balance of conflicting opposites.

40 My addition.

41 Barbara Hannah, *The Archetypal Symbolism of Animals,* p. 52 f.

Fig. 16: The Cat – a pet and a wild animal at the same time.

Part II

The Dog

Fig. 17: Hunting dog of the Pharaoh. Ivory. Ancient Egypt, ca. 1350 BC.

There are so many different types of dog today, large and small in every colour combination, with and without leads, with little jackets, food bowls and dog beds, that we find it hard to believe that the dog, despite being domesticated and among humans, is and remains a wild animal in its heart of hearts. Occasional accidents with aggressive breeds cause the emotions to become heated and can lead to public or political affairs. This is because people forget that living with a dog is only possible because over thousands of years he has adapted to humans. Dog remains have been found in grave sites, their skeletons curled up beside human skeletons, dated at 10'000 to 14'000 years ago, as A. Horowitz writes in her book *Inside of a Dog* (p. 39 f.). In those days it was mainly used for hunting, but even today there are things that only dogs can do: track down people under avalanches or in other dangerous situations, act as ambulance dogs, guide dogs for the blind, watch over sheep or cattle, sniff out drugs and so on (fig. 18). And of course, every dog owner appreciates its natural qualities as a watchdog and protector. All in all, one of the dog's main qualities is its ability to understand us and to cooperate.

Why does the dog do all these things for us? Of course it receives food and warmth, but what it seems to need above all is a *relationship*. Even wild dogs seek out human beings and try to stay close to them. A dog would be totally unhappy if it could not live in the vicinity of human beings. Dogs seem to direct all their efforts towards understanding our wishes and our moods. They symbolically therefore point to an instinct between animal and man, a humanised instinct, so to speak, that can connect the two worlds.

According to Marie-Louise von Franz, the dog is the *essence of relatedness, pure, reliable loyalty, the most faithful eros* (fig. 24). Because the dog is more domesticated than any other animal, it symbolises – as she says – the union of the specific opposites of animal instinct and civilised consciousness. Thus in an Arabic alchemical text, written by a sofar unknown author, the dog is able to mitigate the violence of the fire. This makes colours appear in the alchemical process, which is an image of the different shades of human emotion.[42]

42 Published in M.-L. von Franz, *Psychological commentary on the Book of the Explanation of the Symbols by Mohammed Ibn Umail*, CALA I A, p. 156-158.

Barbara Hannah says that this kind of emotion has to do with an instinctive morality concerning what any particular situation is really like and what is best in any special moment.[43] That does not mean that what is best for the dog is necessarily the best for our own moral standards! If my dog steals meat from the table, it is good for him and he does it completely in harmony with himself, but I hate him for it! If I do not interfere by punishing him he will greet me happily with a big grin, tail wagging excitedly. In the dog symbol, emotions are connected with the instinct. That makes the emotions real and genuine, a prerequisite for any relationship, which is why relatedness to the dog instinct is important wherever eros comes in.

Fig. 18: Rescue Dog at work.

Dreams often bring in the dog symbol when there is a problem with relatedness, be it with animals, be it with those nearest to us. I always made the experience that the unconscious is immensely interested in my relationship to my animals. I remember a young dog of ours that had been given a death sentence by the vets, as he was suffering from a serious growth disorder in his shoulders. I was quite willing to accept the authority

43 B. Hannah, *The Cat, Dog and Horse Lectures*, p. 100.

of the vets, but luckily I threw an I Ching, the Chinese oracle which Jung used to refer to when talking about synchronicity.[44] It came out No. 52: 'Keeping still'. The changing sign, which points to future possibilities of development, was Nr. 53: 'Gradual progress'. I understood the message that perseverance and inner calm was necessary to give the unconscious a chance for the healing process. So we postponed the euthanasia and took the dog for a final vacation to our mountain home, giving him all the love and care we could. Later in his life he always remembered, that he had even been allowed to sleep on the sofa! On our return two weeks later, it turned out that – miraculously – the healing process had started. We had this dog for another 13 years! Another of our dogs, a German shepherd, already 15 years old, had all the difficulties old dogs have, which is also quite a burden for those who take care of it. I could not help running out of patience sometimes, and I was in a real quandary about the right moment to have her put to sleep. This was the dream that came at this moment of painful insecurity (fig. 19):

Nr. 20: Dream about Ascha:

There is a man who is pulling Ascha, my dog, on her leash, as if she was to be tamed, in the rough way dog instructors sometimes do. I protest, take her to my side and make clear to him what a wonderful dog she is and always has been. I go on to say that she does not need such treatment, as she knows everything and has always done her best, and after all she is old and weak. I am proud of her.

This dream helped me to tame my own animus and to go on caring lovingly for this animal until the moment for the final decision revealed itself. It is usually the animus, thoughts, considerations, scruples and fixed ideas that enfeeble a woman's natural feeling and lure her into taking precipitate decisions. It is sometimes a difficult task for her to find out what her own feelings are, and what is interfering with them. A decision might be the right one from a rational standpoint, but if it does not feel right, it is still wrong. Asha, symbol of my dog eros, had to be defended against the harsh dog instructor animus.

44 See C. G. Jung's Introduction into the *I Ching*, translated by Richard Wilhelm.

Fig. 19: Friendship between dog and cat.

How helpful the dog eros can be is shown in the following dream of a young mother in the third month of pregnancy with her third child. As she had lost her second child during pregnancy, she felt restless and uneasy this time and worried about the check-up scheduled with her doctor. In fact, soon after this dream she also lost this child.

Nr. 21: Dream of the dog Sissi:

In a dark, unfamiliar room in our house I want to lay the table for us to eat. My son comes out of this room, saying: «There is my mama». He does not mean me, which seems strange to me. But then I can see Sissi, the old farm dog that died last year. She looks just the same, big, strong, with her dark coat, and she walks very slowly. I am a bit scared, because I do not know how she will behave towards me. Following a spontaneous impulse, I crouch down in front of her on the floor like an embryo. She seems to like that. She approaches me and places herself in a way that I am completely surrounded by her. It is an incredible feeling of being safe. It is as if she were my mother!

The young woman woke up with a great feeling of happiness. The dream conveyed to her a deep feeling of safety and protection. Although she could not know it, she was being prepared for what lay ahead, the loss of her child with the ensuing serious threat to her self-esteem as a mother. The dog in this dream is a protecting, loving mother, the instinctive basis of feminine life. Nothing else is needed at this moment other than the confidence in the animal soul of the body, which has always known how to deal with such feminine life circumstances. Crouching down in front of the dog like an embryon puts an end to all rational reasoning and brings her in harmony with the laws of nature. The dream stayed with her as a great consolation during the painful experience of losing her child

The very positive side of the dog has corresponding dark aspects on the archetypal level as well as in external reality. Male dogs can forget about all good behaviour when following a female in heat, sitting in front of her house, yowling their lungs out all night long. So the negative side of eros-nature is a kind of love madness. In the already mentioned Arabic alchemical text by an unknown author we read «that the dog brings out the water like the great flood».[45] This is an image of the overwhelming nature of the unconscious coming up when eros violently intervenes in one's life.

Apart from that, dogs can also be thievish, gluttonous and disobedient. Therefore in mythology and folktales, the dog commonly features as a *thief and cheat*. A story from central Asia tells us that God had asked the dog to protect man, who he had just created, from the Devil. But the dog was seduced by God's evil enemy, the Devil himself, who promised him a beautiful warm coat. So the dog allowed man to fall into the hands of the Devil. The dog was responsible for this fall, just like the snake in the Bible. The dog had extricated man from his union with God (in Paradise) and forced him into the awareness of his own imperfection.[46]

45 See M.-L. von Franz, *Psychol. Commentary to the Hall ar-Rumuz*, CALA I A, p.159.

46 J. Chevalier and A. Gheerbrant, *Dictionnaire des Symboles* Vol. II, p. 25.

In various tales, the dog is described as the *thief of fire.* A tribe in Biafra says that the dog stole fire from heaven and brought it to man. In a New Guinea legend, the dog stole fire from his first owner, a rat (a nocturnal animal with devilish features). In the upper Nile region, fire was stolen from a snake, or from the gods, or from the rainbow.[47] From all these myths we can see that the dog, even in his dark aspect, serves the development of consciousness. Like Prometheus, who stole fire from the gods and brought it to mankind, the dog commits the sin of disobedience. Yet, it is this very animal which will later on become man's best friend and helper.

The first production of fire must have been an extraordinary event for man. Jung says: «By that mankind has snatched or stolen a secret from nature […] so to say he has allowed himself an illegal intervention in nature and incorporated a piece of primeval unconsciousness to his consciousness. Like a thief he has acquired something precious and did harm to the realm of the gods [...].» In the same text, Jung also explains that the making of fire, which has even been celebrated ritually throughout the millennia, has to do with the transfer of libido to another stage of life. If life is no longer in a state of flow «things have lost their splendour and plants, animals and human beings may not grow any more.»[48] When joy of life and energy are missing, then a life-saving and redeeming fire is needed. In former times, for hunting and gathering societies, fire was essential for protection at night from wild animals. The same holds true for protection from the unconscious animal side. Together with language, fire turned out to be the strongest magical means of handling the constantly threatening daemonic powers of the unconscious. Controlled fire means light, warmth, nourishment, while uncontrolled fire might well destroy the whole house. The dog instinct can cause both.

The dog in Western alchemy is identical with the lion, which is an animal of the sun. Thus the dog in alchemy also has to do with the illuminating light of consciousness. It is the instinct itself that brings up a possibility to handle the instinctual powers by greater consciousness. And this means new life energy.

47 J. Chevalier and A. Gheerbrant, *Dictionnaire des Symboles* Vol. II, p. 18-26.

48 C. G. Jung, *Symbols of Transformation* [Coll. Works 5], § 250.

But as fire is also a symbol for fiery emotion or sexual passion in its dangerous, overwhelming aspects, the dog instinct, which brings all of that up onto the level of consciousness, may be experienced as threatening. The result is often an irrational hatred of dogs. A 50-year-old woman, who absolutely disliked dogs, was afraid of them and always expected every dog in the street to attack her. She refused to touch our dog, even if it showed its most friendly side. An analyst will pay special attention to such cases, where there seems to be an inner resistance to the dog instinct. The projection of these unfriendly dog sides onto the outer dog becomes a fixed idea that cannot be changed by any rational argument. Oddly enough, such people are often bitten or barked at by dogs. Later on it became obvious that this woman had a strong resistance against developing an awareness of her unconscious shadow sides.

We could now say that when the positive side of the dog instinct is constellated in the unconscious, it can bring up new light, an opportunity of seeing things in a new way. The stories about fire and light brought from the other world by a dog show that such an experience cannot be forced from outside. It seems to be possible only when it is sustained and carried by an instinct that is friendly and helpful. In analysis, it is often a matter of patience to wait for the dog instinct to manifest its helpful intention! Then it might 'click' and a problem can be seen from a new angle, or a dream can enlighten the situation.

A 42-year-old woman had this amazing dream, which speaks about the special kind of dog-consciousness:

Nr. 22: Dream of the dog turning like the finger of a clock:

I saw a dog lying on the ground. It turned around like the finger of a clock. When its head faced me its eyes were closed, when it faced the other side, the side of the witches' house, its eyes were opened.

The dreamer herself came up with the interpretation that the instinct, while looking towards the shadow realm, could see, whereas looking toward the ego, it was blind. Through the dream, she realised that it was the dog instinct that could recognise evil and see into the depths of the unconscious, whereas directed towards ego consciousness, it was blind. This might point to the fact that if we let ourselves be guided by the dog instinct when it comes to decisions of the ego, it might sometimes not be a help, and could lead us the wrong way because it is too unconscious or too automatic as a drive. Then we have to take conscious responsibility for what our instinct brings up and see it through our own eyes. Dreams, for instance, can rarely be taken literally. Just because we had a nasty dream about our neighbour, we do not normally go outside and hit him over the head. Bringing the hint of that dream into consciousness would mean realising – at least partly – that same neighbour in ourselves and assuming responsibility for this uncomfortable fact. Nature can be our guide if we know how to how to follow her, says Jung. It is like the needle of a compass which orients us to the North, which is useful if we have a good ship we know how to steer. Nature is not human, it always follows its own collective goals and never serves the personal destiny. Our destiny is the result of a cooperation of conscious and unconscious.[49] Like the ship and the compass, our relation to the dog is an appropriate image for this cooperation.

Where the cooperation is missing, the autonomous acting of an instinct can have the strangest results! Our dog used to come with me to the train station to fetch my husband on his way home from work. Even before the arrival of the train he used to get excited, wagging his tail, trampling nervously on all four paws. However, on one occasion my husband happened to go to the station with him in order to collect something from the post office nearby. Just at that moment a train arrived and the dog as usual started to get excited. Nothing could convince him that no husband would get out of this train, even though that same man was holding the other end of the leash!

Once, while in charge of a regional development concept, my husband had a dream that mirrored a necessary renewal by reconnecting the conscious to the unconscious world. At the end of this dream he was urged to sacrifice our dog! In this dream, the dog symbol seemed to point to a *conservative, unreflecting perception*, even if there was a lot of feeling in it. It had to be sacrificed in order to be transformed into a new reality, as is so often necessary in fairytales. The dog instinct that had accompanied development until then and had brought all the instinctual impetus and feeling necessary to break up old conscious structures, now had to be

49 C. G. Jung, *Letters* Vol. I, letter from 20.5.1940.

sacrificed. The dog's perception will remain conservative and limited if the ego relies on it exclusively. The ego has to take responsibility for the instincts, otherwise it will miss the living connection to the deeper flow of the transforming unconscious, the objective psyche that compensates the natural one-sidedness of the conscious perception. The decision as to how far one has to follow the dog instinct and when the moment comes to sacrifice it, remains one of the most difficult ego tasks. Speaking about the horse symbol, we will later come back to the topic of the animal sacrifice.

The aspect of the *dog as a guide* comes from his relatedness to humans and his very finely developed sense of smell, his 'scenting nose'. This has made the dog in mythology so competent at both finding and showing the way to the spiritual world. In Egypt, where dogs seemed to have been the subject of special attention and sincere affection, the most important canine god was Anubis, patron of embalmers and protector of the necropolis, who guided the deceased and participated in the divine judgment. Therefore Anubis is shown in the embalming rituals, which were a condition for the soul to attain immortality. The priests who did the embalming wore a mask of an Anubis head, thus creating an identity. Anubis is also depicted as a jackal-headed human. Later, in his funerary role, he was identified with the Greek Hermes psychopompos, who guides the souls of the deceased to the Beyond.[50] Hermes is also shown with a helmet or a cap that resembles a dog's head (fig. 20 and 21).

In some places, the dog has a function comparable to that of Saint Peter, who according to popular belief, decides who may go to heaven and who may not. Anubis also takes part in the divine judgement. In India, the god Yama, in the form of a dog, is the guardian of the way to heaven. Psychologically there seems to exist an instinct in man that can distinguish whether someone lives 'properly' or not. It would mean that we could receive an instinctive moral signal from deep down as to whether we live properly according to our life pattern, i.e. whether or not we are true to the self and to our own individuation. Morality here is not to be understood in the dogmatic Christian sense of the word but rather as being true to an inner judgment that is based on more than just outer moral restrictions.[51]

50 *The Oxford Encyclopedia of Ancient Egypt*, Vol.I, 97 f, p. 229 f.

51 See C. G. Jung, *Civilisation in Transition* [Coll. Works 10], § 825-857.

As a guide to the Beyond, the dog always has to be followed. The idea of the dog as a guide for the deceased is also known by the North-Asian Smojedes. They kill a dog and hang him over the grave with his tail above the head of the dead person. In this way the soul of the deceased can grasp the tail and can be guided by the soul of the dog to the Beyond and to new life. In India, the dead are sometimes given a dog's leash in their hand. It seems as if the way to the spiritual world could not be found without the dog. In the psyche, this is an instinctive wisdom which can connect us with the unconscious and the unconscious with our consciousness. The dog is familiar with both worlds. «The dog is the Sheikh», as the earlier mentioned unknown Arabic alchemist says, the guide on the path of individuation.[52] This instinct needs a direct and simple feeling relation such as dogs in outer life are in need of. Without that, even the most refined intellectual approach will not be able to make the realm of the unconscious

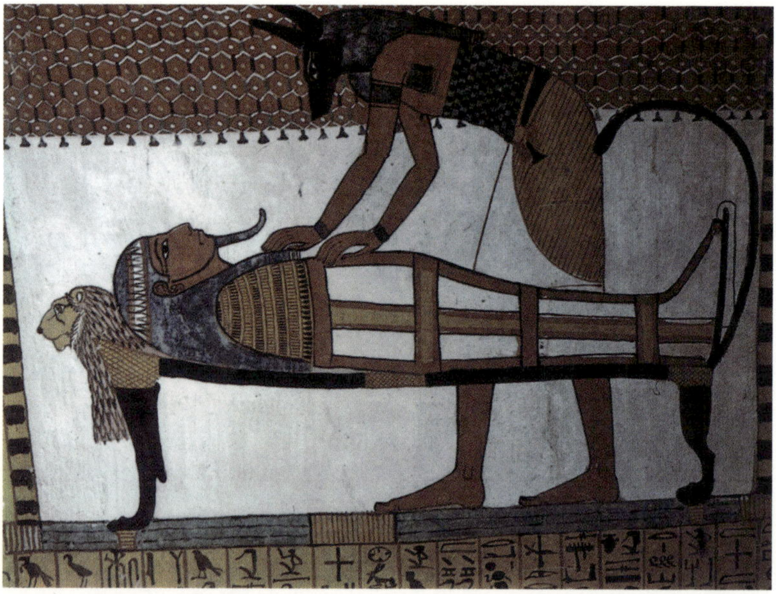

Fig. 20: The priest who does the embalming ritual wears the mask of Anubis. Ancient Egypt, 19th Dynasty, 1292-1188 BC, Tomb of Sennejem.

52 M.-L. von Franz, *Psychol. Commentary to the Hall ar-Rumuz*, CALA I A, p. 157.

a matter of reality in everyday life. Some people seem to know everything about the unconscious and their dreams, but suddenly they give up and fall back into their old way of life. They literally lack the dog, that is an instinctual feeling relation to what the unconscious has given to them.

The dog is also an instinct that is able to find the way to the inevitable end of life, when the frontier to the great and dark unknown has to be crossed. In his article about "Soul and Death", Jung says that the unconscious soul does not seem to bother a lot about death, but it does bother about the conscious attitude towards death.[53] It makes a big difference if this attitude is in tune with the natural unconscious transformation process towards death, or if it is rational, intellectual, superficial, too much looking back into the past, too youthful etc. and therefore cut off from the helpful way of nature. It makes sense that nature has provided us with an instinct we can trust to deal with this situation. It is infinitely older than our consciousness and has the experience of millions of years. Men's intuition has seen it in the image of the guiding dog.

A woman who had just had to put her beloved little dog to sleep had the following dream. It seems to be one of those dreams where one is not sure if it does not also mirror an objective reality. Deciding this is usually a matter of feeling. The dream is striking because of its archetypal symbolism and the familiar images surrounding death.

Nr. 23: Dream of the deceased dog leaving over the bridge:

My dog is lying on the vet's table, dead. There is a warm light on her, even though there is darkness all around. Where does the light come from? Does it come from her? Suddenly she gets up, jumps down from the table and runs around the field in leaps and bounds. Her ears are flapping and she looks happy and cheerful. I run after her. I am out of breath when I reach her near a bridge. She is standing on the bridge and turns to me. I want to step onto the bridge, but I am thrown back by a huge power. I get back onto my feet and I see that around the bridge, everything is on fire. Fire is erupting as if from a volcano, but the bridge itself is not on fire. My dog is standing there and sends me back. I am not allowed to follow her. I

53 C. G. Jung, *The Structure and Dynamics of the Psyche* [Coll. Works 8], § 809.

am offended, sad and do not understand the reason for this rejection. My dog says: "I will always stay with you." And then she is gone. I can see her leaving in her lovely, dancing way of moving.

This dream does not seem to distinguish between an animal and a human being. If we look at the symbolism about the death of the dog, there is no difference between that and what the unconscious of man, his instincts, his dreams and death experiences say about the fact of impending death. It is clearly one of those «dreams, which symbolically indicate the end of bodily life and the explicit continuation of psychic life after death. The unconscious 'believes' quite obviously in a life after death.»[54] Barbara Hannah once joked that one day in the other world we might even be able to have all the dogs we ever loved at once in our lap, as subtle bodies!

Let us have a look at the symbols of this great dream, since they are also well known in mythology, religions, alchemy as well as in many death dreams and death experiences. First of all we have the darkness, which expresses not only the dreamer's grief and depression after the death of her beloved dog, but also has to do with the dark passage into the land of the dead. According to ancient imagination, the rejuvenation and rebirth of the dead took place in the darkness of the grave. This was the mythical place of a birth passage, where the dead person is born into a new life.[55] Today we would say that the deceased disappears into the darkness of the collective unconscious, just another word for the great unknown where all new life has its origin.

The next well-known motif is the light. In the middle of the darkness our dreamer sees her dog lying on the vet's table, dead, but there is that strange, warm light over her. In numerous death dreams and death experiences, light is mentioned. Light phenomena accompanying death or in relation to ghosts are also common in parapsychological literature. In legends as well, we have a great many light apparitions and phantoms that are connected to death. In her book *On Dreams and Death*, M.-L. von Franz says that the image of light appears more often than any other image in her quoted material, which is vast.

54 M.-L.von Franz, *On Dreams and Death*, p. ix.

55 Ibid., p. 60 f.

Jung gives an explanation of the light phenomenon near death that is not easy to understand, but it might help us to grasp intuitively some of the depth of this image. M.-L. von Franz quotes Jung, who «expressed the assumption that psychic reality might lie on a supraluminous level of frequency, that is, it could exceed the speed of light. 'Light,' in this case, would appropriately enough be the last transitional phenomenon of the process of becoming unobservable, before the psyche fully 'irrealises' the body, as Jung puts it, and its first appearance after it incarnates itself in the space-time continuum by shifting its energy to a lower gear.»[56] M.-L. von Franz illustrates this hypothesis of Jung's with many examples. Through following her, we might understand that all those experiences of light near death have something to do with the transformation of the psyche from her highest perceivable limit of extensity to only intensity in the moment of death. More on this can be found in her groundbreaking book *On Dreams and Death.*

As the dream goes on, the dog jumps from the table and runs across the fields towards a bridge, which is surrounded by fire. The motif of the bridge that has to be crossed to the other world is known, for instance, in the Islamic tradition, where the deceased must cross over so-called Chinvat Bridge, «thinner than a hair, sharper than a sword and darker than the night».[57] The ancient Persians believed that an evil person was not able to cross this bridge and would fall down into the world of demons.[58] In North mythology, there is a bridge across the river which divides the land of the living from Hel, the land of the dead. It is watched by the aggressive and dangerous dog Garm, also called The Hel Dog.[59] So the bridge symbolises the transition from our world into the Beyond, a road of no return that is not to be approached by the living. Many reports of near death experiences speak of the existence of a threshold, from which, once transcended, there would apparently be no return.

This bridge in the dream is surrounded by fire as if from a volcano. The Beyond is often described as fiery, in either the positive or the negative

56 M.-L.von Franz, *On Dreams and Death*, p. 146.

57 Ibid, p. 61.

58 Ibid, p. 73.

59 Helle Helseth, *Some Animal Images in Fairytales and Dreams.*

sense. In Catholic tradition since the 12th century there has been the idea of a Hell, where the sinners are punished in hell fire or tested in the purgatory fire. A fiery Beyond is mentioned in the Book of Henoch, which points to Egyptian influences.[60] In the Egyptian Amduat, a Pharaonic Book for the Afterlife, painted on the walls of the Pharaoh's tombs in Thebes-Luxor, the Sungod on his night journey passes the "Lake of fire", a place of punishment for sinners. The blessed deceased, however, drink cool water from the same lake. «It is the paradoxical 'fire water', a well-known feature of the living emanation of the unconscious that can be a blessing or sheer destruction, depending on the attitude of the person towards this other world.»[61] As there is a bridge in the dream, the association of water might be at hand which would make very much sense in the light of this amplification. In alchemy, fire has to do with cleaning and transformation, but also with a fiery reanimation of the dead.

For the dog in our dream, the fire around the bridge is not dangerous. We could imagine animals belonging to the "blessed deceased" anyway, as no developed consciousness has thrown them into the conflict of good and evil! But this fire seems to be destructive to all vegetative life and is not to be approached by a living being. In dreams, fire usually has to do with psychic energy, namely with fiery affects and emotions. What happens really in the moment of death we do not know. From a psychological standpoint we only know that coming too close to the other world in the event of a death, can be dangerous for the living. It can bring somebody close to the dark border of death as well. This border to the underworld, to Hades, is not to be transgressed by living mortals. The dreamer is thrown back by a huge power that seems to be connected to or to be coming from the fire, and the dog itself makes it clear that her mistress cannot follow her. Anubis is the one who guides the deceased to the other world. In the dream, he makes it clear that the moment for the dreamer to leave our world has not yet come. On an objective level, we must leave the door open to the possibility that in this case also the real dog might be meant, although hardy any scientist would approve this hypothesis. It is a matter of feeling. «I will always stay with you» is the last word from the dog, before it disappears to the other

60 M.-L. von Franz, *On Dreams and Death,* p. 80.

61 Th. Abt and E. Hornung, *Knowledge for the Afterlife*, p. 72.

side. Is it the dog itself in a kind of subtle body form, or is it somehow a personal instinctual connection to the Beyond, which we call the collective unconscious, that will remain true to this woman?

This dream is full of archetypal images speaking about death and the transition to the other world. We must consider that it can only partly be explained in a psychological way. To a large extent, it also seems to be one of those archetypal dreams of which Marie Louise von Franz says in her book *On Dreams and Death*: «Somehow they cannot be interpreted very well on the subjective level, that is, as symbolic representations of subjective inner processes. This means that they cannot [...] be 'psychologised'. One feels compelled to leave them in space as a symbolic statement about another reality from which we are separated by a mysterious and dangerous barrier.»[62]

What strikes me with this dream is that it speaks about the dead dog with the light shining on it, just as it would about a human being, as if animals had a psyche like humans. This seems only natural to us, who identify with the happiness of a playful dog, or with all the emotional expressions of animals we can share with our feeling, or when we observe our pets and horses dreaming. However, this fact was certainly never taken into account by the Christian church, where animals were supposed not to have a soul. They therefore had not to be treated according to the Christian ideal of charity, but have been left to the mercy of human stupidity, egotism and cruelty to this day. In the light of such a dream, the evil we inflict on animals, consciously or unconsciously, intentionally or out of necessity or for other reasons, would be a crime no less serious than if we did it to humans. We cannot know whether an animal has a soul or not, but if, as appears from such a dream, we had the idea that it had, it could make all the difference in the world to our attitude towards animals. Although we cannot not avoid becoming guilty just by living life, as Jung says,[63] the burden of being conscious of this fact could at least make us more humble and more related to animals. It makes no difference whether this animal is a dog or a cat or just an ant or a grasshopper, as long as we realise as much as possible what we are doing to them. Ultimately we would have to realise

62 M.-L. von Franz, *On Dreams and Death*, p. 157.

63 C. G. Jung, *Mysterium Coniunctionis* [*Coll. Works* 14], § 200. «The opposites are the ineradicable and indispensable preconditions of all psychic life, so much so that life itself is guilt.»

Fig. 21: Canopic chest of Queen Nedjmet. Ancient Egypt, Late 20th Dyn., 1188- 1075. BC.

that all animals are also part of our own psyche. Animals correspond to our innate modes of instincts, which we bring into life as human beings. They belong to us as part of our own nature. This insight is so revolutionary, so divorced from our usual collective and individual attitude towards animals, that we obviously need such great compensatory dreams as that of the deceased little dog.

The next dream is from a 50-year-old woman who had also lost her dog. At the time of the dream, she was in despair about a situation where she could not see any solution, but when the darkness is deepest, the unconscious sometimes comes up with an enlightening dream.

Nr. 24: Dream of the deceased dog coming back:

I do not remember the beginning of the dream and its circumstances. What I remember is seeing a being, (perhaps a human being but I am not sure) or some other worldly creature who is able to morph itself into other creatures in nature. I not only see but also experience this being as it transforms itself into a bee buzzing through the leaves of a thick tropical forest. I see and feel the leaves that seem gigantic when one moves or flies through them like an insect.

This process continues and the being takes the form of other creatures in the wild and I am right there with it but I know that this is not happening to me but to it. I am just participating in this magical event in a direct and yet indirect way which is hard to articulate. But the only creature that I remember now is the bee.

Now I am standing in the kitchen of my house (not actual house or kitchen) that is located in a beautiful sunny meadow-like place close to the forest. I see my dog, which is completely rejuvenated and looks like a young dog again, run into the house. I know that she was involved in the earlier scene and she may even have been the creature that was morphing into other creatures or closely associated with it. My heart is brimming with indescribable joy, love and excitement at the sight of her excited-looking, beautiful face.

She has a wild look on her face and is panting heavily, which makes me realise that she is extremely thirsty. I look for a dish to fill with water for her and am nervously fumbling through the dishes trying to find one deep enough to hold sufficient water for her. As I am reaching into the drawer below the sink, I see her standing on the kitchen counter next to the sink (to my right) staring at the running water impatiently.

I know at once that her journey through the forest and the experience of morphing into different creatures are what has healed her ailments and renewed her completely. I even have a sense that she has indeed come back from the dead. My heart almost stops beating from joy and gratitude that my beloved companion has come back to me renewed like this because now I can have many more years with her.

Here the dead dog seems to have come back into the life of the dreamer instead of leaving her. On this journey back into life it is morphing through the tropical forest from the insect into different creatures until it reappears renewed in the dreamer's kitchen. Death has somehow been a starting point to re-creation. The tropical forest is an image of the part of the psyche near the somatic, the bodily processes, for the autonomous (vegetative) nervous system. Bees and insects only have a sympathetic nervous system, which is a part of the autonomous nervous system. The sympathetic nervous system sustains the equilibrium of life without sense organs, regulates the vegetative functions of the body, where emotions have their roots and triggers off processes in the body like the heightening of the heart rate, blood pressure etc.[64] It is located in the spinal cord. When we are furious, for example, the blood rushes to the head and we start to sweat, without being able to do anything about it. Thus the roots of the emotions lie in the sympathetic nervous system and so body and psyche are, in a certain sense, still undifferentiated. This helps us to understand better the psychological significance of the bee or insect as a symbol. They are connected to the innermost area of the collective unconscious, where psyche and matter unite and where the emotions are generated.

This first part of the dream already conveys the fact that the revived dog is somehow part of the dreamer herself. In the beginning there is this uncertainty about the «human being or otherwise worldly creature», and a sort of identification with this being. *«I cannot only see but I also experience this being as it transforms itself into a bee buzzing through the leaves of a thick tropical forest. I see and feel the leaves that seem gigantic when one moves or flies through them as an insect.»* And: *«I am just participating in*

64 C. G. Jung, *Archetypes of the Collective Unconscious.* [Coll. Works 9/1], §41.

this magical event in a direct and yet indirect way which is hard to articulate". The whole process of transformation also seems to be part of her, developing out of the deepest emotional level of the psyche. So one could try a first interpretation and say that an instinct, that has to do with eros and relationship, projected onto the real dog, seemingly lost with its death, is now coming to life in the psyche of the dreamer.

The revived dog that has emerged from the tropical forest, i.e. from the collective unconscious, cannot live without water. So we have to look at the symbol of the water. In antiquity, water was always associated with the origin of life and with the creation of the world. In its mysterious flowing, reflecting, changing quality, in its eternal movement, water is one of the most important symbols for the unconscious, from whose invisible depths all psychic life feeds and develops. According to the Arab mystic and alchemist of the tenth century, Mohammed ibn Umail, known in the West as Senior, God created all things from water. «It is the one living thing that does not die so long as the world lasts, and which revives all dead things [...]. Every man needs this water, *which is within him, and without which he cannot exist.*»[65] This water is an image for a source of life in man's own soul.[66] The dreamer herself has it – so to speak – in her hands to keep this renewed instinct alive, by giving it water. By her own relation to the unconscious, she can provide her dog with water of life, with soul water, so that it can stay with her as a living psychic reality.

However, the process of re-creation seems to be an exhausting and painful one for the dog, like all childbirth. One explanation might be that all transformation of unconscious contents into consciousness is, seen from the part of the unconscious, a deprivation or a loss. This is why the fire, the light of consciousness in many myths and legends, had to be stolen from the gods, and it was even severely punished by them. The suffering of the dog can be seen as the suffering of nature itself arising from the process of becoming conscious. Instinct is nature and wants nature. Consciousness, in the first instance, means opposition to nature.[67] Still there is somehow in nature this longing for and focus upon consciousness, evident, for instance, in the amazingly clear guidance of many dreams. Jung explains that in

65 M.-L. von Franz, *Psyche and Matter*, p. 177.

66 R. Abt, I. Bosch, V. MacKrell, *Dream Child*, p.17-44.

67 C. G. Jung, *The Structure and Dynamics of the Psyche* [*Coll. Works* 8], § 750.

looking at hundreds of dreams, he could trace a sort of underlying concept or plan. The dreams seemed to be linked to each other and to be «subordinated to a common goal, so that a long dream-series no longer appears as a senseless string of incoherent and isolated happenings, but resembles the successive steps in a planned and orderly process of development. I have called this unconscious process spontaneously expressing itself in the symbolism of a long dream-series the individuation process.»[68] Our dream of the re-creation of the dog seems to be one of these individuation dreams.

The dog in the dream had also something to do with the dreamer's feeling function. We must therefore say something about the four functions of consciousness, that is sensation, thinking, intuition and feeling, which each person seems to develop in his or her special way. Jung's view of the four-fold structure of consciousness was initially a matter of experience and of verifying by observation. He pointed out that «it seems to be an inborn disposition of the human being to build up a four-functional conscious system.»[69] Later he found the confirmation of this idea in the fact that the four-fold structure of the psyche appears everywhere in myths and religious symbols. Usually one can see that even children tend to do the things they like to do more often, and so one side becomes more differentiated. So if one does not influence a child, he or she will automatically develop one conscious function more than the other ones. If we imagine the four functions on a quartered circle, we have on top the most developed, the most conscious, the main function, for instance thinking (fig. 22). On the opposite there would be the place of the inferior function, the one that we have hardly at our conscious disposition, in this case feeling. In between there are the auxiliary functions, here sensation and opposed to it intuition. Within these four functions, there are innumerable possibilities of combinations. As the dreamer sensed herself, the dog in her dream had to do with her feeling function. As she was a thinking type with a good auxiliary intuition, feeling was her inferior function, which means that feeling is deeply connected to the unconscious. Thinking in connection to intuition would be her usual way of dealing with life, while feeling was her weak spot.

68 Ibid., § 550.

69 M.-L. von Franz, *The Interpretation of Fairytales*, p. 56.

We might recall here the dream mentioned above of the other thinking-type woman about the dog *«which turned around like the finger of a clock. When its head faced me its eyes were closed, when it faced the other side, the side of the witches' house, its eyes were opened.»*

Facing the side of the witch, the unconscious shadow side, the dog, the inferior feeling side, can see and can show the way, whereas facing the ego consciousness, it is blind. So the inferior feeling function can be a soul guide, because it can connect us to the unconscious, but its coming into

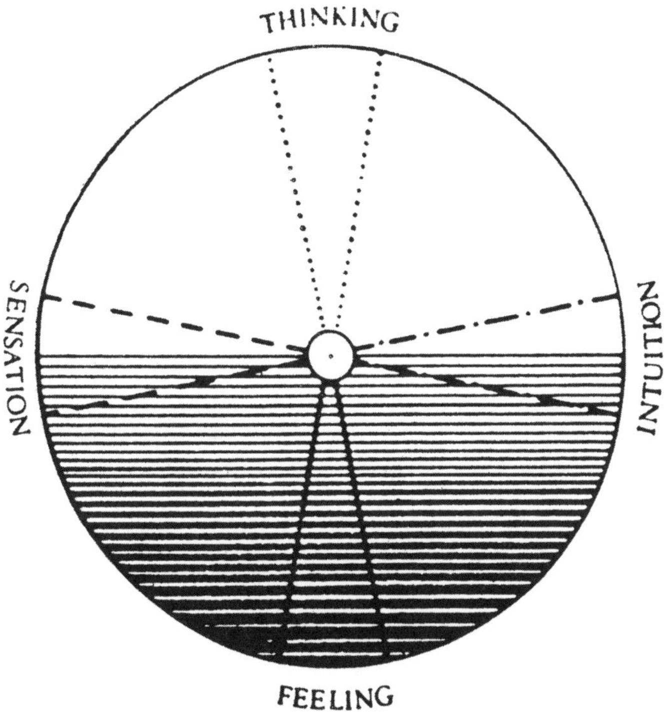

Fig. 22: The four functions of consciousness according to C. G. Jung. The main function here is thinking, while, in this case, the feeling function below in the dark is the inferior function.

consciousness might imply trouble, because there it is blind. When unconscious feeling comes up it usually appears as uncontrolled or 'blind' emotion. To give it water, to let it live, is therefore not without the risk of losing control. Obviously the dreamer's attitude towards the unconscious was healthy and the feeling for her real dog helped her to welcome the experience without cutting it off by a too rational or analytical standpoint. So the dog, her instinctual feeling, could undergo a natural transformation and appear in her conscious life, which gave her the comfort a real dog would.

With all these amplifications we can only approach its meaning up to a certain point, but what really happens in the deep levels of the psyche remains mysterious and also must be seen in connection with other dreams of this woman. The dream had a great emotional impact on her. When she woke up, she felt deeply supported by the self and assured that she was not alone. She felt that while she was doing her work, the unconscious was undergoing regeneration at a deep level and as such, she knew that all would be well.

I would now like to bring a shortened version of a German fairytale which mirrors the problem of the correct behavior towards animals. The title could be translated as "The cake" (Da Guglhupf). The motif of this fairytale is well known all over the world in innumerable versions.[70]

There was once a vicious mother with two daughters. One of them was kind and diligent, the other one evil, like the mother. The mother loved the nasty one and hated the kind one. She sent this girl out to bake an ash cake in an empty castle.[71] *When she had baked the cake, a little dog, a cat and a cock appeared and asked for a piece of the cake. The girl gave it to them, the animals thanked her and assured her of their help. Then they left. Soon afterwards, two black devils appeared and threw a sack of money at her feet. She took the money home and of course the mother sent the other*

70 For instance in "The Three Little Men in the Wood". The Complete Grimm's Fairtytales, Nr. 13.

71 It is not quite clear in the text of the tale, whether if this is a cake that has to be baked in the ash in a baking pan, as it was usually done, or if it is a cake done made out of ash. The latter seems more probable, as the fairytale teller seems to put weightstress onto this detail as something extraordinary. It makes also more sense symbolically.

daughter to the castle to get some money too. This daughter, though, when she was asked by the animals for a piece of the cake, wanted the money in advance to make sure she got enough. When the devils appeared she called for help to the animals and promised to give them something in return, but they said that she had not given them anything earlier and that they did not trust her. So the devils tore her to pieces. The mother went mad and disappeared, and the kind girl married and was happy ever after.[72]

In this version, evil results from the greed and avarice of the mother and her nasty daughter. There is obviously the cake lacking in this feminine trinity, the warm nourishing eros. Baking an ash cake means using up the most worthless left overs that in fact cannot be eaten. It is the prima materia of the alchemists that ultimately has to be transformed into gold. It looks useless at first, but nevertheless the work with it is obviously desired by the animals, by the unconscious and ultimately there might result not only something nourishing, but also money, or – in alchemical language – gold out of it. The baking of the ash cake may have something to do with accepting the seemingly worthless rubbish of one's life, all the failures, shortcomings and one's own shadow nuisances, and taking up the hopeless task of transforming it into something nourishing by giving it warmth, emotion, feeling. While the one daughter honestly and without questioning takes up the task of baking a cake that seems to be inedible and relates fondly to animals, the other one is greedy and calculating and is therefore grabbed by the devils. A calculating attitude towards the unconscious in all the fairytales of this type is severely punished. If there is no honesty and devotion in taking up what appears from the unconscious, there is no help from the instincts against bedevilment and fragmentation of the conscious personality. This is what happens to the evil daughter.

The two devils seem to be in collaboration with the three animals. They can be seen as an embodiment of the alchemical "Mercurius duplex", who was also called the hidden spirit of the truth, good with the good and evil with the evil, as he appears in this fairytale. In his dark appearance, Mercurius is often identified with Lucifer and the Devil. Today, following Jung, we call Mercurius the spirit of the unconscious. Whether or not the

72 "Da Guglhupf" in: *Deutsche Märchen aus dem Donauland*, p. 25 (shortened by me).

spirit of the unconscious appears in his benevolent or in his destructive form obviously depends on how the ego relates to the animals. Animals represent instinctive impulses whose intention cannot be understood from the beginning, just like there seems to be no point in baking an ash- cake.

Fig. 23: Mummy Tablet with Anubis, wearing the keys of the Last Judgement. From the necropole of Trithion, Upper Egypt, Roman Times.

In every life there are situations where one asks oneself why things have to be as they are, looking worthless and meaningless, causing nothing but trouble and suffering. One cannot understand why the old witch with her daughter, the unconscious itself, has provoked such a problem. We might just realize that there is a goal-oriented meaning behind it that might grow out of the ambivalent nature of the unconscious. Fairytales, though, confirm that without a truthful and loving attitude towards the instincts, there is no help from them against the shadow. There is no money which would symbolize energy to deal with material existence, nor gold that can be understood as meaning the indestructible value of higher consciousness.

The following dream of a 49-year-old woman, who for a long time had no relation to dogs, seems to show a reconciliation with the dog instinct and a partial sacrifice of the dominance of consciousness:

Nr. 25: Dream of having to beg for the dog's help:

Someone has brought me a dog – or introduced me to a dog – because it was an honour to meet it, and I had to learn how to cope with it. First I tried to treat it 'normally' by giving orders, but this did not really work. Then the insight came to me like a flash: I had to beg for the dog's help! I, the human being, had to beg the dog, the animal, to help me. This was the truth, even if it turns the world order upside down. I promised to do it that way from then on. But what did it mean?

The dream says that she has to learn to cope with the dog. She cannot master it. Only when she can accept the basic autonomy of this unconscious instinct and accept its superiority might it become helpful. Indeed the unconscious *is* a reality, not just a theoretical construct, and this turns our extraverted world upside down! But with the help of a dog, a relationship to the unconscious becomes possible. That was a clear message which remained with the dreamer! It helped her to stay connected to the world of the unconscious with her feeling.

Sometimes dream images are threatening or more or less opposed to the conscious tendency. Jung used here the term 'compensation' for the restitution of the normal psychic balance.[73] This means that if the attitude of consciousness towards the life situation is highly one-sided, the dream is putting weight on the opposite side. If we are striving too much to the right, the dream will pull towards the left. If we are too high up, the dream might put us right down on the ground etc. To recognize the compensation in the dream, one has to know about the conscious situation of the dreamer. On the other hand, compensating may "illuminate the patient's situation in a way that can be exceedingly beneficial to health. They bring him memories, insights, experiences, awaken dormant qualities in the personality, and reveal the unconscious element in his relationships. "[74]

73 C. G. Jung, *The Stucture and Dynamics of the Psyche* [Coll. Works 8], §545 and §547.

74 Ibid, § 549.

There is a dream of a 45-year-old woman at the beginning of her analysis. During the analysis, this woman had many dreams about losing her dog which seemed to have to do with her negative mother complex. She was suffering in everyday life from her very old, mischievous mother and did not seem to be able to free herself from her. This mother, as a parson's widow, hid a terrible witch shadow behind her Christian attitude of always being good and helpful. As a child, the dreamer, unbeknown to the parishioners, had suffered cruelty and mistreatment from her and also from her pious father, behind the thick walls of the parson's house. As a grown-up woman, she tried hard to be good, as if she could cause life to show its more positive side towards her. At the same time, she could not bear any insight into her own witch shadow. For this woman, horses and dogs, belonging to the positive aspect of Mother Nature, had acquired life-saving importance, compensating the destructive influence of her negative mother complex.

Nr. 26: Dream of the dog falling from the roof:

I am walking with our little dog up a steep hill which ends on the horizon. I wonder what will be beyond the horizon. The dog advances by himself and suddenly disappears behind the summit. I run after him, because I want to know where he is going. As I reach the summit, I see my dog on a brick roof. Underneath the roof there is deep, green water. The dog is sliding down the roof towards the deep water. I cannot save it because my arms are too short and I might fall down myself, by leaning too far forward. I cannot see the dog falling, because I wake up in horror. I am very sad and resigned to what has happened.

From the dream we could understand that her dog instinct, her scenting nose, was to guide her to new horizons, where new spiritual perspectives or insights were possible. But the dog ends up in a dangerous situation. Houses often symbolically mirror the ego personality. Little children paint houses like human beings, with the windows as eyes, the roof as a hat on the top of the head etc. The roof protects the house from wind, snow and rain. It marks, so to speak, the border between the conscious realm and the spiritual world. We can say, that the guiding instinct, instead of being able to open the way to a new view, is somehow blocked at the personal limits of consciousness. At this dangerous point of transition, this important instinctual impulse gets lost and disappears from the level of consciousness. The dreamer is not able to get hold of it and to save it. In trying to hold it, she, too, might even be pulled down and drowned in the unconscious.

The dream mirrors a dangerous situation. The dog instinct, which could compensate the darkness of the motherly unconscious and be a guide into a new standpoint in life, is swallowed back by the unconscious, and the dreamer, despite her great struggle, is in danger of falling back into regression and depression. A later dream by the same woman, which is clearer in its compensating tendency, goes as follows:

Nr. 27: Dream of the signpost in the shape of a cross:

I am walking through our garden. Suddenly I see a great signpost made of dog excrement in the shape of a cross. Additionally there are some footprints, also consisting of dog excrement. The signpost points to our kitchen and somebody says that my mother has died.

The dog, in contrast to the frightening end of the last dream, has not disappeared but leaves its footprints in a weird way! Yet stinking and disgusting excrement in dreams often has the meaning of a creative product and as such can be quite positive! They are, so to speak, *prima materia,* the dung which, according to the alchemists, contains the gold. They belong to a strong instinctive power one has to deal with in everyday life, namely the shadow sides we usually prefer to hide more or less from our nearest and from ourselves. Through trying too hard to be decent, we are cut off from our roots, our instincts, and it starts stinking. The shadow brings us into a serious conflict. Depression might ensue, because with the shadow we also repress instinctive life energy.[75] That was the case with this woman, whose puritanical education cut her off from precisely this instinctive life energy. Her ethical Christian attitude, of course, would never have admitted that she had in her unconscious anything other than honest striving for the good. As a compensation, the dream placed this whole lot of stinking, revolting 'shit' into her garden.

75 M.-L. von Franz, *Shadow and Evil in Fairytales*, p. 69.

Now what about the kitchen? In olden times the kitchen with its stove was the centre of the house, protected by the mother goddess Hera, and the setting for the house cults. It was the place of feminine creativity, the warm and nourishing motherly centre for the whole house and family. The signpost indicates that the dreamer has, so to speak, to follow the tracks of the dog's excrement to get to what could be the place of her own nourishing feminine creativity, until now dominated by her negative mother.

The signpost has the shape of a cross and it consists of dog excrement, a very strange image. After having looked at each of the three symbols separately, the excrement, the cross and the signpost, we might be able to suggest their one meaning. First of all, the repulsive connection of excrement and cross was not acceptable to the dreamer, nor is it really for us. We therefore have to consider the wider meaning of this most important symbol of the cross. Jung defines the cross as one of the most primordial symbols that has always meant *mana* or life- power.[76] As an eternally living symbol, it is already found in the Paleolithic Age, and it has not lost its value through the ages. It is by the four cardinal points that man marks an orientation in space. It is therefore a most archaic symbol of order and orientation. The symbol of the cross is found all over the earth, even in Mexico, Peru and Central America before Christianity reached there. There it can also have the meaning of 'the world tree', the 'tree of life', the 'cosmic tree'.[77] Christian legends, too, made the cross, 'tree of death' to a 'tree of life' and as such, it is also a mother symbol.[78] In Christianity, it symbolises the divine suffering for the salvation of mankind. The cross for the good Christian also has the function of banishing the Devil. The symbolic meaning of the cross would in this case have to be understood, as Jung pointed out, not as a means of getting rid of the Devil but of integrating him into the Christian trinity as the fourth aspect of the divine. There he had to have his place as the anti-Christian side of God, integrated rather than constantly threatening to seize control. In the personal psyche, this would mean not repressing the devilish destructive complex nor, on the other hand, letting it take over, but accepting it as belonging to one's own psyche, and consciously suffering

76 C. G. Jung, *Dream Analysis*, p. 340-365.

77 Ibid, p. 346 f.

78 C. G. Jung, *Symbols of Transformation* [Coll. Works 5], § 411-415.

Fig. 24: Aztec dog. The dog is «the essence of relatedness, pure, reliable loyalty, the most faithful eros.» (M.-L. von Franz, CALA I A, § 327.)

from the resulting conflict. So the cross symbolizes the suffering from the opposites of good and evil in one's own psyche.

In this context, we might remember the shock Jung had in his early vision of the cathedral of Basel: «I gathered all my courage [...] and let the thought come. I saw before me the cathedral, the blue sky. God sits on His golden throne, high above the world – and from under the throne an enormous turd falls upon the sparkling new roof, shatters it, and breaks the walls of the cathedral asunder.» This vision left its imprint on Jung's whole life because it shattered the Christian image of a good god and raised the question of what this would mean for empirical man.[79] The everyday actuality of this problem is mirrored in our dream, dreamed by a woman of our days, who in her childhood had experienced the hard way the dark and incomprehensible backside of Christian goodness. The cross made of dog 'shit' in her garden has to do with this unsolved conflict in her own personality.

As a universal symbol of order, the cross has the function of an order-creating centre in the psyche in which the opposites such as good and evil, above and below, spiritual and material world, consciousness and the unconscious, sky and earth etc. are united. "Carrying one's cross" also has the meaning of carrying the burden of one's own self and destiny.

Keeping the dream of the dog on the roof in the back of our mind, we can understand the cross as the dreamer's suffering from the conflict of opposites of 'above and below', with her longing for the spiritual realm above, and the water of the unconscious with the danger of overwhelming depression below, with her Christian ideal of striving for the good above, and the threatening shadow below. With the dog falling from the roof, the conflict reaches a dramatic climax. The cross could be the uniting symbol that connects the two realms.

A signpost has the function of pointing one in a certain direction. It shows us the way to go. So the signpost/cross of stinking dog excrement pointing to the kitchen, might be an image for a creative – albeit hard to accept life impulse from the unconscious. Despite its terrible appearance it means salvation and gives direction to the feminine self. Consisting of

79 M.-L. von Franz, *C. G. Jung – His Myth in our Time*, p. 158 f.

excrement, it has to do with the problems of the shadow, the *prima materia* of psychic development. The 'shit' is a crude image for the fact that in the 'shit' of one's own unconscious shadow, the footprints of the guiding instinct and a uniting order can become visible. The signpost/cross of dog 'shit' is the guiding symbol left by the dog to the dreamer, even if it seems utterly unacceptable. It points the way for the dreamer to accept the unacceptable in her own soul and to the insight that this also belongs to God.

The fact that the negative mother is announced as dead does not relate to the real mother, who went on to live for many years. It means that the negative mother complex could now lose its destructive influence. If the dreamer could have grasped the message of the dream, the dog might have had a healing effect on her eros and her relationships, which were so damaged by her mother. Unfortunately there was probably too much shadow 'shit', so that she could not stand it and her suffering continued for a long time. At that time, and we can empathize with her, it was too much of a strain for her to follow the footprints of the dog instinct, the soul guide which could have guided her through the devilish shadow problem and might have enabled her to leave behind the tragic background of her childhood. Maybe the dream was just hinting at the strain and could be understood as a signal to the analyst.

The dog instinct that knows how to deal with the shadow is described in the great Norwegian 'dog-tale', the fairytale "Prince Ring" that M.-L. von Franz dealt with in depth in her book *The Interpretation of Fairytales*.[80] There, the dog Snati-Snati is an enchanted prince, a helpful character for the hero Prince Ring through all his trials. It is only from him that the knowledge comes about how to deal with evil, with threatening shadow sides. The gloomy shadow consists of all the dark emotions and impulses that have still not been integrated, such as envy, jealousy, hatred and murderous greed. In this fairytale, all this is contained in the character of Rauder, the evil minister of the king. Snati Snati is a helpful watchdog, a mediating instinct that can warn about and deal with such destructive shadow tendencies. This is – in the end – healing for the whole psyche.

80 M.-L.von Franz, *The Interpretation of Fairytales*, p. 115f.

Being connected to the instincts always has a healing effect, and it is especially true for the relationship to a dog, because the dog is more related to men than any other animal. Never have I been made more aware of the *healing function* of a dog than when I saw our German shepherd dog take care of a little kindergarten girl. This girl had been a victim of abuse by her stepfather. When she came to the kindergarden, she hardly spoke a word for more than a year, nor did she play or laugh with the other children. Once a week our daughter, who was her teacher, took our dog along for a play morning with the children, out into the forest. The girl, after first being scared by the dog, slowly approached it all by herself, each time a bit more closely, until she was able to touch and caress it, which the dog tolerated with patience and gentle consideration. From then on, the girl always tried to stay close to it and I could see them sitting together in the wood, the child with her arm around the dog. Although the dog sometimes would have preferred to stroll around, it stayed patiently sitting with the girl, with an expression of 'I am fulfilling a dog's duty' on its face! For this girl, the dog signified a warm eros relationship, free from worries, and the beginning of a first hint of trust, also in humans. Within another year she also learned to play and to laugh more with her schoolmates and she started to speak normally. The dog certainly played a crucial role in that process. There was also an extremely difficult boy in that group who developed amazingly in his ability to relate to other children through the contact with this gentle dog. There is growing appreciation nowadays of the importance and the benefits of introducing dogs into education and therapy (fig. 25).

We find this healing function in a dog's character but also within the psyche. Dogs and snakes were associated with Asclepios, the Greek healing god, who was nourished with dog's milk as a baby.[81] Although a human, he even brought a dead man back to life and was killed by a thunderbolt as a punishment. It seems that in the Aesculapian temple of Epidaurus, sacred dogs as well as serpents took part in the healing ceremonies and were, so to speak, the living repository for the healing power of the god.[82] Because dogs can heal themselves by licking their wounds, people believed they could do this for human beings too (fig. 26). This idea is based on the psychological fact that sometimes we just need simple, warm,

81 Angelo De Gubernatis, *Die Thiere in der indogermanischen Mythologie*, p. 358.

82 B. Hannah, *The Cat, Dog and Horse Lectures*, p. 104.

Fig. 25: Ascha with Kindergarden children.

loving care to feel good! And this is healing. The little girl whose feminine personality was so badly wounded was comforted by being accepted by that big dog. The faithful dog in dreams and fairytales symbolizes a soft inner voice associated with trust in one's own soul. To realize such a 'dog-impulse' is not always easy because what it does for our soul's sake is often so inconspicuous and unpretentious. It is easily underestimated by extraverted activity and the demands of daily life.

We know that the dog as a healing figure in Europe was even the subject of a pagan cult. In an article, Regine Schweizer [83] reveals that in pagan Europe a sacred dog named Guinefort was worshipped until the 13th century. The forest of the holy Guinefort still exists. The legend tells that

83 R. Schweizer, "Anima animalis. Der heilige Hund", *Jungiana* Band 8, p. 49 f.

a dog killed a snake that was threatening the lord of the castle's baby in its cradle. When people found the blood-spattered dog above the cradle, they assumed it had killed the baby and they murdered it. Only later did they saw that the baby was still alive and that the dog, which had been killed, was innocent and had saved the child's life by killing the snake. They buried the dog and planted trees on its grave. This shrine became an object of worship, a worship that has continued in one form or another up to modern times, despite being suppressed as heresy by the Church. The story of the faithful dog that has been killed despite its innocence is a common motif that may have its origins in the Orient, says R. Schweizer. It can even be found in China. In medieval times there were about 60 Guinefort shrines in Europe, where he was considered to be the arbiter of life and death – either he healed or he sent death: «A Saint Guinefort, pour la vie où pour la mort.» (To Saint Guinefort, for life or for death.)

According to the story of the faithful dog, it seems as if consciousness had a tendency to misunderstand this instinct or even to accuse it of evil. This can only be made up for by worship. The dog signifies the «instinctive basis upon which to be faithful towards one's own nature and soul.»[84] This instinctive basis is healing and determines whether life may flow or come to a complete standstill. «Pour la vie où pour la mort.»

In the following dream, the dog has a guiding function. He is leading the way to a spiritual world or a spiritual development that ultimately also means healing.

Nr. 28: Dream of the pilgrimage:

Together with my parents we are on a holiday trip. We want to climb the highest and only mountain in this region. We are accompanied by friends of ours from the Spanish pilgrimage, the Way of St. James. Halfway up the mountain we stop; maybe the others don't want to go on because the path is too steep...

This time I'm alone, climbing up the same mountain but on another path. In contrast to the first one, this path goes up to the left. Possibly there is a dog with me. The path is so steep that it is difficult to go on. On the left-hand side there are old steps made of concrete, perhaps constructed by

84 R. Schweizer, "Anima animalis. Der heilige Hund", *Jungiana* Band 8, p. 71.

Fig. 26: Lazarus with wound-licking dogs. Burgundy (France), ca. 1100.

M.-L. von Franz. There are banisters on the left. I decide to venture up these stairs. It is not so easy to keep my balance, because my left hand is not free. I am carrying something – or holding a dog's leash. I come to a crossroads on the path, to the right and to the terrace in the direction of where the others are. I wonder if I should go up to the peak alone or if I should try to approach the others. But I could get lost in the wilderness. I decide to continue up this way, because I definitely want to go up the mountain.

In real life, the dreamer had made the pilgrimage to Santiago de Compostela on foot through France and Spain. This dream speaks about another pilgrimage and the goal is the mountain. Because the top of a mountain is close to heaven, it became a symbol for revelation and spiritual self-understanding. In myths and fairytales, it is often the goal of a long quest or the passage to eternity. Climbing a mountain in dreams often points to the life goal of individuation.

The left path in the dream is the way of the unconscious, which Marie-Louise von Franz has improved by making steps, thus facilitating the climb to higher consciousness and self-understanding. This section of the path is very steep and has to be taken alone. It is not a collective or popular way, like the Way of St. James, and it is difficult to keep one's balance while also holding onto a dog's leash. Luckily there are banisters on the left-hand side as well as the concrete steps. We have here the motif of Jacob's ladder, which means that the way towards a higher consciousness must be accomplished step by step. The dream describes beautifully how we could get lost on this way if we were to get diverted by the crossroads. For the dreamer, the books and the life of Marie-Louise von Franz were the stepping-stones in her quest for consciousness. She did not know Marie-Louise von Franz personally but she had heard a lot about her and read her books.

Today the pilgrimage to Santiago de Compostela in Spain has an increasingly important meaning for many people as a spiritual quest. They feel that something essential is missing in their lives and therefore they embark on this highly symbolic pilgrimage. Many of them are not members of the Catholic Church. This dream emphasises that for the dreamer her quest has to be of an individual nature, accompanied by the invisible dog to the left – her own instinct. The main problem is finding her balance as the dreamer's left hand is not free. This is the side of the unconscious. Indeed, the path of individuation means the balance between the inner and the outer world, between the demands of the unconscious and those of outer life. With every dream we have to make a new tricky decision about how much and how far we shall, can or must go with the dream's realisation in our life and what might be right in each specific situation. This is one of the most difficult things to do. The dog's leash on the left-hand side in this dream could be a guide in the sense of a connection to an instinct, helping the dreamer to make the right decision.

Sometimes the invisible or inner dog seems to draw us to the wrong side. In such a case we might have understood a dream too much in accordance with to our own expectations and desires. The dog therefore has to be watched carefully! This brings us to some other aspects of the dog symbol that are not helpful at first sight, because they have to do with *laziness, greediness, sexuality and aggressiveness.* Dogs are pretty lazy. They could sleep the whole day, only exerting themselves during short intervals of exercise. And indeed we can always be misled by laziness, but also by sexual greed or seductive scents!

It is the subtle task of consciousness to find out and then to decide whether or not it can accept the way of the dog or what he is doing. In fairytales and myths, the dog is promiscuous and a real *trickster.*[85] The Indians of North America have a lot of tales about the coyote, who loves to pull the wool over people's eyes. Whenever we meet the dog in the ancient world, we also find erotic promiscuity. In its erotic aspect, the mythological dog is part of life and creation. As we have seen, it is a bringer of fire. But if we want it to enter our real life, we must be careful. Its guidance in the unconscious is undoubtedly precious, but if we do not understand the symbolism in the right way it can mislead us. Relying too much on the dog in blind confidence might put us onto the wrong path or even into a kind of obsession. An instructive example of this is the following dream of a woman. It shed light onto a difficult marriage situation. The dreamer's husband was at that time involved in an affair with another woman.

Nr. 29: Dream of the dog stealing a cake:

Our dog has stolen a big golden-yellow cake and is running away with it, scampering around in the garden. My husband acts as if he wanted to beat it with something though in fact this is not really his intention. But I think the dog should really be punished and the cake should be taken away. I'm getting angry.

Here the dog is connected with an instinctive greed that transgresses the boundary between the world of humans and that of dogs. Naturally this man's wife is getting angry. After she had told her husband this dream, he couldn't help thinking about it. It was his gluttonous dog, a sexual instinctive

85 C. G. Jung, "About the trickster's psychology" in: *The Archetypes and the Collective Unconscious* [Coll.Works 9/I], § 456-488.

greed which kept him too much involved with the 'sweet cake' of the other relationship. The dog in the aspect of a thief suggested to him that this was his food, allowing and encouraging him to go ahead on the physical level. The dream was really enlightening. Also this dog, although a greedy thief, was in the service of self-awareness.

Another aspect of the dog symbol has to do with the dangerous barrier between the living and the dead, which we have already mentioned. In Greek mythology, we have at this barrier the three-headed dog *Cerberus*, originally also a god of death and the furious watchdog of Pluto, the god of the Underworld. No one enters the Beyond without passing Cerberus. Symbolically this dog instinct blocks the door to the unconscious. Why is that so? During the development of consciousness, the instincts had to be tamed and hence have been more and more suppressed and devalued. Thus the conscious attitude has become disconnected or even in opposition to the unconscious, which provokes an angry reaction of the inner nature. The dog, which could connect the two worlds, becomes aggressive. The instinctual reactions of our dreams become threatening. Moreover, as mentioned before, becoming conscious, stealing the fire from the gods, is an act *contra naturam*. In nature, that is in the unconscious, the opposites lie dormant together. There is no separation between good and evil. The laws of nature do not bother about moral concepts. It is consciousness which tears the opposites of good and evil apart. The more one-sided and rigid the attitude of consciousness, the more dangerous the reaction of the unconscious. It is therefore a matter of wisdom always to be aware of the furious Cerberus. If there is also a certain weakness of the ego, the approach to and the invasion of the unconscious might result in dangerous inflation, confusion and panic. With a weak disposition, this can even lead to psychoses.[86] It is obvious that we cannot fight Cerberus, nor should we offend him. He is a powerful god, who can only be appeased by sacrifice.

In Greece, it was the custom to give honey cakes to the dead for their path to the underworld; this was in order to calm down Cerberus.[87] Honey has to do with the sweetness of eros. The gift of honey would mean an approach to the unknown with loving devotion. This attitude is also important in analysis. It is the only way to get along when we are, for

86 C. G. Jung, *Mysterium coniunctionis* [Coll. Works 14], § 178.

87 C. G. Jung, *Symbols of Transformation* [Coll. Works 5], § 577.

Fig. 27: Dog in front of the offering table, greedy for food. Ancient Egyptian humorous painting. Ancient Egypt, New Kingdom, 1540-1075 BC.

example, not successful in understanding our dreams in a satisfying way or when we are confronted with threatening shadow qualities.

The following dream of a woman, interpreted by M.-L. von Franz, mirrors a dangerous reaction of the dog instinct, and we will see that here it has to do with a wrong attitude towards the feminine.

Nr.30: Dream of attacking Doberman dogs:

In the dream I am lying on an enormous king-sized mattress. I mean huge! It is suspended, floating in the air. There is nothing else around it. No sheets, nothing. Over to my right I feel that something is approaching. It's a woman walking along at a distance with two Doberman dogs on leashes – black Dobermans. As she comes toward me, I keep watching her. She comes closer and closer. When she gets to about three feet, she looks straight down at me with disgust. (She has a babushka tied around her head.) She looks at me, lets go of the leashes, and the two dogs leap – zap!- right at my throat. And then I woke up. I couldn't breathe. I sat up in bed gasping for breath.[88]

[88] M.-L.von Franz, *The Way of the Dream*, p. 216.

M.-L. von Franz says that this woman's problem has to do with her floating in the air. Instead of having her feet on the ground, and being rooted in her instinctual feminine life and body, she floats in the realm of ideas, illusions and theoretical conceptions of life. The woman with the dogs is a mother figure, as she reminds the dreamer of her mother with the babushka on her head. The mother's realm is the earth, the body, the feminine life, the whole instinctive basis. In this case, the mother's fierce, aggressive dogs have to do with an instinct that has become hostile, because of the unnatural floating of the dreamer in mid-air.

In mythology, the dangerous side of the archetypal mother is mirrored in the figure of Hecate. Hecate is the howling goddess of the Underworld with a dog's head, who in late antiquity and the Middle Ages became the mother of all witches and demons of the night. Death, insanity, poison, treason, magic and black magic, all belong to her. This dark chthonic goddess is also often described as three-headed, being herself either a dog or accompanied by barking dogs.[89]

We find the dog as a ferocious beast everywhere in mythology and legends. Equal to the wolf, he then represents *untamed aggressiveness*. Our German shepherd dog, also known in German as the *wolfshund* (wolf dog), gentle though she was, transformed into a furious beast when confronted with a simulated burglar. If such dogs are not properly trained, they can easily become dangerous. When the Spanish came to the New World, they are reported to have used dogs to kill the inhabitants of the new country so that the dogs could be fed with their corpses. This aggressive, dangerous dog instinct can be misused for power. Although, or maybe precisely because German shepherd dogs are in fact the most benevolent animals, they became the favourite helpers of the German Nazis, who brought out their dangerous wolf-side by specific training. Hitler loved his German shepherd dog. The dangerous wolf/dog side appears in the dream of a 40-year-old woman. Here it is connected to the animus.

Nr. 31: Dream of the German shepherd dogs attacking a cat:

On the first floor of my parental home I was looking down on the meadow behind the house. At the boundary of the garden I saw how two

89 C. G. Jung, *Symbols of Transformation* [Coll. Works 5], § 577. Originally Hecate was a cosmic goddess of nature, a moon goddess, powerful in the ocean, the sky and on earth, and then, like all moon goddesses, a goddess of fertility, of marriage and birth.

German shepherd dogs (which look like wolves) were attacking a cat. They came closer and closer to it until at a certain point the cat jumped into the face of one of these Alsatian dogs. I knew that this was very courageous but also extremely dangerous because there was still the other dog that would now attack the cat from the rear. I had to help this cat somehow for it might have been my own cat and I couldn't just stand there and watch. I had to draw the dogs' attention to something else. So I started barking as loudly as I could. I was astonished myself at how I could bark. Just like a very big, dangerous dog. Well, I could almost bark like a wolf. The barking didn't really seem to come from myself but it came out of me and was most effective. The dogs were startled and finally backed off so that the cat could slip out between their legs and come to the house. In fact it wasn't my cat but a robust tiger cat I hadn't really known before. I was very relieved that it wasn't my cat, which would have had to fight for its own life. But I was also a little bit astonished that I had got so involved with a strange cat.

For the dreamer, German shepherd dogs were associated with the police, the army and the negative masculine fatherly aspect which was constellated in the relationship between her father and her timid, unhappy mother. The dreamer had in reality experienced her mother as extremely obstructive for her own development. In the dream there is a fight between the big dogs and the cat. The cat, which has to do with the positive mother and feminine independence, is being attacked by an unconscious aggressive impulse, the German shepherd dogs. In fact these mirrored not only her own animus, but also the animus of her mother. The problem of the mother was in this sense also her own. Her own animus could pose a threat to her independent, feminine side by sudden attacks. If an animus appears as an animal, this means that he is unconscious, and therefore hardly controllable. It can then occur, for instance, in the form of conceptions and opinions about how the world and how oneself should behave. Women thus sometimes build themselves a rigid set of prejudices, which can completely destroy their female cat-independence. Some women outwardly show an almost excessive conformism, a reluctance to draw attention to themselves, but lurking in the unconscious lies a malicous animus, which, to the astonishment of those around them, can sometimes rise to the surface as aggressive opinion tyranny. The cat in the dream indeed is very brave but the domination of the dogs is dangerous. The female side is too small, too weak even if it musters up all its courage and strength.

If we consider the cat as being her own independent feminine side, associated with the joy of life, the dreamer now has a great opportunity to understand how this cat quality of her soul is sometimes really endangered. Her mother's problem is also her own. But what can she do? Would we even try to get involved with two hostile German shepherd dogs? According to this dream, it can only be done successfully because the dream ego herself starts barking like a wolf.

In mythology, wolves also belong to the dark side of Apollo, to Mars and to Wotan. Wolves and black dogs in our legends rush along in the wild hunt with Wotan and the souls of dead people. They are daemonic dogs and linked to wild, unrestrained emotions and aggressions. The dreamer in this dream neither turns into a German shepherd dog herself nor does she plunge into the fight, but she can bark like one. It is a female wolf quality that surprisingly emerges in her and is able to fight the aggressive animus attack.

In Clarissa Pinkola-Este's book *Women Who Run with the Wolves* the author writes 540 pages about the wolf character in women that should be lived out to a greater extent to the benefit of their independent femininity.[90] This author must have catered for a deep need if we consider the enormous success of this book. Marie-Louise von Franz says that in the dreams of modern women, the wolf often represents the animus, or that strange devouring attitude women can have when possessed by the animus.[91] The danger of a book like *Women Who Run with the Wolves* could be that women misinterpret it as describing something on the outer level. As a consequence, the animus might capture the wolf image and just bring out more aggressiveness and greediness instead of a natural firmness of the feminine personality.

Because of the ambivalent nature of these archetypal symbols, it is important to face the German shepherd dog instinct as consciously as possible. Giving it free rein in the outside world can be dangerous. What happens in the dream mirrors an *inner* process.

Our dreamer can suddenly bark and in doing so, saves the cat. This is how we woman could handle evil. In this case, it is an instinctive reaction;

90 C. Pinkola-Estes, *Women who run with the Wolves*.

91 M.-L. von Franz, *Shadow and Evil in Fairytales*, p. 255.

the dreamer cannot do this by will power alone. It comes from inside and is as surprising as if she suddenly could really bark. *Simila similibus curantur* – likes are cured by likes – is the homeopathic principle. Our consciousness might have problems barking as wickedly as the wolf-dog instinct does when dealing with evil, inside or outside, even if it is the only possible course of action. Our Christian morality is far too much of an impediment. We are supposed to be good and not act in an evil way! So we are usually either too rational, which is sometimes not a bad thing, considering the dangerous Hecate wolf-instinct. Or else we are too sentimental. In fact there is on the one hand the danger of our becoming a wolf, which means to become possessed by our rage and aggression. On the other hand we tend to attract evil by too much consideration and kindness. The surprising solution is the barking from the instinctual basis. It is, so to speak, a *humanised wolf nature* that is able to chase its evil part away and to rescue the relationship to the cat. Women who are able to bark like a wolf will radiate a strength of personality that is less likely to provoke attacks from their surroundings than if they were always trying to be good, never to hurt anybody nor do anything wrong. Women who constantly have to defend themselves against the world's evil might try to listen to the instinct which enables them to bark like a wolf!

The next dream was dreamt by Barbara Hannah. It is not a dog-dream, but it deals with the problem of evil and the feminine in a most impressive way. It is one of the big dreams that needs to be told again and again.

Nr. 32: Dream from Chichester Cathedral and the Devil:

At the beginning of the last World War, I dreamt I was in Chichester cathedral, which contained an unfinished chapel where stones and other things were stored. There I met the Devil. I said to him: what's that bullshit you're doing to the world with this war? He said: sorry, but this is not my fault – it's yours. I denied being responsible and he said: of course I don't mean you personally. I mean women in general because women could handle the dark side and evil but they don't, and so it is placed in the hands of men, who are absolutely unable to handle the dark side. But if women don't make their own effort, then wars are inevitable. [92]

92 B. Hannah, *The Cat, Dog and Horse Lectures*, p. 99.

One of the church fathers, Athanasius, says that devils talk about things which are true, but we should be careful not to be too open-minded towards them, *even if they talk about true things!* «So my brothers, we should be armed with the armour of justice…as the devils are nothing…»[93] This mirrors the masculine Christian attitude that denies the reality of evil. In Barbara Hannah's dream, the Devil is real; he even explains his presence. If a dream talks in such dimensions it is also a collective dream, referring to all of us. We women could feel flattered by the responsibility the Devil assigns to us if it were not so shocking! But of course the dream also addresses the feminine side in men! Nowadays in all of us, the male attitude has to be completed by a feminine receptivity and openness to the dark manifestation of the instinctual background. Today we have to listen to what the Devil is telling us. And we have to learn how to bark! Women who can bark from the bottom of their heart, can put up respectable opposition against masculine predominance and aggressiveness. It may be important for women to know that they are capable of doing this!

I want to remain a little longer with the dangerous wolf side of the archetype of the dog, because it so often turns up in dreams. In reality, some wolves are coming back to our civilised country, crossing mountains and frontiers, and the problem people have with them gives rise to vehement discussions in the media. The irrational fear of this shy and wild animal, which most people will never ever meet, is typical of these discussions. Of course this holds true for other wild animals too, such as the lynx and the bear, but the wolf has by far the worst reputation. Taking into account that at the roots of our civilisation, the wolf, with his connection to Wotan, symbolises wild daemonic emotions and aggressions, the projection these animals must still carry, will hardly promote their peaceful acceptance in the near future. If the wolf cannot be understood for what he also is, namely an inner reality, the outer animal will not have a chance to survive in our culture.

In his article on Wotan,[94] which Jung wrote in 1936, before the outbreak of the Second World War, he speaks about this powerful psychic

93 Quoted by C. G. Jung in *Psychological Types* [Coll. Works 6], § 77 from: "Life of St. Anthony" in *The Book of Paradise*, by Palladius, Hieronimus etc.

94 C. G. Jung, *Civilisation in Transition* [Coll. Works 10], § 391-393.

factor that he considered then as the greatest threat to Western civilisation and peace. His warning was not heeded, and the erratic and violent god of wind and thunderstorm broke out, bringing war and destruction in its wake. As an archetype, the Germanic god Wotan is an autonomous psychic force that acts collectively at times and captures the masses in collective emotion. In mythology and sagas, Wotan is followed by grey or black dogs or wolves with fiery eyes. Wild dogs and wolves are also often a manifestation of the god Wotan himself.

A woman of 62 years, who was deeply concerned about the current political situation in Europe, which seemed to evolve more and more along the lines of mass psychology, dreamed:

Nr. 33: Dream of the attacking wolf:

I see a wolf coming down the wood, a big, grey animal. My cat walks in his direction blithely unconcerned. I fear for her and want to keep her with me. Further up in the wood, a young man appears with a few dogs that are playing together. As he approaches, he recognizes the wolf, but to make sure that it is really a wolf, he looks into his eyes from close up. The wolf attacks immediately and bites his throat and chest. The young man is seriously hurt and there is a lot of blood. I run to the house to get help, but I cannot find the telephone number of the ambulance. The man will bleed to death if there is no help immediately. I wake up in terror.

What is threatened in this dream is the cat, the dogs and the young man. We can take the cat as the individual that goes its own way and the dog as the principle of relatedness and playfulness, but maybe also of greediness. The young man seems to be naively unfamiliar with the dangerous side of the wolf. All three of them are completely surprised by the appearance of the wolf. The young man, who wants to look into the eyes of evil from too close, could mirror a naïve and careless attitude of the dreamer herself. The result is a life-threatening attack of the animus, with whom the feminine ego cannot cope. In fact the collective problem, which worried the dreamer so much, occasionally seemed to cut off her breath (the throat) and to attack her feeling (the breast, the heart), so that she was in danger of losing all her life energy (the blood).

Apart from the dreamer's personal situation, this dream must also be understood as a collective dream. Wolves as 'Wotanic' animals that prowl and hunt in packs, are an image for the mass instincts. Whenever the archetype takes over, for instance Wotan and his wolves, human relatedness fades away. This is the great danger of a mass movement. Probably every single one of us is quite convinced that we are individuals with a certain amount of common sense, who would never take part in such madness. But Jung, in his *Essays on Contemporary Events* made clear that in the deep collective layers of our psyche, underneath our Christian education, we all take part in the collective evil, Wotan and his wolves, and we are all threatened by it, from inside and from outside.[95] He wrote these essays with his heart and soul, though his thoughts have not prevented the same unconsciousness and the same danger from seeming to threaten this present age.[96] These facts, which Jung presented to his time, are so frightening that to this day they have been repressed by collective consciousness. Today Wotan and his wolves are lurking in dreams again. So when the wolf surprisingly reappears, there are no precautionary measures in place for defence, and there is no chance for an ambulance to arrive in time. People believe in rational agreements between states, and naively underestimate the danger that comes from the collective unconscious psyche, the wild and untamed instincts of the masses, and the psychopathology of the political leaders. The dream seems to clarify this collective situation. It points out that juvenile naivety, combined with the instinctual greediness of our fun-loving society (here the playing dogs), is most dangerous, given the non-perceived Wotanic wolf power in the collective unconscious, which might be constellated once more in our time.

Underestimation of the destructive instinctual forces of the collective unconscious is also the topic of a most impressive archetypal dream, dreamed in 1790 and reported 22-years later by John Adams, the second president of the United States of America in the years 1797-1801. It is the merit of the American Jungian Analyst Sheila Dickmann Zarrow, to have

95 C. G. Jung, The articles "Wotan" and "After the Catastrophe" in: *Civilisation in Transition* [Coll. Works 10].

96 See also in this book dream Nr. 3, "The cat Cleo and Wotan".

brought it to our knowledge in her book about John Adams and Benjamin Rush.[97] It goes as follows:

Nr. 34: Dream of John Adams:

I dreamed that I was mounted on a lofty scaffold in the center of a great plain in Versailles, surrounded by an innumerable congregation of five and twenty million, at least, of the inhabitants of the royal menagerie. Such a multitude is not to be described or enumerated in detail. There were among them the elephant, (the) rhinoceros, the lion, the hyena, the wolf, the bear, the fox, and the wildcat, the rat, the squirrel, as well as the calf, the lamb, and the hare. There were eagles, hawks and owls of all sorts, and storks and cormorants and crows, and ducks, geese, turkeys, partridges, quails, robins, doves, and sparrows. There were whales, sharks, dolphins as well as cod, mackerel, herrings, and even minims and shiners.

My design was to persuade them to associate under a free, sovereign, 'annimatical' ('self-acting' or 'self-animated') government, upon the unadulterated principles of liberty, equality, and fraternity among all living creatures. I had studied a long speech, arranged it in exact method, with a beginning, a middle, and an end, with an exordium and a very pathetic peroration, according to the most orthodox rules of the most approved rhetoricians. Throwing my eyes round and gracefully bowing to my respectable audience, I began:'

My beloved brothers! We are all children of the same Father who feeds and clothes us all. Why should we not respect each other's rights and live in peace and mutual love!'

I had not pronounced all these words before the elephant pouted his proboscis at me in contempt, the lion roared, the wolf howled, the cats and dogs were by the ears, the eagles flew upon the turkeys, the hawks and owls upon the chickens and pigeons. The whale rolled to swallow twenty at a mouthful, and the shark turned on his side to snap the first he could reach with his adamantine teeth. In a word, such a scene of carnage ensued as no eye had ever seen and no pen or pencil ever described.

Frightened out of my wits, I leaped from the stage and made my escape – not, however, without having all my clothes torn from my back

97 Sh. Dickmann Zarrow, *Friendship and Healing – The Dreams of John Adams and Benjamin Rush.*

and my skin lacerated from head to foot. The terror and the scratches awakened me and convinced me forever what a fool I had been.

The dream action takes place in Versailles at the time of Louis XVI, where in fact in these years the outbreak of instinctual forces had swept away almost the whole aristocracy and drenched the country in the blood and terror of the French Revolution. Nationwide there was a violent outbreak of destruction of the poor, so long starved out, mistreated and repressed; lofty scaffolds and guillotines were erected all over the country, with thousands of heads falling.

So the place of the dream and the scaffold already refer to the conflict between upper and lower level, between head and body, between ruling consciousness and unconscious instinctual powers. John Adams was caught up in the throes of this conflict, which also threatened the young states of America with their new collective identity, based on the principles of liberty, equality and fraternity. The Constitution was only signed in 1787, and the Bill of Rights, a series of ten amendments to the Constitution which John Adams was deeply involved in, was ratified in 1791. «It was hoped the amendments would be responsive to the needs of the individual states and would fill in what they saw as missing from it. The Constitution, coupled with the Bill of Rights, would be a container large enough to hold a union of the opposites – individual differences and collective identity.»[98]

This was the conscious standpoint and hope. John Adams's dream, by way of contrast, mirrors the point of view of the unconscious concerning the problem of the opposites. It makes quite clear that the ideal of peace and mutual love does not appease the animal instincts. The opposites of the conscious idealistic goal and the reality of the animal instincts cannot be united by "pathetic peroration". On the contrary, this attempt at persuasion instantly provokes the outbreak of instinctual emotionality and destructive aggression. It was only much later, in the year of the outbreak of the Civil War between North und South in 1812, that John Adams reported the dream to his friend Benjamin Rush. Amazingly enough for his time, he seemed to have considered dreams and the unconscious a source of knowledge, and equally relevant to the collective and the culture as well as to the

98 Sh. Dickmann Zarrow, *Friendship and Healing – The Dreams of John Adams and Benjamin Rush,* p. 47.

individual.[99] He therefore probably understood the warning of this dream in an intuitive way. The insight might have dawned on him that human nature was not to be changed collectively by a persuasive rational concept of an ideal world, an ideology, however good it might be. According to the dream image, this was like naively trying to convince an uncountable congregation of different animals, the whole instinctual basis of the collective unconscious.

Such an accumulation of different species of animals would be quite unthinkable in the wild, where every animal is given the space to live its life according to its own law, and where killing usually has its well-defined and limited function, exclusively serving the survival of the species. The unnatural conglomerate in the dream already mirrors a dangerous collective psychic situation. Moreover the animals of the dream are inhabitants of the royal menagerie, until now suppressed and kept in cages, obviously liberated all together for the event. Disaster is inevitable and John Adams's speech merely triggers it off.

So the dream compensates a too optimistic view in respect to a transformation of collective consciousness. It points out the danger that results from suppressed or underestimated animal instincts and a naïve attitude towards the mass phenomenon of the collective unconscious. The dream was dreamed close to the beginning of the 18th century, the age of rationalism, at a time when in France the reign of the *Déesse Raison*, the "Goddess of Reason", was proclaimed. The American constitution and the Bill of Rights had a tremendous influence on the world, with the notion of Human Rights, anchored for the first time in a constitution. However, even at this stage, the unconscious suggested in a compensating way the insight that it is in the final analysis only in the individual, where instinctual behaviour can be influenced. It is only in the individual where the opposites of consciousness and unconscious instincts can find a way of cooperation that sustains life. This conclusion could be drawn from the dream, long before there was a C. G. Jung to outline the problem in his scientific work. The alternative to the total liberation of the animal instincts, which ends up in revolution, in blood and terror, is the liberty for the individual to live in accordance with its instincts. After this dream, John Adams might have

99 Ibid., p. 45 and 49.

realised that the protection of this liberty was to be the highest goal of a constitution.

As a result of this dream, John Adams apparently «changed his working tactics, [...] he began, more often, to approach and convince individuals who represented a union of attitudes similar to his own.»[100] He had obviously learned something essential about human nature, which made him act with greater caution and insight. And it brought him down from inflation so fittingly described in the dream:*«I had studied a long speech, arranged it in exact method with a beginning, a middle, and an end, with an exordium and very pathetic peroration, according to the most orthodox rules of the most approved rhetoricians. Throwing my eyes round and gracefully bowing to my respectable audience, I began.»*

It ended with: *«The terror and the scratches awakened me and convinced me forever what a fool I had been.»* Considering that John Adams was deeply rooted in his Christian background, he was not a fool, but just trying to overcome by reason and will power what the church judged as sinful, namely the animal nature of men. Jung says that where there is a church, the Devil is not far away! And: «Nobody has such hellish dreams as a saint. It is the pair of opposites, the law of *enantiodromia*. In such a place one is apt to become aware of tremendous opposition if one is clinging strongly to one side. One becomes aware of very ancient animal instincts, for instance, which is a rather terrifying experience.»[101] John Adams's dream illustrates this fact in a most accurate way. After this digression into the whole of the assembled animal world, we now go back to the topic of this chapter, the dog.

In the next two dreams, the dark dog appears in a very different context, one which is not easy to understand. The first of these dreams goes like this:

Nr. 35: Dream of the frozen dog:

I'm in Africa, in the grasslands. Many animals are around. My mother is there. She is shaving my dog and then freezes her and prepares to dissect her frozen, shaven body. I intervene, hoping to defrost my dog and bring her back to life. I believe I've heard such things can be done.

100 Sh. Dickmann Zarrow, *Friendship and Healing*, p. 50.

101 C. G. Jung, Dream Analysis, p. 324.

In the days before this dream, she had just left her husband and begun the process of separation and divorce. Three months later there is the second dream:

Nr. 36: Dream of the dog growing out of another dog:

I have moved and recognize that something has happened to my dog. She is no longer herself, something is different inside her skin. There is another dog in there, a black dog whose markings are plainer than my dog's markings. This dog is trying to grow through my dog's skin. Its head is discernible as it is attached to, and also inside my dog's body. This other dog is looking at life and living it through my dog's eyes.

Then I realise that the other dog has successfully grown inside my dog and so is now living as a complete, whole dog attached to my dog. I hope to be able to get my dog back but think it is probably not possible. Then, however, as I make this wish, someone comes and cuts the two dogs apart by slicing the skin attaching them. They are separate now. I go to my dog hoping for a response but I get none. My dog is like a living hollow shell. I wonder about the possibility of taxidermy for keeping my dog in my new home but this idea is wearisome and problematic. I'm left sad that my dog seems to have gone forever.

The dreamer had both dreams at a very difficult time of transition. Her marriage, for various reasons, had grown void of both physical and emotional intimacy. In later reflection, she knew that her personal development depended upon the break-up despite the fact she loved him. She experienced both difficult and successful times in the years following and began to re-train. She saw herself as having a negative relationship with her mother.

Looking superficially at these rather uncanny dreams, one could easily jump to a negative conclusion concerning the dreamer's decision to break up her marriage. I must confess that I myself first fell into that trap. But then it seemed to me all too easy, just to blame the negative mother complex for all that had happened. Moreover, the dreamer was quite aware of this complex. So where would the new message of these dreams then be? There must be more to it. And indeed, after elaborating on the archetypal symbolism of the dreams, I saw the horizon broaden into a deeper understanding of the whole situation. The first thing that suggests itself is to take a closer look at the central figure, the mother.

This mother figure lives in Africa, the land of animals and of nature, as it is still perceived by most white people. She is clearly an image of the great mother and nature goddess, mistress of the animals. In the dream, she is identical to the dreamer's mother. In the psyche, it is she, the archetypal mother, who is always behind the personal mother. She has the power either to make the daughter's instinctual life blossom or else to dry up and freeze it to death. It is she who bestows on the personal mother the power to influence the daughter's whole life. Psychologically the effect of what we call a negative mother complex is in the first instance a bad instinctual basis. This means an unfavourable psychic condition and hence a curtailment of life's possibilities.

In fairytales this problem is mirrored in all the dangers that occur to the hero or heroine through the influence of a witch or evil stepmother. We do not know why one person's life is destroyed by the dangerous influence of the motherly unconscious, while the other one reaches the goal precisely because of this danger. It sometimes just seems to be a matter of the hero's or the heroine's destiny. But there is another remarkable fact: if we look at many fairytales, we can see that it is quite often precisely the dark feminine figures that bring positive feminine values to light.[102] In this context, Jung's statement makes sense when he says that – of all the forms of mother complex – a woman with a negative relationship to her mother has, if she can overcome it, the greatest chance to combine femininity and masculine reason in a beneficial way.[103] She does not want to live unconsciously, because the unconscious is for her not a warm mother, but rather a realm of threat and confinement. In the mother she «negotiates also all the darkness, drives, ambiguity and unconsciousness of her own being».[104]

Back to the dream: the dark mother now wants to freeze, shave and dissect the dreamer's dog. She is clearly a dark mother goddess like

102 S. Birkhäuser, *Die Mutter im Märchen*, p. 48f.

103 C. G. Jung, "The Negative Mother Complex" in *The Archtypes and the Collective Unconscious* [Coll. Works 9/I], § 184-186.

104 Ibid, §186.

Hecate, Hel, Kali, Persephone. Witches in fairytales sometimes kill their victims by either burning them or leaving them in the cold. Old stepmothers, witches, too, often attack a young queen's child, the future king or queen because they are against renewal. Here the dog is attacked. The danger is great that the negative mother complex, behind which dwells the great archetypal mother, could freeze the dreamer's instinctual eros to death. Shaving the dog also means depriving it of the last natural warmth-giving coat, so that it remains completely unprotected. Luckily the ego intervenes. The love, the dreamer's warm feeling for her dog is all she has to maybe help it to escape from the death mother. She asks herself if it will be possible to warm up the dog before the great mother can slice it up. It is important that under certain circumstances one resists the unconscious, although it seems nearly hopeless that there will still be life in this dog. The dreamer in this case has to fight – for her dog, for her feeling and for her sense of being related – against the negative mother, which attacks her instinctual life possibilities and wants to keep her unconscious.

7 years she has been married, when she leaves her husband. Her goal is to follow her own way to her own self. Even though she takes her beloved dog along into the new life, something terrible seems to happen to her instinctual eros. The great mother seems to be infuriated, she who is not only the great renovator, but also the one resisting transformation. M.-L. von Franz says that a woman who has the first intuition of the self will immediately be attacked by the inner 'stepmother', the persistence of the old collective role image of the feminine, a regressive inertia that always tends to pull us back onto the easiest way.[105] This means a terrible problem that might bring the fairytale heroine into great danger. But it seems to be a rule of nature that there is no creation without darkness and destruction. They even seem to be a condition for renewal. So the terrible attack of the dark mother figure in the dream might in the end not be only negative. The negative effect of the mother figures in fairytales is often followed by transformation and renewal, as mentioned above. Looking at it in that light, we might take the dismemberment, cutting and slicing up of the dog as a motif of a possible transformation, as we know it from

105 M.-L. von Franz, *Das Weibliche im Märchen*, p. 151. Also compare: *The Feminine in Fairytales*, p.172.

certain North American, African and Siberian shaman rites or dreams, where a symbolic death and resurrection with different ways of dismemberment, cutting, slicing, opening the body etc. is a condition for the healer's initiation.[106] We find a motif with a similar meaning in Russian fairytales, where Baba Jaga, the dark mother and nature goddess, comes along on a mortar, grinding to dust all that is wrong in the old ego attitude.[107]

Let us recall the second dream:

I have moved and recognise that something has happened to my dog. She is no longer herself, something is different inside her skin. There is another dog there, a black dog whose markings are plainer than my dog's markings. This dog is trying to grow through my dog's skin. Its head is discernible as it is attached to, and also inside of my dog's body. This other dog is looking at life and living it through my dog's eyes.

In this dream, the topic of transformation leading to renewal is not easily visible from the beginning. Once again amplification helps. In connection to mother figures, as we have seen, the black dog symbolically belongs to Hecate, the great goddess of the underworld, who devours humans and inflicts madness. At the same time, she is a moon goddess, a goddess of fertility and of birth and renewal. Dogs were sacrificed to her and like the corpses of the executed, were placed at crossways.[108] The crossroads is the place where the decision has to be taken as to which road to follow, symbolically a place of transition. It has to do with a crossover into a new time, a new attitude, a new life, any new outlook. It is also the place of the union of opposites, where contrary directions converge. At this point, evil spirits and death are close, as we know from popular belief. Psychologically this can mean that the negative mother might linger in the unconscious as a depression, or even a suicidal tendency. The black dog, the new one that appears in a dark instinctual form, can only be perceived as destruction and threat. The dream image is crude.

106 Mircea Eliade, *Schamanismus und archaische Ekstasetechnik*, p. 65.

107 M.-L. von Franz, *Das Weibliche im Märchen*, p. 154 (this does not appear in the translation of this book, *The Feminine in Fairytales*).

108 C. G. Jung, *Symbols of Transformation* [Coll. Works 5], § 354f.

And it goes on:

> *Then I realise that the other dog has successfully grown inside my dog and is now living as a complete whole dog attached to my dog. I hope to be able to get my dog back but think it is probably not possible. Then, however, as I make this wish, someone comes and cuts the two dogs apart by slicing the skin attaching them. They are apart now. I go to my dog, hoping for a response but I get none. My dog is like a living hollow shell. I wonder about the possibility of taxidermy as a means of keeping my dog in my new home, but this idea is wearisome and problematic. I'm left sad that my dog seems to have gone forever.*

In a painful growing process, the old dog is now replaced from inside by another one. It is like a cruel destructive birth process, a paradox. The new dog looks at the dreamer through the eyes of the old dog. One could say that the darkness of nature itself looks at ego consciousness from inside. That the ego is in a way seen by nature is a fact that we experience again and again in the meaningfulness and relatedness of our dreams. «Another inner subject watches us in dreams; it sees us as too anxious, too reckless, too immoral, or too anything else that seems to be a deviation from the norm of wholeness.»[109] But at first glance there does not seem to be any meaning in this crude dream image. It is just scaring the wits out of the ego.

The two dogs are finally cut into two by somebody else, a side of the dreamer that is able to discern, to analyse, to bring into consciousness. Taxidermy is a temptation, but it would mean keeping something seemingly alive that in fact is already dead and nothing but a hollow shell. This might also shed light onto the dreamer's relationship with her husband, which had lost substance and warmth. Such an insight is painful and sad. In such a situation, the old point of view is shattered, and consciousness is darkened.

The death of the beloved dog in the dream is a terrible shock for the dreamer, and the new one is still unknown, uncanny and maybe even threatening. But further amplification makes clear that the black dog in the dream might even have an important healing function. As we said above, the dog in Greek mythology is also the companion of the healing god Asclepios. Moreover, the dog in Ancient Egypt helped Isis to rejoin together

109 M.-L. von Franz, *Projection and Re-Collection in Jungian Psychology*, p.165.

110 C. G. Jung, *Symbols of Transformation* [Coll. Works 5], § 354f.

the pieces of Osiris.[110] Therefore he was closely linked not only to death, because of his feeding on corpses, but he was also a *helper in joining things together and thus helped to regenerate and resurrect.* In Persia, it was the custom to bring a dog to the dying person's bed and he or she had to give the dog something to eat. Jung assumes that this, besides appeasing Cerberus in a symbolic way, was also a resurrection rite. In a footnote, he also mentions a moving little text where obviously somebody addresses himself to a friendly person: «I beg you very much to paint a little dog at the foot of my statue […] so that thanks to you I might live after my death.»[111]

A modern image is revealed in following story, which I was told some years ago. A physiotherapist owned a little black dog which she used to take along when visiting her patients. One day a dying old woman, who had always been looking forward to seeing the dog, asked her to let it lie on her bed. After some time, while the dog stayed patiently on the bed, the physiotherapist had to leave the room for a short time. When she came back, the woman, still holding the little dog in her arms, had just passed away. On her face there was an expression of peace and serenity. Amazingly the agile little dog had stayed close to her. – Today in Switzerland, dogs are used in terminal care, and amazingly enough, it seems that most dogs have the tendency, even of their own accord, to seek closeness to dying people. If this is really a common feature of dogs, known from time immemorial, we can understand even better that in Ancient Egypt and in many other cultures, the dog has become the guide to resurrection into the other world.

Back to the dream. The strange image of the black dog entering the body of the old dog reminds us of the common fact that death was seen symbolically as entering the mother's womb for resurrection.[112] Therefore it might have something to do with the death of an outlived instinctual attitude and its renewal, albeit in a still ominous form. In spite of its awkward appearance, it mediates hope for a new possibility of eros and relationship, growing out of difficult life experiences, suffering and

111 C. G. Jung, *Symbols of Transformation* [Coll. Works 5], §354.

112 Ibid., §354.

loss. Nor must one forget to mention the fact that the dreamer's beloved real dog lived with her for a further nine happy years!

During this time, it appeared in dreams again and again, showing a slow process of psychic development in the relation to the dog instinct. Here is another of these dreams:

Nr. 37: Dream of the baby puppy:

My dog is a little baby puppy and I am cradling her in my arms, bonding with her. Then she transforms into a newborn human infant, and I know that I am seeing my own newborn infant. But also, she looks like me, as if I am the infant.

This beautiful little dream does not need much interpretation. It is a confirmation and also an encouragement to take care of this instinct, whatever this means in the personal life situation of the dreamer. The little baby puppy is also depicted as the dreamer's own newborn infant or even herself. One's own child in dreams in its positive aspect usually has to do with one's own future life and possibilities, with what 'it' wants with us in life. This 'it' is often perceived by the individual as something like destiny or destination. The child is a symbol of the self, the unknown centre of the psyche that seems to lead and regulate the inner process of development. That the dreamer also senses it as being even herself points to the fact that the self, although it is the archetypal and impersonal basis of all life, can only be experienced and realised by the individual. The new child is born in the psyche of the individual, even if sometimes it does not look like a child yet, a human content close to consciousness understanding. It can even be experienced in a little dog!

Various ensuing dreams mirrored time and again the threat to the dog instinct by the complexes. They showed that through all the fear and pain and caring for the dog, the process of becoming conscious about and dealing with the complexes was going on. There was for instance a dream in which the dreamer could could miraculously save her dog unharmed from her burning house. Through the suffering or other reaction of the animal in our dreams, we learn what, for instance, a negative mother complex can do to us. The dog, because it is more close to men than other animals, in this regard specially is a guide to higher consciousness and thus to a change in the whole life situation.

I would like to add a last dream from the same dreamer. In the meantime, her old dog had died and she now had a young dog.

Nr. 38: Dream of the dog with diamond-shaped patterns instead of eyes:

I see my new dog's litter mate across the way. I go over to look at her. In particular, I want to see her eyes as I hear they are two different colours. I lift open the lids but see diamond-shaped geometric patterns instead of eyes. I learn that her eyes are still forming and this is the stage they are currently in, as if a "pre-eye" stage. It seems like one side is blue and white and the other pink and white. (Fig. 28)

The litter mate was in reality the second puppy in a litter of two. The dream with the litter mate brings up the duplication motif, which is common wherever something new is coming into consciousness. « [...] when unconscious contents are about to become conscious and differentiated... they split, as often happens in dreams, into two identical or slightly different halves corresponding to the conscious and still unconscious aspects of the nascent content.»[113] Irmgard Bosch, who was working on pregnant women's dreams, discovered that the duplication motif in her collection came out clearly, although none of the dreamers were expecting twins. It pointed in a symbolical way to the fact, well known also from mythological twins, that with the birth of something new, there is always an individual aspect as well as a super-individual aspect, which is deeply rooted in the other world, in the unconscious. There is, so to speak, a human and at the same time a divine aspect of the new child to be born.[114]

While the dreamer's own puppy symbolizes, so to speak, what can become conscious of this archetypal content, the litter mate has to do with its divine or unconscious aspect. As we love our animals, we tend to forget that they have their double, so to speak, in the unconscious psyche. The psyche itself supports an attachment or a relationship to the outer dog by projecting the archetypal image onto it. Psychology knows that such

113 C.G. Jung, "The Negative Mothercomplex" in: *The Archetypes and the Collective Unconscious* [Coll. Works 9/I], § 608.

114 R. Abt, I. Bosch, V. MacKrell, *Dream Child*, Chapter "The Duplication Motif", p. 381 f.

Fig. 28: The dog as represented by the dreamer after the dream.

unconscious projections affect our whole world-view and determine our relationship to the outer world. A projection, however much it might interfere with our outer life, can have the effect of bringing out a new content into consciousness the moment it can be recognized as such.[115] The dream gives us a hint as to what is constellated in the unconscious.

The eyes of the dream puppy are of special importance. Looking into the eyes of the litter mate means relating to an inner reality, a 'pre-eye' or a pre-conscious stage. But it is not only the ego that looks at the unconscious; it is also looked at by the eyes of the unconscious. M.-L.von Franz calls it "an inner eye of self-recognition, which mediates a different view of ourselves than does the ego".[116] For the great alchemist Ibn Umail, the eye of the animal is another symbol for the stone: «The eye is elsewhere known as a name for mercury, the spirit and light of nature. It symbolises a latent consciousness or luminosity that is unified by the stone in the same way as the eye collects everything that it sees. *To look into the eye of an animal gives human beings a hint of that preconscious totality that is longing*

115 See in general: M.-L. von Franz, *Projection and Re-Collection in Jungian Psychology.*

116 M.-L. von Franz, *Projection and Re-Collection*, p. 165.

to become conscious. To reach this wholeness on a conscious level is the quest of the alchemist.»[117]

The dreamer wants to connect to these inner eyes, as she is interested in the two different colours, something unusual in the animal world. Looking more closely, she can see that they show diamond-shaped geometric patterns, one in blue and one in red or pink, the two opposite sides of the colour spectrum. Diamonds are highly precious stones, not only because of their shining beauty, but also because of their hardness, which is why they are used in all sorts of techniques. They seemed to be indestructible and have therefore become a well-known symbol of the indestructible and immortal core of the self. Diamonds and jewels, difficult to attain, symbolise the eternal substance in man, the essence of individuation. For the alchemists, the diamond became the symbol of the stone of the sages as well.[118] With these amplifications, we can therefore identify the diamond patterns as abstract patterns of the self in matter. This is what seems to be at the bottom of the new insight in this dream. These eyes are still forming. The new insight, a possibility of reflection, grows out of matter.

We can only try to approach this amazing statement of the dream with the help of the concept of the *unus mundus.* The term was used by the alchemist Dorneus in the 16th century for the unity of the psycho-physical reality and was taken over by Jung. He assumed that all new consciousness emerges from this realm, where psyche and matter are one. The latest insights in physics and brain science seem to confirm the hypothesis of such a unity. But the breathtaking consequence of such an insight is a living matter, inconceivable for a world-view which is still based on Newton's clearly defined consistency of matter and the principle of cause and effect. And it is doubtful whether modern physicists and brain scientists will be able to admit such a conclusion, because this would open the door to the psyche. A disturbing prospect for most scientists!

The diamond pattern in one eye of the puppy is blue, in the other one red or pink. Red, as the colour of blood, has always characterised the emotional and instinctual realm of the psyche. Blue, as the colour of the sky, though, is connected to the spiritual world. We can say that the red

117 Th. Abt, *Psychol. Commentary to the Hall ar-Rumuz*, CALA I B, p. 134 f.

118 M.-L. von Franz, *Individuation in Fairytales*, p. 133 f.

pattern symbolically has to do with the basis of our instinctive and animal drives, and the blue one with the spiritual realm of the psyche. When we look at the painting the dreamer has done of this puppy, we can see that between the two eyes there is a white blaze, separating them. The eyes with blue and red diamond patterns are not only separated, but are actually opposites, though united in one animal. They represent those opposites of human nature that can only be united in the self. The little dog is therefore not just a symbol of an instinctual drive, as we might expect, but a symbol of the self, uniting instinctual and spiritual life. The dog is still a puppy, and its eyesight has not yet developed, but with the appearance of the self symbol, a process is set in motion towards recognising that this important content belongs to the dreamer's own personality. It appears in the form of a still unconscious new instinctive life feeling. If the dreamer patiently stays with it, it will grow and, looking at her, will be able to open her eyes to what it means in her life.

A dog, being a symbol of the self is also the topic of the next dream. It comes from a young man who was in training to be an analyst.

Nr. 39: Dream of the bishop:

A bishop in a green-coloured garment actually made out of grape leaves says: 'Priests should listen to what God says.' But God is a dog. Is it my dog whose name he mentioned?

I will first amplify this amazing dream by a story at the end of the Indian epos Mahabharata. It goes as follows:

The five heroic brothers Pandava are ready to die. Together with their common wife and a dog they climb up the Himalaya's holy world mountain, Meru. On their way, the wife and four of the brothers die, one after the other. Yudhishthira, the eldest brother, is said to be the only one mature enough for the honour of being accepted in heaven with his body. Therefore he goes ahead, accompanied only by his dog. Then, with thunder and lightning, Indra, the king of heaven, appears in his carriage to take Yudhishthira with him to heaven. But he steps aside and first allows the dog to jump into the carriage. Indra is shocked. Never could a dog be accepted into heaven. They can never be holy and would therefore be out of place. He asks Yudhishthira to send the dog away. They argue, but

Yudhishthira does not give up. He says his dog had always been faithful and devoted and that it would be the worst sin to leave it behind. With this heavy burden on his mind, he could never live happily in heaven, and for the dog's sake he would renounce the idea of going there. At that moment, the dog transforms into Yama, the radiant god of the holy order of life, of death and absolute justice.[119]

From this story we can see that the idea of god being a dog is not new! In reality no Christian bishop would say that God is a dog. In medieval times he would have been burnt as a heretic. If in official Christian doctrine an animal is mentioned, it is usually reduced to the embodiment of devilish instincts and greed. But popular feeling has always assigned animals to defined places and personalities. The patron saints often have animals as their companion, one example being Saint Anthony, the hermit with the pig. And there are countless customs, rituals, special blessings that serve to protect animals. Historically, an animal was fundamental to life. People owed them their livelihood. Now let us look at this very special bishop.

In the Roman Catholic hierarchy, the Pope, the cardinal and the bishop are of the highest-ranking spiritual authority. In the dream, though, the bishop is wearing a green garment that is made out of grape leaves, which makes him a man of nature. The grape leaves are attributes of. Dionysos, the god of wine, the son of Zeus and the earth goddess Semele. The myth tells that because of Hera's jealousy and intrigue, Semele was burnt by Zeus' lightning bolts while Dionysos was still in her womb. Zeus took the prematurely born child and sewed it into his thigh, from where a second birth took place. As an adult, Dionysos retrieved his mother from Hades and made her a goddess of Olympus. The child Dionysos was raised by motherly, nursing women. They all lived together in the forests. Later those women became the torch-bearing maenads who, like the nymphs in later times, accompanied and worshipped Dionysos, as did many enthusiastic female priests and also normal women. As a god of vegetation, a phallic god of fertility, Dionysos is shown with flowers and fruit. Ecstasy,

119 In Hindu mythology, Yama is the first human being, an Anthropos figure who later became the judge and ruler of the Underworld.

Fig. 29: Stele with dog. Abydos, Ancient Egypt, Predynastic, 3100 – 2686 BC.

drunkenness, orgiastic worship, spiritual inspiration but also confusion, hallucination and delirium were all associated with him. In Delphi, Dionysos was originally worshipped as a god of death but also as a god of oracle, like Apollo. As a god of oracle, he expresses himself through dreams. Such dreams and healing oracles were also assumed to have sprung from the contact with solitary earth spirits, for the earth was considered to be the mother of all dreams.

Now we have to connect the bishop with Dionysos! The bishop could be understood as a spiritual guide connected with our culture and development of consciousness. He is closer to the people than the Pope is. With the green grape-leaf garment he is complemented by aspects of nature and therefore the feminine. This points to a different attitude towards dreams and inspiration from the depths of the unconscious, also to the realm of death, the earth and the dark and dangerous side of nature, which have been neglected in official Christian doctrine. Despite being an archetypal part of human nature, they could no longer be addressed in ritual and worship, as was and still is the case in all pagan cultures.

In this context we might insert the dream of a priest, mentioned by Jung:

Nr. 40: Dream of the priest, the church and the vine grapes:

He came into his church at night. There he saw that the whole wall of the choir (chancel) had collapsed. The altar and the debris were overgrown by vines full of grapes, and the moon was shining through the opening created by the collapse. [120]

Jung comments that the Dionysian «element has to do with emotions and affects which have found no suitable religious outlets in the predominantly Apollonian cult and ethos of Christianity. The medieval carnivals and *jeux de paumes* in the Church were abolished relatively early; consequently the carnival became secularised and with it, divine intoxication vanished from the sacred precincts. Mourning, earnestness, severity, and well-tempered spiritual joy remained. But intoxication, that most direct and dangerous form of possession, turned away from the gods

120 C. G. Jung, *Psychology and Alchemy* [Coll. Works 12], § 182.

and enveloped the human world with its exuberance and pathos. The pagan religions met this danger by giving drunken ecstasy a place within their cult.»[121]

Today we have on the one hand an irrational fear of the unconscious, with the whole aversion to everything that cannot be grasped rationally. On the other hand, there is the fascination with all sorts of esoteric theories and irrational movements, with science fiction and fantasy in films and art, with the virtual world of the internet, not forgetting alcohol and drug abuse, but also in contagious so-called visions of a new and better world divorced from reality, often playing a leading and destructive role in politics.

In our dream, however, all the parts of human nature are contained in the image of the Dionysian bishop, who represents a spirit of wholeness and who could play a new leading role on the level of consciousness.

I think Jung must have had something of this spirit. He loved wine, laughter, pleasant company; he descended to the world of death and brought back a relationship to the Beyond; he reacted intuitively and he connected people with fertile seeds in their dreams. It is said that he could also be ruthless and even rude, but he always seemed to be in harmony with his inner nature. As Marie-Louise von Franz once said, he could be completely at one with the person sitting opposite him and at the same time he had this instinctive way of reacting that was quite unpredictable.

Our dream, as well as the Mahabharata story at the end, reveals the godly nature of the dog instinct. A Christian bishop would hardly have found out about this dog god. It is Dionysos, a god of nature, who completes the Christian one-sidedness. To experience the dog instinct would correspond to a feeling of harmony, of inspiration from one's inner nature and a connection with the deepest regions of the natural spirit, where animals are gods. The dog, however, like no other animal, is *in between nature and mankind* and therefore provides perfect qualities for maintaining the connection between the unconscious and consciousness - if we listen to what it tells us! We might think that the dogs in our dreams are simply our real dogs, which need to be cared for and fed every day. However, according to this dream the dog is also a god, an awesome psychic power that deserves the utmost respect and daily care. Without

121 Ibid., § 182.

man's attention, this archetype is as lost as a stray dog without a human being. In the Mahabharata, absolute faithfulness and voluntary self-sacrifice are needed for the sake of the dog - even the willingness to give up heaven.

In the dream, the Dionysian bishop tells us that 'the priests should listen to what God says, but God is a dog.' According to the dream, the young man must be modest enough to listen to this gentle voice from the unconscious talking about eros and relationships and the respect for our real nature. We should be able to accept this voice as if it was God who is speaking. This gentle voice could once again open the gates to the unconscious and help the young man to find his way down to the rejected unconscious world of the darkness, of the drives and shadows, but also of the creative seeds. It could help to connect the unconscious realm with the world of consciousness. A new spiritual attitude communicated by the Dionysian bishop could create the opportunity for a true understanding of the divine nature of this dog instinct. Analysts, in supporting the connection of the human individual with this dog, need some of that Dionysian spirit!

Not only the priest, whose task it is to care for the soul, but also every individual who has started his or her quest, could begin to realise that the spirit of God is at hand, namely hidden in one's own dog, in one's own animal soul. We could argue that God cannot be a dog and that this is heretical nonsense. But who knows how and who God really is? We can only see what our unconscious shows us of Him. Therefore Jung always pointed out that he was talking about the *images of god* and not about what God is really like. This is the theologian's job. We can only see what the psyche shows us of God and we can assume that God as a dog is a compensation for the dreamer's image of God, which was too lofty and airy and cut off from the instinctual side, which is nowadays true for most people in our Western culture.

An unknown Arabic alchemist says: «And on the dunghills you will find (the dog) thrown away. Thus do not deny it for the sake of God. It means that it (the dog) is thrown on the dunghills of the sages. And the dunghills of the sages are their earth which is in the bottom of the vessel. And the dunghills are also from the names of the ashes which are inside of the vessel. Thus you must understand that and you must be subtle.»[122]

122 See M.-L. von Franz, *Psychol. Commentary on the Hall ar-Rumuz*, CALA I A, p. 159.

In her interpretation of this text, M.-L. von Franz states: «Sigmund Freud stumbled over the symbol of the dog: on the one hand he saw that on the dunghill of repressed contents lay the important life principle of the psyche, but at the same time he denied its being the power of God by not seeing the divine aspect of love, but calling it only a biological drive. Our author (a sofar unknown alchemist) is fully aware of the paradox of eros. The symbol of the dog stands for what we reject and throw away because it seems useless. It is also what we take as being banal and self-evident, the naked facts of life so to speak. Within that dung or ashes lies hidden the creative activity of God, which constantly sustains our existence. It is through the experience of love that we most frequently discover this hidden miracle of being.»[123] This paragraph summarises perfectly the whole meaning of the dream! Indeed, the dog in the language of our Western culture is still the rejected one, the 'Schweinehund' , as we say in German (the filthy pig-dog), the lazy dog, the son of a bitch etc., and 'dog racism' is gaining more and more ground in industrialised countries. Thus the dog symbol in dreams in all its aspects is often far from being understood in a natural way. It is the love of whatever or whoever happens to be a part of our destiny in everyday life that brings the dog's secret numinosity up to the light.

M.-L. von Franz in her book *The Way of the Dream* interpreted a dream of a woman that is very close to the dream of the Dionysian bishop. The dream and her explanations are so important that I want to bring it into our collection. The dream goes as follows:

Nr. 41: Dream of the dog with gold eyes:

«In this dream I was swimming in a very dark, deep cave. At the far end of the cave there was an enormous rock. On the rock there was a small, ginger-coloured, furry dog with gold eyes. The animal was smiling at me, and I knew that this little dog represented the Christ. I don't know how I knew that, but I knew it.»[124]

In her interpretation, Marie-Louise von Franz explains that the dog is a symbol of the inner Christ in the depths of the soul, «not out there in

123 Ibid., § 332 f.

124 M.-L. von Franz, *The Way of the Dream*, p. 276 f.

the sky, as Christian teaching wants to have it or in some metaphysical spiritual realm. He is in the depths of the earth, and the earth is an image of matter, of our body, of our physical existence. The cave has always been a sacred place in former ages. Long after man no longer lived in caves, they remained sanctuaries. They were, so to speak, the womb of the earth goddess, or the goddess of nature. So the cave symbolises the depth of the inner nature. Now, this dream says that Christ is not some model figure you have to follow as you have been taught. On the contrary, he is a being which you find when you go into the depths of your own being. You find him in the womb of Mother Earth. But he appears in a strange form. He appears as a dog.»

Now we know about the dog as a guide to the other world. «What mythologies and religions describe as the land of the dead is what we would call the unconscious. [...] In relation to the dream world, he (the dog) is the guiding god in the unconscious. That is why in our dream it is very fitting that Christ is a dog, because he is a guardian of souls. He watches over the dreamer's soul and guides her in the darkness of the unknown.» «The golden quality which is stressed in the dream refers to immortality. Gold is the only metal ancient people knew which is not corroded by old age or by acids. Gold can be buried for five thousand years, and be absolutely unaltered, while silver, copper and iron rust and disintegrate. And so gold has always carried the projection of immortality, eternity, the substance of highest value. In most civilizations, divine figures and statues are painted and decorated in gold. This stresses that they are eternal, shining, immortal, everlasting. In the dream, the woman realizes that the golden dog is Christ. It is the way Christ appears within her. He is an image of what we call the self, the inner guiding principle.»[125]

And this eternal, shining, immortal, everlasting self, which is usually extremely difficult for us to understand as an inner reality, is so close to the human being, like a little dog, even smiling at the dreamer as if he was human itself! He has to do with these little, seemingly unimportant impulses from our unconscious and meaningful everyday synchronicities that remind us of this hidden benevolent golden friend smiling at us and guiding us.

In summarizing some of the aspects of the dog symbol, we can say that first of all the dog has to do with *eros*. It appears whenever the quality

125 M.-L. von Franz, *The Way of the Dream*, p. 280.

Fig. 30: The dog, man's best friend. 'Kay'.

of feeling enters. With its 'scenting' nose it is an instinct showing us which way to go, a *guide* to the Beyond, to the spiritual world, to the unconscious. In this respect, it is also a *healer*, even more so than the cat, because it sniffs out healing impulses for us from the depths of the unconscious psyche. As a *god of death and hell*, it has to do with the perils of the unconscious, which can only be resisted with a genuine sacrifice and with an attitude of devotion and respectful modesty. Entering the unconscious with the selfish intention of enjoying an advantage in outer life means risking being savaged by Cerberus. Today scientific experiments are trying to prove that the seat of religious experience is located in a special part of the brain structure where such experiences can therefore be provoked at will artificially. Only time will reveal whether it will be possible to trick out Cerberus and to enter the Underworld without sacrifice.

The dog as the *bringer of fire* signifies warmth, protection, light and consciousness, but in its shadow aspect, possession by overwhelming emotion as well. Aggression, covetousness, greed and a conservative attitude are other shadow sides of the dog instinct. We need to develop a relationship to this instinct in order to avoid becoming possessed. Then this fiery energy is purified from the shadowy aspects, just as fire means not only destruction but also light and warmth. This goal of containing the fire inside was the goal of alchemical work. It all depends on our way of dealing with it. The *wolf-instinct* can be dangerous unless we find the right approach, but it might also release unknown forces. The dream of the Dionysian bishop, the dream with the dog as Christ and the story from Mahabharata make clear how much we tend to underestimate this dog instinct. Why else would we need such great compensatory images? In the dog, *the self* can manifest itself and become visible.

Fig. 31: The Greek goddess Hekate with a hound beside her, placing a wreath on the head of a mare. Marble relief from Crannon in Thessaly, 4th century BC.

Part III

The Horse

Fig. 32: Horse Head. Paleolithic Rock Painting. Grottes de Chauvet, about 32,000 years old.

Before embarking on the horse dream interpretations, I would like to relate a story that is supposed to be a true one. Even if that is not the case, it is something that people have obviously considered worth telling to this day, like a myth or a saga, with all the emotional background thereby entailed.

The woman who told the story was in Belgium in the year 1944 during the terrible bombing of a big town by the Americans. Herself still a girl, she was helping to rescue the injured and the dead from the ruins when she discovered the body of a young German soldier amidst the smoke and dust and debris. He seemed to be dead; his eyes were glazed and his hair sticky with blood. When she touched him, there was suddenly life in his eyes for one brief moment. He looked at his helper in a friendly way, then his glance seemed to move to something behind or above her. And then suddenly a radiant smile lit up his face and he said in a low voice: «Janosh, my horse ... are you not dead?» and passed away as if he was simply falling asleep.[126]

This story needs no interpretation. Even if we maybe judge it to be sentimental, it is nevertheless the expression of the emotional impact of this great archetype. Whether it was really the spirit of the young soldier's horse that came to him in the last moments of his life to guide him into the other world, or whether it was a dream horse of his, we do not know. Nor do we need to.

Before immersing ourselves in horse dreams we would like to take a look at the history and some of the symbolism of the horse. In Europe and Asia three million years ago, wild horses already existed in many different forms. One of the first places of horse worship in Europe, for example, was found in Chauvet in France and is about 32, 000 years old.

However, the domestication of the wild horse up to its development into a riding horse took thousands of years. For countless generations, riding must have been an insoluble problem. Many Indo-Germanic tribes, such as Indians and Persians, had invented wheels and carriages and put harnesses onto their horses long before they learnt how to ride a horse. Horseback riding must be considered as a great cultural leap forward (fig. 33).

126 A. Lindbergh, in: *Journal Franz Weber*, Nr. 90, Dec. 2009.

Fig. 33: Horses with carts. Ancient Egypt, 18th Dynasty, 1540-1292 BC.

It remains a source of wonder to this day that there can be communication or even harmony between man and such a large, wild animal. This must always have exerted a great fascination, because people continue to ride horses, even though they are no longer used for warfare, transport, fieldwork or herding cattle, and despite the fact that physically we are not built for this and riding will never really be natural for us. In European courts, some outstanding riding masters such as F. R. de la Guérinière [127] were highly respected and are still famous today. The whole theory of European art of riding as it is still practised, for instance, in the Vienna High School or the Spanish or Portuguese royal riding school, is based on their theories (fig. 34).

Symbolically, riding a horse in harmony mirrors a reconnection with the fundamental instincts from which we have become separated during the long course of development of consciousness. Thus the harmonious relationship between rider and horse often appears in modern dreams and makes an enormous emotional impact, even with people who do not ride or do not relate to horses. Many people, especially women and young girls,

127 F. R. de la Guérinière, *Reitkunst*. De la Guérinière was "Ecuyer du Roi" (royal riding master) in Paris until 1730.

are fascinated by horses. They clean stables, ride out in all weathers and sacrifice their energy, money, leisure time and freedom to be with horses. One such woman dreamt that *she could clearly see the complete skeleton of a horse through a hole in its chest.* The skeleton is the basic structure of the body, which symbolically means the archetypal foundation. Thus, this whole fascination refers to the *experience of an archetype* that lies at the very foundation of the instinctual libido.

In addition to its capacity to carry human beings, the real horse, as well as the symbolic one, has another important function because of its incredible power and dynamism. Whoever has tried to keep a nervous horse under control, or ride a galloping or even a runaway horse, will know what I mean. The Greeks and Romans believed that only horses could pull the carriage of the sun god from the dark underworld into the new day's heaven. If we try to understand this image, it could mean that here the horse is a symbol for the instinctual dynamism which gives momentum to the development of consciousness.

An old German legend tells of a horse coming out of the sea. This horse helps to plough the soil for man, but then shakes off both ploughman and plough into the abyss and disappears back into the sea.[128] From this legend we learn that for the individual, the natural power of the unconscious libido was not only culture-bringing but also a threat to consciousness, and was potentially highly dangerous. Indeed relating to the horse, that unconscious libido which promotes the evolution of consciousness, has always been a problem for humans. The old German legend shows that the dynamic horse libido supports the achievement of the cultivation of land, 'agri-cultura'. Yet, in its wild emotionality, it can abruptly destroy the weak, little man with his consciousness- and culture-bringing instrument, the plough.

It was Christianity that first introduced the idea of salvation from autonomous instinctual powers. But from then on, these powers of nature were considered the work of the Devil. As a consequence, the destructive side of the pre-Christian oceanic horse-god was damned, and even his helpful and culture-bringing side was considered to be evil.

128 A. von Ström and H. Biezais, *Germanische und baltische Religion*, p. 173.

Fig. 34: Statue of Louis XIV. Bronze.

Psychologically, if a dynamic creative drive, with all its aspects, is shut out by consciousness as devilish, it is one of the most destructive things that can happen to the soul. When the flow of libido is blocked it can lead to outbreaks of destructive emotionality. As they cannot be handled, there is a tendency to suppress them even more or to cut them off completely. Then the whole energy coming from the unconscious can die off, giving way to feelings of emptiness and meaninglessness. Dreams of modern people often mirror this neglect or misuse of the horse as well as of other animals.

A 29-year-old woman had one of those alarming dreams which seem to call for immediate reaction. In a wider sense it had something to do with her body and sexuality.

Nr. 42: Dream of the starving horse:

To my great amazement, I find a starving horse in the cellar of our house, where it is locked in.

In official Christian church dogma, the physical side and the whole range of instincts as carriers of carnal desires were associated with the Devil and thus discredited. With Christian asceticism, the contempt for the lower regions, including the physical aspect, showed its harshest side. St. Frances of Assisi talked about his body as his 'brother donkey', the beast of burden of the poor. He disciplined this body by means of extreme poverty and self-castigation. But before his death, he admitted that he had sinned against his brother donkey, which he had violated too much. Approaching death, by then very ill and almost blind, St. Frances of Assisi was no longer sure about whether or not this extreme asceticism really corresponded to God's will.

The problem with our dream now was that in real life the young woman seemed to be living out her sexuality and care for her body. She was attractive and well dressed and nothing in her life story gave the impression that she neglected the instinctual realm. She was also carrying on a thrilling, clandestine affair and fully enjoyed modern sexual liberty. The dream therefore came as a surprise, as if the horse was still not able to live in the right way. An important aspect of her sexuality was obviously locked in and abandoned in the cellar. This dream also mirrors a collective problem. The liberation of sexuality that started with Freud at the beginning of the last century has so far not necessarily brought a better relationship to the instincts. Having been rejected by Christian morality for so long, they seem to have lost their numinous quality. In the same way as the real horse has so often been and still is misused, this instinct today, in both individual and collective life, often seems to have a function like any other form of entertainment, and has become a crucial factor in business and marketing. While sexuality is omnipresent, the problem of potency is increasing. The instinctual libido, in pagan times worshipped as a godly animal, is still locked off, as our dream shows. Feeding it would mean giving it loving care and respecting it instead of merely using it. It is more than sexuality, it is instinctual life energy! The next dream is of a 25-year-old woman:

Nr. 43: Dream of the attacking stallion:

Our horse, a stallion, is out in the run. We are standing outside and my mother says it is time to bring him together with another mare. Later on I must hide from the stallion because it had suddenly escaped from the paddock and is pursuing me angrily and aggressively. I'm hiding behind a haystack but I know he will find me here sooner or later.

In real life, the dreamer related very well to this good-natured stallion but she saw this dream in the light of her unfulfilled sexuality at that time. In a wider sense, it could also have to do with her physical needs, which she neglected too much by excessive work and activity. The subject of the angry horse often occurs in European Alpine legends. It seems to be connected to the social discrimination against sexuality by country people in recent centuries, owing to strict Christian morality and social conventions. In the old legends, witches' or devil's horses mirror this destructive tendency. In Germanic history and mythology, the horse plays a most important role. Therefore in the psyche it still lingers on just beneath the surface of European Christian consciousness.

In this dream, the horse or the sexual aspect of this instinct becomes dangerous or even obsessive, like any other suppressed instinct. Then it is the Devil. The Devil is also connected to the fire, as he sits in hell together with his hellfire. So the fire attributes of the Devil also belong to the horse and with it the fertilizing side of the old fire- and thunder gods. Fire means also light, as is seen in mythological horses like Helios' fire horses, or Hector's horses, called Lampos, the shining one, and Aithon, the burning

Fig. 35: Horses are often connected to the wind, symbolizing creative energy. Lusitano stallion 'Dourado'.

one.[129] Therefore in a wider sense, the dream of the pursuing stallion probably also mirrors a creative potential that seeks fulfillment.[130]

A woman whose husband had fallen in love with a brilliant but cold 'anima-witch' had the following dream (shortened version):

Nr. 44: Dream of the horses and the ice water:

In our pasture there were unfamiliar grazing horses which had something to do with this other woman. They were dark brown, with a white spot on the forehead. The pasture was green although it was still winter. The ground was torn up by big tractors and there were some men present. My husband went down to ask them what was the matter. But then he fell backwards into an icy torrential brook. With his heavy winter-coat he was dragged down into the water, beneath the snow and ice. I tried to

129 C. G. Jung, *Symbols of Transformation* [Coll. Works 5], § 421.

130 Compare R. Abt, "The Fiery Horse, a Russian Fairytale" in: *Psychological Perspectives*, Vol. 53, issue 3/2010.

get him out, which was extremely difficult because I myself was standing on slippery and unsafe ground. I tugged and tugged, holding onto his coat until at last his head was above water and he could catch his breath (then I woke up from this tremendous exertion).

Here they are, the anima's witch-horses, the energy behind that fascination! The concept of the anima as a dark horse, a horse woman or a 'night-mare' is widely spread. She manifests herself then in the form of a chthonic, elementary unruly power that transcends any conscious approach. In *Man and his Symbols*, Marie-Louise v. Franz mentions a Siberian tale where a lone hunter is persuaded by a seductive woman to cross a river. But as soon he dives into the icy water she transforms into an owl and flies away with a mocking laugh, while the hunter is drowning. Von Franz says that here the anima is the unreal dream of love and happiness, of motherly warmth and protection.[131] These aspects – an erotic fantasy – are also emphasized by the horse symbol in our dream, as the horse, in its life-giving and life-bearing aspect in mythology, is also part of the mother.[132] In her dark aspect, however, she means overpowering unconsciousness, which is expressed in the image of drowning. Just as the hunter finally drowns in the cold river, so very nearly does this unfaithful husband. Obviously he is no longer able to help himself. He needs the full support of his wife. The horses in this dream are brown, the colour of the earth mother, and they have a white spot on their forehead. That means that they carry some light or a possibility of becoming conscious. In fact, the difficult experience of the marital situation of this couple entailed a complete breaking up of the ground as if on a big construction site, which looked like a disaster for their natural habitat. However, it did not end up in divorce but finally led to an enlargement of consciousness and a better relationship. The dream seemed to shock that woman out of her too indulgent and unrealistic attitude concerning the love possession of her husband.

An essential feature belonging to the horse and the horse-symbol is that a horse can easily fall into *panic*. A nurse who suffered from inexplicable physical symptoms had a dream which mirrors this problem.

131 M.-L. von Franz, in: *Man und his Symbols*, p. 178.

132 C. G. Jung, *Symbols of Transformation* [Coll. Works 5], § 425.

Every day at her place of work, bitter conflicts among the nurses were the norm. She suffered badly from this and it was hard for her to tame her hot-blooded nature. She was very religious and had the idea that one should be good with other people even if they place a heavy burden on your life. This is an attitude which is often found among social workers. The suppression of her spontaneous reactions to such quarrels resulted directly in physical symptoms. She had pain in her abdomen and her stomach, fainting-fits, heartache and spasms in her throat. Here is her dream:

Nr. 45: Dream of the train and the coach:

I was on a train. I had to get off and change trains at a crossing where the trains stopped and started. Beside the trains there was a carriage pulled by four horses. These horses suddenly took fright when the guard blew his whistle, reared, crashed into one another and then everything collapsed. The coachman angrily whipped the horses. I wanted to put all the blame onto him. At first I didn't dare but finally I challenged him.

Trains symbolize the collective form of travelling on rails that always keep the train on the same track. That was her situation in the hospital, where everything had to be done in a precisely defined regular and prescribed way. Her being good in the Christian sense, always doing her work according to the highest standard and keeping her emotions under control, led to an enormous amount of pent up aggression in her unconscious. The carriage with the four horses symbolizes the vehicle of consciousness, which is drawn by the instinctive libido, and also by the body. Now an accident happens which has been caused by the man with the whistle, the guard, i.e. the one who keeps everything under control. The angry coachman who blames the horses for the incident is an animus, who aggravates the situation by his behavior. If the instincts are in danger of getting out of control, an angry animus will ruin every possibility to calm them down and bring them to safe ground where they can be taken care of. It was definitely such an animus who would brutally interfere whenever her horses got upset because of unforeseen incidents such as quarrels or extra work. He would then put all the blame on the panicking horses and punish them accordingly. With negative adjustments about herself he would make the situation even worse.

A horse usually panics when it cannot follow its natural fleeing instinct. This causes a stagnation of libido which is often compensated by a dangerous outburst. The more we observe real horses and understand their reactions, the better we recognize warning symptoms and can take precautions. The unconscious libido can be related to in exactly this way. It can suddenly express itself in violent outbursts. 'The horses have bolted with him or her', we say in German if someone has lost his or her self-control. Accumulated destructive libido can manifest itself as sheer panic. «Sudden spontaneous reactions from the unconscious need not be destructive, but when they turn into panic, they are really dangerous», Jung once said to Barbara Hannah.[133] This panic from the unconscious can bring us close to madness. A runaway horse can also be called mad because it may kill itself and others when it is in this state. Our dreamer was often close to suicide. In legends, this destructive libido side is represented by nightmares and sinister ghost-horses.

From the dream we can see that the excited horses have to be calmed down in order to re-establish order. If we shout at horses when they are upset, or hit them, it only makes matters worse. Luckily the dreamer was able to actively intervene in the incident. She learned from this dream that instead of always pushing herself to work hard and be nice to everybody, she needed to allow herself some relaxation and look after herself. Whenever her horses got upset, they had to be calmed down and fed. She took her physical reactions seriously and learnt to take better care of herself. The physical symptoms disappeared very soon. M.-L. von Franz once said in a private conversation that Jungian psychology was often attacked for not considering the body. But if the unconscious is taken really seriously, including the body becomes a natural part of individuation.

The dreamer of the next dream was a 30-year-old woman, a kindergarten teacher and painter. She suffered from a heavy negative mother-complex that used to rob her of all positive warmth and joy in life and hindered her from taking care of herself in an instinctive motherly way.

133 B. Hannah, *The Cat, Dog and Horse Lectures*, p. 123.

Nr. 46: Dream of the white and the brown horse:

A white rider on a white 'steed' dashes towards me, gets off, moves towards me, then mounts again and rides up to heaven, comes back, dashes away – a few times. I am urgently asked to look after my horse. My horse is earth-coloured, reddish brown. I become stressed. Do I own a horse? I am terrified at the thought that the animal could be starving to death because I had forgotten to feed it. Or perhaps that is not the case. But where is the horse? Where should I look for it? And what if it has died of hunger? Maybe I shouldn't have gone to the painting studio so often. I shouldn't have neglected the horse. In the sky I see strange black birds with forked tails. They are completely new to me. Some are small, some are big.

The white horse always and everywhere had a special value. It used to be the riding horse of kings and was considered the most thoroughbred of all horses. For Indo-Germanic races such as the Greeks, Romans and Persians, it was a symbol of the sun. The white horse in the present dream seems to be related to creative energy because it connects heaven and earth. This woman was very creative and intuitive. Strokes of genius came and went in her life like the white horse in the dream. But she suffered when they disappeared and when she had to wake up again to the everyday world. Then she became depressed, and behind this depression there was tremendous unconscious aggression. Depressive thoughts turn up in the dream as black birds.

The dream advises her to look after her own, earthly horse. This can be understood as caring for her body, using her life energy. In the widest sense she had forgotten to pay important regular attention to her unconscious fundamental instinct, which is like a horse that has to be fed every day. Fascinated by the white horse, and the experiences with her work in her painting studio, she was always in danger of neglecting her everyday life with cooking, eating regular meals, sleeping and working as a teacher. But her dreams also complained bitterly when she forgot her work as an artist! It was a constant balance on a tightrope, a continuous conflict between the here and now and the beyond. This is *the* problem of individuation!

Fig. 36: The nocturnal ascent of the Prophet Mohammed on his horse 'Buraq'.

A few years later she dreamt about a big wonderful beige horse which apparently was hers and on which she was supposed to learn to ride. At that time I put her on one of my horses and let her feel the smooth warmth of the animal. After that she did some active imagination in which the horse explained its nature and told her about the importance of staying in regular contact. It also asked her to take her life into her own hands without complaining miserably and reassured her of its support. As the horse as a symbol of unconscious libido has a close connection to the motherly unconscious it appears in this dream as a new positive aspect of the mother on an instinctual level, something which was most painfully absent in her life before.[134]

The horse in dreams often represents creative energy (fig. 35). If this energy is not freed or channelled it becomes regressive and nightmarish, and either sits on one's chest or becomes a ghost horse which carries one away. This motif is widespread in legends. Unlived creative energy can become dangerous because it pushes us out of our own reality into unreal fantasies. We can see this in projections or in inadequate ambition, a specific danger for people with artistic talents whose creative spontaneity is strangled. The nightmarish aspect of the horse is closely connected to the problem of the anima in the male psyche and to the animus of women. And, as mentioned before, blocked, unlived creative energy can transform into panic or even psychosis.

A young man dreamed:

Nr. 47: Dream of the nine black horses:

I see how somebody keeps playing a trick on the banks, and each time when the police think they have caught him, he disappears with the help of nine black horses of which he is the owner.

I would like to look at the nine first. The meaning of the number nine symbolically evolves mainly from the fact, that nine months are needed for the creation of a new child. The nine horses therefore symbolize creative energy that tends to renewal. However, the horses in this dream are black.

134 C. G. Jung, *Symbols of Transformation* [Coll. Works 5], § 421 f.

Black horses are always somehow uncanny. Evil spirits and the Devil himself ride black horses in sagas. They have something chthonic, certainly unchristian. These black horses carry a thief, a robber. This thief, as he owns nine black horses, which help him to escape whenever he is about to be caught by the police, is obviously not a common man, but rather a god, like the Germanic god Wotan with his black horses, or he is a demon. As a demon or a god, he embodies an archetype. He can be seen as the destructive aspect of the archetype of renewal, which the alchemists called *Mercurius*. Mercurius was also the god of thieves! If *Mercurius*, the spirit of the unconscious, is not respected, he becomes a thief of energy, a bank robber, who gives the authorities – the controlling consciousness – the runaround. If he cannot play his role as a messenger of the gods who conveys the will of the unconscious, he acts as a thief of our bank account. The bank account can be seen as energy available to consciousness. He is then incomprehensible and unpredictable, but carried by the brute instinctual energy of the unconscious, the black horses. Looking at this dream one cannot help thinking about the threatening situation of the current world-wide financial crisis with all the unforeseeable future consequences.

On the personal level, the black horses might also have to do with the young man's mother complex and therefore the problem of the anima, as the mother is the first carrier of the image of the anima. In her unconscious state, as a horse, the anima sustains the hidden capricious actions of the spirit of the unconscious which make a man unreliable and erratic (mercurial!) in his feelings and she provokes his creative energy to become destructive. What often comes out as depression, a loss of energy, or else unrelatedness and aggression with young people, in fact often has its source in this problem of creativity, which inhibits development and growth.

The young man in this dream was actually on the point of starting a new creative project, which was causing him a lot of headache as he had no idea where to begin with and where it would lead him. He first of all fell into a depression, but then he decided to abandon it all and just listen to his dreams and give the unconscious a chance. Some time later it answered his attempt with a moving dream of a speaking stone, another image of *Mercurius*, but this time in its most helpful and consolidated aspect. His project then continued in a creative way.

The topic of the creative energy of the horse comes up in another dream of the woman who had the dream about the whistling guard and the panicking horses.

Nr. 48: Dream of drawing a horse and a carriage:

I have to draw a picture for other people. There should be a carriage and a horse in the picture. The most beautiful picture has been made by a little girl. In the picture there is a horse, a big wheel and beside this a big R, the first letter of my name (fig. 37).

Fig. 37: Horse pulling a wheel. Drawing of the dreamer.

The carriage with the four wheels can be seen as the foundation of consciousness with its four functions: sensation, thinking, feeling and intuition. On this vehicle we are driving through our lives! But it also needs the power of the horse to drive our carriage, which is the unconscious instinctive energy. In our dream, in the most beautiful picture made by the little girl, the carriage was not drawn. Only a big wheel is shown, as if this were its most important aspect. The wheel is one of the oldest of all symbols. In earlier cultures, it had to do with time, which was imagined as a circle. The horoscope, which shows the individual's way through the constellation of the archetypes, starting from the moment of birth, is also a wheel of time, as birth means entering time and the chance of becoming conscious. The wheel is also a mandala. The mandala has to do with the order within the personality, but also with re-establishing an order especially after a period of disorientation, panic or chaotic psychic states. It thus has the effect of transforming disorder into a new order. It is an inner re-organization which results from the evolution of consciousness and from reflection. This seems to be the meaning of the wheel in this dream. The horse is like the galvanizing force of this development: in pulling the wheel, the horse symbolizes the instinct which maintains self-awareness and consciousness, i.e. individuation in motion. There is an amazing resemblance between the above drawing and the famous archaic sculpture of the sun disc pulled by a horse, found in Trundholm in Denmark (fig. 38). It illustrates impressively how archetypal structures in the collective unconscious provoke the same images everywhere and at all times.

Apart from the wheel in this dream, the capital R., as the first letter of the dreamer's name, is also important. The name changes a nameless being into one specific individual among many others. The R. therefore represents the beginning of her own individuality. I had the impression that this dream, which came at the beginning of analysis, had an important meaning, like a program for what lay ahead. The little dream girl who has painted the most beautiful picture is a spontaneous creative side within the dreamer, an aspect of the feminine self who gives loving care and attention to these processes. It is this which will make her an individual personality with a name of her own. So the little dream gave her an overview of unconscious libido, development of consciousness and her own role in it!

Horses and riding feature in many dreams – even those of people who have never ridden a horse in their life. Such dreams are important because they tend to motivate the dreamer towards establishing a closer connection to the unconscious. We could even say that riding a horse in a dream has to do with accepting the process of *individuation*. For women, this is often guided or accompanied by a positive animus figure. No wonder skilled riders and riding teachers often carry the fascination of an animus projection!

The dreamer of the following dream was 27 years old and at that time in a transition, personally and professionally which was expected to change her whole life and included considerable uncertainties.

Nr. 49: Dream of the test on a horse:

I have to pass a test on the back of a horse. First I have to pick a postcard from a stand, maybe it shows Paris. Then I have to balance a mirror between my knees, and at the same time I have to hold my necklace in my hand. Although it is quite short, I have to place it into the mouth of the horse, just like a bridle. But as I am still not feeling secure in the saddle, the teacher says I should first just play with the necklace in my hand to become more familiar with my balance on the horse. I move forward in the saddle. The teacher tells me to move backwards to have a more comfortable and safe position. The horse is very soft and compliant, even becoming attached to me. Everything goes well. The teacher is helpful, but maybe sometimes a bit cold or cynical. I feel quite safe, everything seems to be easy. I would like to go ahead. But the teacher says it is enough for today and asks me to get off the horse.

Fig. 38: Horse pulling the sun disc. Trundholm, 14th century.

Let us start with these strange tests. Picking up a postcard from a stand with a view – probably of Paris – reminded the dreamer of her past life there. We can assume that this has to do with an earlier view or perspective of Paris with all that it represents for her. This has to be consciously taken up. The mirror symbolizes self-reflection. Especially in dealing with the unconscious, we need the ability to reflect. Otherwise we can be carried away by the contents of the unconscious like a rider on an untamed horse. Reflection also has to do with prudence because only if we stay in the saddle do we remain conscious and able to realize the meaningful contents and signals of the unconscious. Balancing a mirror when riding could mean a delicate balance of thinking about the unconscious and oneself, and at the same time reacting from the unconscious vital basis of the horse instinct. Too much conscious thinking will violate the horse instinct; too much horse instinct will endanger consciousness.

Now a necklace will be placed into the horse's mouth like a bridle. In fact the dreamer always wore this necklace. It was made of small silver beads or balls, with some black pearls (i.e. also balls) between them. We often carry such things as a talisman for protection. We need those little symbols we love and to which we have an emotional relationship. Often they are symbols of the self, like the ball. The self, the central regulating factor of the unconscious psyche, has many different functional aspects and we always have to work out the specific meaning of its symbols. The ball has the surprising ability to apparently move out of itself. Thus it symbolizes that aspect of the self that has the ability to cause spontaneous motion. This is a divine quality that always has been connected to the world creator. The ball is thus also an old god image.

We experience this spontaneous motion in our dreams. Something from the unconscious psyche has come into motion and has created a dream. And with each dream that we have understood we have gained another ball in a chain that protects us from the autonomous powers of the unconscious and helps us to deal with them. In our dream, the necklace is supposed to direct the horse like a bridle. It contains all these little conscious experiences of the self which enable the ego to give a direction to the unconscious instinctive energy. The horse or the horse energy then will carry us and do great things for us but only – as Barbara Hannah says – if we live according to our inner law and do not abuse our power over the horse.[135]

The dreamer's position in the saddle, however, is not yet secure enough for her to place the necklace into the horse's mouth. This could indicate that the dreamer is not yet secure in her relationship to the unconscious. She has not yet found the right position, her balance towards the unconscious has not yet been established. Furthermore, the necklace is still quite short. According to the advice of the teacher, she should first only play with the necklace in her hands in order to become more familiar with it. Playing has to do with creative spontaneity. Children are creative when they play. Unintentional playing gives the unconscious the chance to enter consciousness through spontaneous ideas.

We must bear in mind that the dreamer was in a transitional and open-ended stage regarding her future life. Because we cannot stand uncertainty, in such situations we are often tempted to focus only on the outer situation or we are obsessed with one certain possibility. There is no connection to the unconscious. If we are symbolically not able to ride we might stumble into something which is not right for us because our instinctive energy has not agreed or has run away with us. One can directly transfer this to creative work, where we have the same problem. The question is always: are we in harmony with our unconscious or not? The dreamer is now told to sit on the back part of the saddle in a secure and comfortable position and she should just play with the necklace. It is like playing with the ideas from her unconscious until she has built up some certainty in connection with her basic instinct. By playing with all these creative impulses from the self she was increasingly able to find more and more the pattern of her life and hence the direction in which her life should be moving. Thus she will be carried in harmony with her horse. Her constructive and knowledgeable riding teacher, a positive animus, can help and teach her the right way. The animus has to do with logos and with the ability to analyze. If, however, he were cynical, then devaluating thoughts would enter the learning process, whereas if he were supportive, he would encourage the dreamer to bear with her uncertainty and to reach

135 B. Hannah, *The Cat, Dog and Horse Lectures*, p. 113.

her goal in accordance with the unconscious instinctive libido. Then she would also be able to take reasonable decisions in a relaxed way. She would feel from inside what is right and would be able to manifest what is in accord with her own nature in a true and powerful way.

A woman, mother of three adult children, had the following 'riding' dream:

Nr. 50: Dream of the horse, the cow and the unicorn:

I am travelling by train. The train stops. I mount a cow and ride on it for some time. Then I continue by train. Again the train stops. I mount a horse and ride on it for some time. Again I continue by train. As the train stops again, I mount a marvellous white unicorn and ride on with it.

In addition to the horse, we now have to enter the symbolism of the cow with this and with the next dream. The cow provides us with a great part of what nourishes us everyday: milk, cheese, butter, cream and all sorts of combined products containing them. The cow's nurturing aspect belongs to the mother and love goddesses such as the Egyptian Hathor with a cow's head, and the sacred Indian cow providing humans with the milk of heaven, which is rain. As B. Hannah points out, the cow's milk is an especially feminine creative product, a product of the eros side of a woman in contradistinction to the masculine creativity of the spirit and of the mind. The whole realm of eros and relationship has in fact a lot to do with creativity because, as B. Hannah says, «it cannot run on recognized rails. It must be individually tailored to each particular relationship, and this adaptation requires a creative effort [...] »[136]

This enables us to understand what the first 'stop over' on the individuation journey of the woman might be, where she has to get out of collective rules and preset goals. She was in fact a welfare worker, where the role of being good is, so to speak, predetermined, much similar to the nurse with the dream about the horses and the train mentioned above. The cow has on the one hand an aspect of humility and acceptance that can be too much for our taste. But its positive side is a quiet attitude of voluntary

136 B. Hannah, *Archetypal Symbolism of the Animals,* p. 378.

docility that makes it a «symbol par excellence of the attitude that finds the precious middle way [...]»[137] So riding the cow might have to do with a very individual feminine eros, a nurturing acceptance that is rooted in the instinctual bases of the psyche and not preset by outer demands and collective convictions. For women this positive cow quality, the mediating side of this sometimes ponderous-looking opposite to the mobility and flexibility of the male spirit and our extraverted culture, is often underestimated by their own animus and by the expectations of men. Modern business life makes it even more difficult, because these cow qualities live in connection to nature and to the unconscious. The image of a cow resting and ruminating has something immensely reposeful and comforting. The cow's mediating quality differs from the cat's by her docility. However, there is nothing servile here; it is in its own way creative and related in what B. Hannah calls "gentle acceptance",

The next stop-over brings to the dreamer the experience of riding a horse. This time there is a lot of energy and dynamism carrying her. It is not only her physical life that is affected; this unconscious libido generally sustains movement and creative impulses. Afterwards she has to go back to the train and continue a while on the collective rails. We can probably never stay on the cow or on the horse for a longer period of time, for this would mean that things would work out, so to speak, by themselves, instinctively. Human consciousness and external circumstances will always throw us out of the paradise, and time and again we lose the feeling of this important connection to the instinct. Yet it is not lost, as the dream clearly shows an inner development.

The third station seems to be the most important one, as the unicorn is an archetypal symbol of great significance in the history of human culture. It is a mystical animal that does not exist in this form. Nevertheless it has lingered on in the fantasy of men throughout the ages. Illustrations have been found from Neolithic times as well as on Assyrian friezes, in Indian-Buddhist legend, in the work of Aristotle, in the Old Testament, in alchemy and so on. It has not only been visualized as a horse with a big straight horn on its forehead, but also as an ass, a stag, a bull, a buck, a fish, a dragon, a

137 Ibid, p. 381.

scarab, in other words as a fabulous being.[138] The symbolism is vast. Jung has written a whole chapter about the unicorn in *Psychology and Alchemy*, showing how it is connected to pagan nature philosophy, Gnosticism, alchemy, to Indian and Iranian spiritual traditions and to the traditions of the Christian church. He worked out that the unicorn is a symbol of the wild, untamed, male, penetrating power of the spirit *Mercurius*. In medieval illustrations, there is the frequent motif of the unicorn wounded by the hunter, captured in the lap of the virgin (fig. 39). This motif is even found in China. In the allegory of the Christian church, the unicorn symbolizes primarily the dark, chthonic, emotional power of god, but also of Christ himself. It is known in Gnosticism as *alexipharmakon*, the all-healing principle, and moreover it has the capacity to bring everything to maturation and perfection. The essence of the power, health and life of the unicorn is concentrated in the secret of the unicorn horn. The attributes ascribed to the unicorn horn were also assigned by the alchemists to their stone, which, according to legend, was found under the horn of the unicorn. [139]

As a possible interpretation of this section of the above dream, we could say that with its horn, the unicorn points to the essence, to the core of a life. Being carried by the white unicorn means being carried towards higher consciousness by an instinct that is at the same time a spiritual power beyond human dimension and understanding. Mounting the unicorn means that the feminine ego is carried by an archetypal goal-oriented dynamism that aims at the religious experience of the self.

The whole dream brings to mind the fairytale where usually three challenges have to be accepted, three steps have to be taken, three tasks have to be completed before the final goal can be reached. In that respect, the dream mirrors the dynamic course of psychic development. On an external level, the three animals could also be seen as connected to the three stages of the life of a woman. The cow would then stand for the biological phase, where family, childbirth, partnership are possible and central and determine a woman's limitation, the horse for a phase where the energy pulls her into outer life again, where she might be able to take

138 R. Abt, I. Bosch, V. MacKrell, *Dream Child,* I. Bosch: Chapter "The Unicorn", 297f.

139 C. G. Jung, *Psychology and Alchemy* [Coll. Works 12], § 518-554.

Fig. 39: La Dame à l'Unicorne (The Lady and the Unicorn). Tapistry.

up new projects, go back to her job or take up some other activity. The unicorn would characterize the last phase, where the energy can change its course towards the inner reality of life, to a more spiritual interest in the demands of the self.

«Jung once likened the human psyche to the colour scale: At the infrared end it loses itself in the depths of the instincts and somatic processes; at the ultraviolet end it reaches into the realm of the archetypes, that is, of the spirit. In the archetypal image, the *meaning* or latent spiritual aspect of instinct is revealed.»[140] So our consciousness moves anywhere along the scale between the animal instinct and its latent spiritual aspect. The instinct as the power which, especially in young people, galvanizes an individual into action from the infrared end, later usually starts to bring up its other side, namely the side of meaning from the ultraviolet end. What in earlier life just works naturally in a dynamic natural flow – the biological life as it were – later begins to weaken. Then the meaning and the apprehending

140 M.-L. von Franz, *Archetypal Dimensions of the Psyche,* p. 90.

of the inner images become more and more important. Cow, horse and unicorn in this dream mirror such a natural development process. This seemingly simple little dream is in fact a great individuation dream.

The cow and horse are connected in the next dream in a different context. The dreamer was a young man of 25 who came to analysis because of an unhappy love story. He was somewhat spoilt by a positive mother complex and too soft to stand up for himself as a man in relation to women.

Nr. 51: Dream of the cows turning into young horses:

I am in a stable. Someone (I think it is my analyst) shows me the cows. She points to a cow in the front row and says that it is a stupid one. It would not be able to bend its neck to the floor to reach the hay there. To be able to eat, it always has to go down onto its knees. The way the cow is eating looks odd. Suddenly, while we move on, all the cows turn into young horses. The woman points out the beauty of these animals and praises them to the skies.

In the context of this dream, one of the cows behaves in a weird way. It is unable or does not want to bend its neck to get its hay from the floor, which would be much easier than to go down onto its knees. For a cow, bending the neck means getting food in a natural way, while kneeling is uncomfortable and humiliating. The cow represents the dreamer's own unconscious feminine side, an anima that behaves, so to speak, like a stupid cow, humiliating herself instead of grabbing what she needs. This probably has to do with the dreamer's love situation, where he is not able to stand up for his own needs and feelings. A positive mother complex sometimes can make a man too much of a softy, an all-understanding and considerate friend rather than a man who grabs for himself what he wants. Of course, women then often make a fool out of him and he only gets attention when he falls onto his knees. The analyst is an anima with analyzing competence that can open his eyes to this fact. Then the cows turn into young horses, the image of wild, untamed energy. This is what he obviously needs to see and to regard as a possibility for himself. The young horses will have to be taken out of the cows' stable into the fields, and once they are grown up they will learn to carry a human being. They represent instinctual energy from the infrared end, and they will carry him into life. This man later got into homosexuality for a while. Dreams made it clear that he was attracted by the virility in other men that he himself was still lacking. Afterwards he gained a foothold in his own life, learned to "get hold of his food" and to esteem and trust his own creative libido, feelings and psychological understanding.

I would like to continue with a further important characteristic of the horse. It is its incredible powers of *perception and orientation*. If we ride through the countryside, our horse will perceive and remember every little detail with photographic precision. Another time, on the same path, the horse will no doubt recognize each change with increased alertness, will be uneasy, break out and snort fearfully. Sometimes falling leaves, a rustling bird in the bush, or a sudden blast may be enough to cause a similar fright. The rider is often surprised by the horse's unexpected reaction as he or she does not usually perceive these little details. The nervous energy of the horse is expressed by sudden movement and is usually communicated from the horse up through the back of the rider like a flash. Every rider has experienced that. This might be the external reason why horses were popularly believed to be able to see ghosts and spooks. And wherever ghosts or powers from the Beyond were present, one had to be careful. The behavior of a horse was often thus interpreted as an oracle. Sometimes it was considered a bad sign if a horse was neighing at the beginning of a journey, and it was deemed wiser to turn back immediately. Psychologically we could say that an *instinctive perception of the invisible* had been projected onto the horse.

We know from ourselves that something within us has a perception for inner and outer things which has nothing to do with consciousness. Everybody has probably had the experience of thinking of a person one has not seen for a long time and the next day there is a letter from him or her in the mailbox. Mothers sometimes hear their children cry before they really do and they often have a presentiment of danger for their child. In the Tsunami flood in Asia in 2004, animals are reported to have left the coast hours and days before the water arrived. People who realized this were alert and many seemed to have had this strange feeling in the pit of the stomach that something was about to happen. In such cases we say that a sound instinct had warned or helped. These would be the *extrasensory perception (ESP)* of the inner horse or the horse instinct which brings the invisible into consciousness.

Legends often tell how the choice of the place where a church should be built or a cross should be set up was determined by a horse. Also the place where the coffin should be buried was, according to some legends, determined by where the horse stopped. Old legends also tell that horses could paw the ground with their hoof and water sprang up, often the origin of healing wells. When Pegasus' hoof hit the ground water sprang up, but also the horse of the Germanic god Balder was said to pump out water from the earth with its hoof. Not only water, but also fire has this fertilizing aspect brought out by the horse. Old fire and lightning gods have fiery horses (fig. 40).

Horses here symbolize future possibilities which may be constructive and healing. Thus psychologically they represent an *instinctive semi-conscious spontaneous creative side*. In *Shadow and Evil in Fairytales*, M.-L. von Franz points out that the horse and its wisdom represents an «immediate spontaneous reaction from the deepest instinctual layer of an individual personality. It is each time unique, because it is always improvised and springs in new form from the spontaneous living basic nature of the psyche.»[141] Consciousness has to be attentive to these inner 'horse reactions' because through this instinct, dangers, inclinations or new vital impulses may become visible.

The following dream is one that mirrors a dramatic reaction of the horse instinct to the dangerous threat of evil. It was dreamt by a middle-aged woman who had heard a man giving a talk. Together with almost all the other women in the audience and quite a few men too, she fell for his eloquence and smart appearance.

Nr. 52: Dream of the horse/cow warning from a criminal:

There is a big room like a cinema or lecture theatre with hundreds of people. A man has invited them all. In the beginning I think he is marvellous and I even want to dance with him. But then I realize, that he has burnt people backstage. I see the black burned corpses lying there. Nobody has realized anything except me. Down the stairs there is a horse or a cow tied to the wall. It is shivering, terrified, because it has realized what is going on. Then there is a courageous little woman who asks questions in a

141 M.-L.von Franz, *Shadow and Evil in Fairytales*, p. 249.

Fig. 40: Fire attributes belong to the horses of old fire-and lightning gods. Lusitano stallion 'Dourado'.

loud voice and warns people. After that the doors, which had been locked so that nobody could escape, open and it is possible to escape from this place of horror.

With this dream, the woman realized the inflation and destructive fascination of the man she and the other women had fallen for. The dreamer was deeply impressed by how easily women can fall for such a man because he embodied such an animus figure. The suffering of the horse or cow had shed light onto the hidden terror behind the stage. It was indeed only the instinct that knew and could warn, an instinctual feeling of suffering deeply in the unconscious she had not listened to. After the dream, the reality of his inflation and superficial and even incorrect statements seemed so obvious that not only she but everybody else asked themselves why they had not seen it before! The most frightening was the insight that women collectively, for instance in politics, might support the most awful men if they were not conscious about their own negative animus they are dancing with. It was the instinct, the animal that would indicate that something was wrong and therefore help towards a more adequate view of the inner and outer reality. Courage and standing up against evil by the individual is in this case suggested by the dream.

The wisdom of the horse instinct is the topic in the Irish folktale of 'The Prince and the Bird who sings so sweetly', which Marie-Louise von Franz interprets in *Shadow and evil in Fairytales*. Summarized it runs as follows:

A king sends out his three sons to catch a mysterious bird for him. The two stepsons do not succeed because they are wicked and have no courage. But the real prince finds out that the bird is a queen's daughter. Her father is a magician, killing all the princes who want to take his daughter away from him. The hero, who has been given a magic white horse by a helpful old woman, has to face the challenge of a magic competition against the old king. The king hides himself three times, in an apple, in a fish and in his daughter's ring. The hero has to hide himself from the old king three times, in a hole made by a hair pulled out of the tail of the horse, in a hole made by a nail pulled out of the horse's shoe and in a hole made by a tooth that has been pulled out. Even the blind seer of the king cannot prevent the hero from taking the princess away with the help of the horse, which tells him exactly what to do. In the end, the wisdom of the helpful horse overcomes the magical book knowledge of the evil king.

The horse's advice even overcomes the blind seer and the king with all his books and traditions. The wisdom of the horse instinct is obviously superior to all traditional established knowledge. From a psychological perspective, this is, according to Marie-Louise von Franz, a semi-conscious reaction and the only thing that can conquer the onslaught of evil. This spontaneous reaction from the unconscious is each time a creative moment and comes as a complete surprise [142] – a gift we should accept thankfully, for example, if suddenly the right words come to us in a critical situation. This is experienced as genuine enlightenment.

The next dream (shortened) of a 45-year-old man is about this illuminating quality of the horse symbol:

Nr. 53: Dream of the phosphorous horse:

I am riding my wife's horse through the countryside. Suddenly I realize that thorny tendrils have torn open a triangle in the horse's coat. Through the hole I can see that the whole horse is phosphorous inside. I realize that this hole has to be closed again, as the divine quality of this horse should not be visible to people.

In the woods one can sometimes see phosphorous stumps glowing in the dark, a weak but distinct light. White phosphorous has this illuminating power when ignited by air. The phosphorous horse is thus a carrier of such a symbolic *lumen naturae*, as this enlightening capacity of the unconscious was called by the medieval medical doctor, philosopher and alchemist Paracelsus. This illuminating instinct is connected with the dreamer's wife or with his anima. As an unconscious vital base, the horse with the phosphorous inside bears a dim light, which symbolizes creative potential. It is important that this potential remains hidden because extraverted forces might try to get hold of that numinous power and exploit it for personal claims to power. As a consequence it would mean falling into the dangerous trap of inflation that lurks around creativity. The dreamer understood the message.

142 M.-L.von Franz, *Shadow and Evil in Fairytales,* p. 249.

The topic of inflation in connection with the horse is also known in the mythological tale of the Greek winged horse Pegasus, the son of Poseidon. Bellerophon, a mortal, wanted to ride with him into heaven to sit together with the gods at their table, but they sent a horsefly that stung Pegasus, so that he threw off his rider, who from then on was lame. Other mythological winged horses are Wotan's eight-legged stallion Sleipnir or Mohammed's horse Buraq, which, according to the myth, carried him up to heaven. These winged horses have to do with creative *intuition and inspiration* that can carry to heaven, but can also lead to dangerous inflation and fall. That would then mean the total loss of the creative drive and the paralysis of the ego. The Siberian shamans used sticks with a horse's head on them during their journey through the Beyond. They also symbolize the inspiration which carries the shaman during his trance.

We keep this ancient symbolism in mind, when we now plunge into a series of dreams of a woman around 45 years old. These dreams contain the horse symbol in an amazingly broad range of meaning. They are clearly connected, which is why they are here discussed as a whole. The dreamer was a nurse and physiotherapist for people, but out of her great love for animals she had also become an animal therapist. Besides her work with humans, she was working with dogs, cats, especially with horses, and whatever animals needed her help. She was a gifted healer, not only because of her expert knowledge, but also because of her closeness to the unconscious. This entailed a remarkable instinctive understanding of animals. She had a negative mother relation, which very nearly cost her her life when she was a child. She survived, but courageously escaped the situation, left her family and country at the age of sixteen, and found her own life.

The dream is in two parts, following each other with an interval of three months.

Nr. 54: Dream of the country inn and the horses on the wall:

I am travelling by car. I have to look for accommodation for the night. I drive through the woods and on little country lanes. After some time I discover an inn, rather secluded, on the edge of the wood. An elderly lady welcomes me and gives me a key for my room. In the morning I go to the breakfast room. It is a big room with wooden tables and benches. It reminds me of a great hall in a castle. Attached to the walls there are large and small heads of horses, with necks and chests, as if stuffed, but one can see and hear that they are living. There are 8 horses, ranging from a light Arabian horse to a heavy workhorse. It is very impressive. I sit down to have my breakfast at one of the big tables. Suddenly the door opens and the elderly lady comes in with an enormous wheelbarrow filled with hay. She starts to feed the horses and to clean the stable. The horses are very lively. The room fills with horse sounds. I drink my tea and leave the inn, with the feeling that I must come back.

Nr. 55: Dream of the country inn and the black horse, 3 month's later:

It is like in real life. It is early in the morning. I am riding with my horse through woods and fields in lovely weather. We are enjoying the ride. At the crossroads, I want to turn right to slowly go back home. But my horse just wants to go on. I cannot stop him, he goes on and on, very determined. He seems to have a definite goal.

Suddenly we arrive at the inn from my dream. My horse does not wait for me to get off, but just walks into the inn and into the breakfast room. I dismount and want to leave through the nearest door. But he stands in my way, so that I cannot leave. The same happens on the other side of the room. All the horses are still there and look at me expectantly. After some time I choose the fifth horse on the wall. It is a black horse, about 7 years old, with a lot of radiance, but still fragile in his physique. This horse holds an enormous attraction for me; it is powerful, beautiful yet at the same time a little frightening. I then try to open up the wall to get out of the room. I even use a hammer and chisel, but without success. The old lady appears and says casually: «There are other ways!» (to get out). I look at the nervous and impatient horse. Suddenly I know what I have to do. I must plead. I beg the black horse to come. And already he passes me, crosses the room and walks out through the door, out of the inn. I am stunned. The old lady says:«Hurry up, it is important!» I follow the horse. Later I am riding on my horse, galloping after the black horse. We find him standing in a meadow, eating grass. Each time we approach him, he runs away. This game goes on until the evening. I give up, but I have a feeling that things will be okay.

Later I am in my bed. I wake up because I hear the wheezing of a horse. I first think of my horse, but I know he is in his stable. After some time I go to the window. There is the black horse on the veranda. He is shining in the light of the full moon, beautiful, powerful and fragile at the same time, black-blue, full of confidence. The smell of roses and lavender is in the air. The white rambler roses are opened and smell sweetly. There is an overwhelming feeling of love in me. This is love!

The dreamer travelling by car, looking for accommodation for the night, comes to a fairytale-like inn. The whole beginning of the dream already reminds us of the beginning of many fairytale situations, where the hero or heroine is on his or her way, when something unexpected happens that opens up new outlooks. The dreamer enters that strange inn, where an old lady feeds her magical horses, the living heads on the wall. She obviously has special knowledge, because, as can be seen in the second dream, she knows what has to be done. Strangely enough she does not explain what she is doing nor does she make it clear from the beginning what the dreamer is supposed to do. She just feeds her horses, but she is clearly not a normal woman. She is like a mother-nature figure, mistress of the animals, appearing here as the hostess of an inn which is at the same time a stable. In her house, one can get shelter, rest and food, and animals are fed. At first glance, she is not interested in the human being entering her house at all, although she provides her with food.

Now what about these horses heads? They are fixed on the wall, like a hunter's hunting trophies. Yet they can eat and live as horses in stables do. This is something that can only happen in the miraculous dream world of the unconscious. So we try to understand the deeper meaning of this image. The horses live, but they are blocked in an unnatural state. It is implausible that the lady herself should have fixed them onto the wall in this position. We would then have to consider her as a witch, who has put a spell onto these horses. But she is not evil and her helpfulness speaks in her favor. I would rather conclude that in the magical world of the great mother, in the unconscious, a most essential life instinct is blocked by a wrong attitude in collective consciousness. This does not seem to be a personal problem only, as the archetypal setup of this dream shows. Obviously not even the great mother can change this unsatisfactory situation. She is only able to keep the horses alive by feeding them. If we look at fairytales, we can see that there, too, the archetypal figures only assist towards redemption, but it always needs a hero or a heroine to complete the process. In fairytales, the hero or the heroine is the unconscious role model for a conscious ego acting in the right way. The archetypal world of the collective unconscious needs ego consciousness, but ego consciousness without the help of the archetypal world will not succeed either. Only in relation to each other can the process of development of consciousness move on. This dream seems initially to be about the liberation of the horse instinct.

In the Grimm fairytale, "The Goose Girl", there is the speaking horse Falada, whose head is cut off by the old king and nailed onto a wall. It is alive and it speaks and helps the goose girl to her true destiny, to be the new queen. It belongs to the mother archetype, but in the end it is not redeemed itself. So in this fairytale there remains something unsolved and not quite satisfying. If we take fairytales as something like collective dreams that are not yet understood in collective consciousness, as M.-L.von Franz suggests, we realize that the first dream section throws our dreamer into the middle of a collective problem that remains unsolved to this day. It has to do with the unredeemed horse instinct. But she realizes that at that moment

Fig. 41: Urartu horse bit from 8th-7th century BC, from a burial chamber in Altintepe, near Van (Eastern Anatolia).

she cannot do anything and leaves the place, knowing that she will have to come back. The time has not yet come. It looks as if it was just by chance that she came to this place by car. In fact it was probably meant to be, because in the next dream there is a definite instinctive drive that brings her there.

She is now on her own horse. The car as a vehicle of consciousness with its four functions is now replaced by her own instinct. This instinct is close to her personal life. Something inside her knows the way she has to go. Her old horse, a white horse, was in reality found abandoned in a field, just skin and bones, on the verge of death. Although she had neither money nor time, and her life situation was unsettled and problematic, she took him to a stable and looked after of him with total commitment. There he lived for another ten happy years. He also played an important role in her dreams and fantasies.

It is this horse who, in the second dream, brings her back to the inn with the old woman. He does not allow her to go to the right, the side of consciousness, but he wants her to trust him and let herself to be carried to the place of the old lady. Although the old lady is not a witch, the situation brings the dreamer close to her terrible mother problem and it looks to her as if there was no way out of it. Such a powerful complex has the quality of being seemingly unchangeable, so that one seems to be locked in it forever. Her horse, her own instinct, prevents her from escaping from this place and running away, as we usually do when we get close to the open wounds of our complexes. Raging around with hammer and chisel – the tools of consciousness – does not help in this situation of confinement and anxiety. All the horses are looking at her expectantly. There is this unexpressed expectation in the unconscious, a longing for liberation and redemption that is greater than her personal problem. But there is also that very powerful and yet fragile black horse, the fifth in the row, which holds an enormous attraction for her. Her personal horse is a white horse, this one is black. While the white horse symbolically is connected to the light, the sun and the daylight, the black one belongs to the night world, to the unknown, to the dark mother. It is the fifth horse in the row. So the number five must be looked at more closely.

The direct relation of the number five to the human body (we have five extremities, head, two arms, two legs, and five sense organs) «helps us to understand why this number is so often symbolically connected to natural man and to the microcosm, since human beings used to be looked upon as being a small cosmos. In Christianity, the five therefore became associated with everything corporeal and thus especially with lust, drives and sin.»[143] It makes sense that the black horse is somehow connected to the dreamer's own microcosm, to her own personal life, even if he belongs to the archetypal world of the collective unconscious. He is, so to speak, the part connected to both worlds and he can be contacted by her as a human being. He is in that sense a *mediator*. This corresponds to what alchemy describes with the number five, the quintessence. The alchemical quintessence is a mediator in the middle of the four, the two pairs of opposites. This «gives the number five a specific erotic dimension, as it is by 'loving attraction' that opposites join together, as the old masters of alchemy described that unifying quality.»[144] The number five also seems to be connected to the course of the planet Venus.[145] The fact that in Christianity the five, that is everything corporeal, has been put on the side of sin, has its consequences to this day in the unbelievable lack of understanding of the animal world, be it the instinctual level of the unconscious psyche of men, be it the external animal living besides us. Our dreamer meets this problem everyday in her work with her animal patients and their owners. While people usually nowadays at least consciously care for their body, if not for their psyche, the relation to the animals and also to horses, is often cruel, heartless, ignorant, without compassion and eros. So the number five in the dream already announces the deep dimension this symbol of the black horse is leading into. Above all, it has to do with the collective problem that Christianity and the development of consciousness have brought upon us, namely an alarming alienation from the instinctual world.

Now the old lady comes and says that there are other ways, without saying what sort of ways. The 'hammer-and-chisel-method' is obviously not the right way to proceed in this situation. The dreamer suddenly realizes

143 Th. Abt, *Introduction to Picture Interpretation*, p. 133 f.

144 Ibid, p. 134.

145 Ibid, p. 135.

that she has to ask the black horse for help. As in so many fairytales, the help of the animal has to be sought and accepted and the claim to rational will power solutions has to be given up. With that, the dream ego of this woman demonstrates an attitude of devotion and respect in front of something bigger than herself, a truly religious attitude. This, and her wish to be close to him, seems to free the blocked animal. She begs him to come and this is what he does. And then all the doors open and he steps out into freedom. It is now the old lady who tells her to hurry up and follow him, because «it is important». The dreamer obviously needs this kick.

This could be a moment when consciousness might miss the continuation of the process of realization. It is a feeling of being stunned and even helpless in front of the unexplainable power of an hitherto unknown realm of the psyche that sometimes even prevents people from continuing with analysis. They cannot see that «it is important» to go on. Some unknown intention in the unconscious sometimes seems to try to activate or motivate the ego to follow its hints, to reflect on them, think, brood and chew them over until they eventually reveal some of their origin and meaning.

It is again the dreamer's feeling for that beautiful black horse that makes her react immediately to the lady's challenge. Feeling and emotion is intrinsically tied to the individuation process. Wherever a conscious realization of importance takes place, we are emotionally touched. Sometimes it is a shocking dream or other manifestation of the unconscious

Fig. 42: The dreamer's white horse with a black companion.

world that makes one wake up and realize that «it is important». The encounter with that black horse provokes a feeling in our dreamer that it is something that belongs to her intrinsically, which makes her choose it and follow it, even if it now seems to be playing a game with her. She has to follow him alone, she cannot free all the other horses, too. She is obviously not meant to solve the problem collectively, but just has to go where her own destiny wants her to go. To follow the instinctive impulses from her unconscious, which entice her onto the individuation path, is her contribution to a renewal of the collective, although for the time being she does not seem to be very successful. The horse escapes again and again.

Anybody who has ever tried to catch a horse that does not want to be caught, knows what that means! It's frustrating! In fairytales it is eventually a deer or a stag that provokes the hero to follow it and then he gets lost in the great wood, and this is the beginning of the story. The misery of not being able to get what one wants not only belongs to the hero's quest, that is to psychic development, but it is even a *conditio sine qua non*. If the hero had now just turned back and gone home again, knowing that he would anyway never get that stag, he would have missed the princess in the end! Our dreamer does the right thing. Being carried by her white horse, she does not give up, although she is not successful at the start. Even though the contents of the psyche cannot just be grabbed, it is important to stay with them. Dream symbols so often cannot be understood, though eventually they touch us deeply or else repel us. The white horse is a libido that helps with the continuation of the growing process of nature in the psyche, while the goal is out of sight again and again. It also conveys the confidence that things will be okay, so that one can let go and settle for the night. Then, when conscious effort comes to rest, the object of the whole endeavor can appear by itself. It is a common experience that after a long and desperate struggle, a solution sometimes comes unexpectedly from nowhere the moment we can let go. It is as if the unconscious needed this emptiness to bring up the new impulse. But it does not appear without the preceding effort!

We could ask why the black horse runs away at all and why sometimes it has to be so hard to understand what is meant by all the detours and what the whole suffering should be good for. As mentioned before, «there is like an inner eye of self-recognition, which mediates a different view of ourselves than does the ego».[146] This eye, which looks at us from within, was understood by the alchemist Gerhard Dorn, a pupil of Paracelsus, as an image of god planted in the human psyche. Seen from this angle, the right moment, which is also so important in fairytales, is hardly ever what we expect, but might only come when this inner subject considers the time to be ripe.

The last part of the dream brings an image of utmost beauty and numinosity. There is the black horse, shining in the light of the full moon, with the smell of roses and lavender in the air and there is this unimaginable feeling of love. It is difficult to say something about this image, as it speaks for itself in its radiance and beauty. Roses in antiquity were sacred to the mother- and love goddess Venus-Aphrodite and Dionysos. In the antique tale of "The Golden Ass" by Apuleius, the hero figure, Lucius, is finally redeemed by the roses of the Egyptian goddess Isis from having been turned into an ass. So the smell of roses belongs to the invisible presence of a god or a goddess. Roses, as the attribute of these gods, symbolize eros in its widest sense as a principle of relatedness and love. Lavender is used against all evil powers, bedevilment, the 'evil eye', the demons of decease etc. and is also a healing plant.

So the black horse turns out to belong to the archetype of the great nature and love goddess, with all her instinctual and healing power. The blackness belonging to the nature goddess is still present in the black madonnas we find in many churches. In their blackness, the instinctual eros aspects of the great pre-Christian mother goddesses have survived, although often not really accepted as such by the church. One used to say that the Black Madonna originally was just burned in a fire, but black she remained in countless copies all over the world. It was by the simple people that she was worshipped through the centuries although it was prohibited. Male church authorities often threw black madonnas out of the churches, although people loved them, and installed white and pink madonnas instead. She is black, because she dwells in the shadow of the Christian Virgin Mary as a mother of nature, of the earth and of the instinctual feminine life, unperceived, like the lady in the inn with her horses on the wall.

146 M.-L. von Franz, *Projection and Re-collection*, p. 165, see also C. G. Jung, *Memories, Dreams, Reflections*, p. 67 f.

Black horses in sagas, as we mentioned before, are often devils' or witches' horses. They are usually destructive and represent repressed instinctual energy. But this one is not evil. It is even to be followed with all endeavor, until finally in the moonlight it will approach and be visible. The moon belongs to all mother goddesses and to the feminine. Its light can only be seen in the darkness of the night world. It is the world of the unknown psyche, the unconscious, of whose wisdom we can only get a hint through its symbolic images, like the one of the black horse. There it reveals itself in all its radiant beauty and is an omen for the goddess, as is the lovely smell of roses in the air. The dream culminates in the overwhelming feeling of love, which is described by the mystics as the utmost fulfillment and experience of the godhead.

M.-L.von Franz says that the development of relatedness to our fellow creatures and to mankind as a whole, a process that always accompanies individuation in the single person, is a relatedness that proceeds not from the ego but from a transcendental inner center, the self.[147] The goddess with the black horse as her messenger and visible embodiment is an image of the self. It conveys a feeling of eros that is beyond words.

This great individuation dream might impart meaning to the dreamer's whole life and destiny. It connects her with the healing centre of her instinctual psyche, which means healing for her own soul. Realizing the deep background of such a dream can enlarge a personality, bring it into a new balance of the internal and the external, render it more whole. Healing and wholeness are connected. Wholeness, the goal of individuation, is healing. And being healed in the original meaning of the word means whole. In the German language, the words 'whole' and 'healed' are one and the same: 'Heil' means being whole and also healed. It is also at the root of the word 'holy'. The saints in their holiness embody the archetype of human wholeness. They are usually regarded as healers, too.

Only in relating to the nocturnal realm of the unconscious will this woman be able to get over the terrible mother experience of her childhood and connect to her healing feminine self, which provides a foundation for her own way of life and gives meaning to it. The symbol of the black horse

147 M.-L. von Franz, *Projection and Re-Collection*, p. 174.

seems to assign highest priority to the instinctual level of the unconscious psyche, where the contradictory opposites in the mother image can be bridged and old wounds can be healed.

To understand the next dream of this woman, we have to look at an active imagination first, as the dream takes up some of its motifs later. Her question before the imagination was: Where is my eternal soul in the shamanistic upper world? She had attended a shamanistic seminar, with the well-known risk of estrangement from one's own personal relation to the unconscious.

In this imagination (shortened) she is taken to an ice castle by an eagle or buzzard, a friend of hers from other dreams and imaginations. Left alone by him in front of this castle, she enters through a big door. She follows a path with many people passing and realizes that what seems to be snow or ice under her feet is in fact all salt. She arrives at another door with carved animals on it. When she touches the animals on the door, the door and the animals somehow vanish beneath her hands and she can enter. Behind the door she finds a great room all made of salt, like a church but with much more light and with the salt reflecting all the colors. Later she realizes that this room is at the seaside, and it is directly connected to the water, which comes and goes in a spectacular way. She sits down near the edge of the water with her feet and legs dangling in it. Around her there are animals all over the place, flamingos, crocodiles, scorpions, dogs, sea lions, cats, horses, just everything, all in complete harmony. They all communicate with each other and with her. There are no barriers. Later she desperately realizes that she has to go back, which she several times refuses to do. At the end of the active imagination she feels the sharp claws of the buzzard, who brings her back into real life.

She remained upset for several hours after this active imagination. Unexpectedly the question about the place of the eternal soul in the upper world brings her down to the animal world! The door to the unconscious seems to be wide open for her. That could also be dangerous, because who would like to leave such a paradise to return to the hardship of everyday life? Luckily there is the buzzard, guiding her and bringing her back into conscious reality.

Now the dream following this imagination. The old white horse was still alive at that time. His owner used to make sure every night before falling asleep, that he was okay in his stable. This happened in the form of a fantasy, where, so to speak, she entered the horse to see if everything was okay. This night she had the alarming feeling, that something was wrong with his eyes. She got up, jumped into the car and rushed to the stable, where she found him in pain with an ablation of the retina. Thanks to her quick reaction and the swift response of the vet, they could save some 5 percent of his eyesight, which was already a miracle. There was no hope that it would become better. After the dream and the following fantasy work in the evenings, it even slowly improved up to around 30 percent.

Nr. 56: Dream of working inside the horse:

In my dream I am asleep. My buzzard has come to fetch me again (like in the fantasy of the salt castle). He lifts me out of my bed and brings me to the lane of the salt castle. The lane is now like a bobsled run, with walls on both sides. I am rather calm and cheerful. There are many such paths to the castle. I want to go to the wooden door, but then I suddenly slip and go speeding down the run like a bobsledder. I expect the wall to appear and me to crash into it, but I simply glide through it and land in the stable in the hay besides my horse. «Ah there you are finally», he says, «get down to work!» He does not explain, but it is quite clear, that I have to work on his eye. So I go into his eye. I start chiselling, hammering, scraping, painting the retina new in all the necessary colors. The whole night I am at work on the retina, repairing, sewing, painting, attaching it again, a complete overhaul! I am inside the eye for all that, in a good atmosphere, working away. When I have finished, I tell the horse, and ask what I should do now? He says that I still have to go to his reins, and that will be all. I scrub the reins a bit. Then I fall asleep besides him in the hay.

The ice or salt castle of the imagination is repeated in her dream, but now the path leading to it is depicted by the unconscious as dangerous and slippery. So the dreamer does not arrive where she actually would like to, in the paradise of the salt castle, but instead lands in the stable with her horse, where she has to do hard work. The whole situation, though still miraculous, is now connected to her horse, her own instinct, which makes her work!

The closeness to the unconscious could carry a human being into having his or her head in the clouds and into inflation. The dream now seems to attach great weight to her instinct and her healing mission, which is very much down to earth. It is hard work, as was her job in reality. She was a small and slender woman, treating those big horses with her hands. In fact it seemed that a lot of this work was sustained by her shamanistic intuition, symbolically the eagle/buzzard and the horse. Entering into the horse to mend what is out of order could be an image for the empathy necessary for all healing, also for psychic healing. So it is ultimately the eros and the will to work hard that stand behind all healing capacities, also when it comes to the healing of one‘s own psychic wounds. But after all it needs a going inside. Let us elaborate a little more on this statement.

With such a shamanistic dream one could easily lose the ground under one's feet. Human beings are not able to create miracles. It is in fact the matter of the self, the goddess, which is much more than a personal gift. The identification of the ego with the self would lead this woman astray, as is the case with some of these well-known inflated modern healers. She would then probably soon lose her empathy and eros, because identification with an archetype always spoils human relatedness. The same is of course valid for a true relation to animals. Inflation would therefore endanger her genuine capacity for healing. We can easily transfer this insight onto the analytical situation. Fortunate are those who have a buzzard with sharp claws to bring them back into the reality of the personal life!

The dream of the horse that has to be healed by work in his eye is so closely connected to the personal situation with the dreamer's sick horse that it is difficult to discriminate the archetypal meaning from it. However, from this dream it seems as if the instinct itself would call upon consciousness for its healing. For that purpose, a complete union with the animal is needed. The union with the animal is an archetypal motif. According to Jung, it symbolizes the removal of the separation between consciousness and unconscious, which is the real source of life, and a reunion with the matrix of the inherited disposition.[148] The animal, if not disturbed or violated, never deviates from what it is meant to be or to do. Healing the eye of the animal by uniting with it, means healing an instinct that can see what is meant for us, because it is rooted in our inherited disposition. So the eye has, besides the real, also an important symbolical meaning.

The role of consciousness in the process of this healing union with the instinct is an active one. Hammer and chisel, needle and brush, saw and

148 C. G. Jung, *Psychology and Alchemy* [Coll. Works 12], § 174.

file must be used. It is hard work with these tools of consciousness, which have to do with understanding and reflection. The only motivation to do that comes from eros and compassion, the love for the dreamer's horse. The negative mother complex of a daughter means fighting against the mother and with that the negotiation of all the irrational sides of her own instinctual nature. On the other hand, a woman with this sort of mother complex, as mentioned the interpretation of dream Nr. 36, will always look for the safe, the clear, the reasonable. She can have an objectivity and clear personal opinion, which might help her to overcome the destructive effect of the mother or the maternal unconscious on the psyche. She can overcome the frustration and irritation, which could inhibit a new forward-looking attitude towards the reality of life.[149] Instead of reacting in an unconscious way, she can, as it were, work with hammer and chisel and contribute to the recovery of her life instinct. So the deeper meaning of "entering into the animal" is the active union with the unconscious, the dreams and fantasies and the conscious work on them, in an attitude of loving devotion. If the feminine principle of love is connected with awareness and understanding, the world of the mother, which is the unconscious, can become the fertile soil for new life.

Working in the eye of the horse to mend the *iris*, the 'Regenbogenhaut', the 'rainbow-skin' of the eye, is a task of healing eros. Although this 'rainbow-skin' is also a matter of the dreamer's real horse, it is worth the effort to look at its symbolism. The reason for this is that the outer events with our dreamer's horse coincided synchronistically with what was going on in her psyche. Synchronicity means that inner-psychic events coincide with external concrete events or they agree in their meaning, without causal relation or even simultaneity in time and space. Jung has added synchronicity as a fourth principle to space, time and causality, to explain nature phenomena that are not explainable by these three principles.[150] An example would just be the strange connection between this dreamer and her horse. We cannot say that there is a causal relation between what went on in her psyche and her horse's illness. But there is a relation of meaning, which gives weight to both. Its source is the absolute knowledge of the unconscious, which is also the creator of meaningful dreams.

149 C. G. Jung, *The Archetypes and the Collective Unconscious* [Coll. Works 9/1], §186.

150 C. G. Jung, *The Structure and Dynamics of the Psyche,* [Coll. Works 8], § 951.

The rainbow contains the whole spectrum of colors. So the rainbow skin in the eye of the horse could be interpreted as the wholeness of the outlook on life through the eyes of the instinct. When this all-embracing instinctive sight or attitude towards life, damaged by the negative mother complex, can be healed by loving care and conscious work, a great step on the individuation path has been accomplished and life can become full of colors.

Another dream by the same woman is the following. It came after the white old horse had died and for many weeks the dreamer had felt only half herself:

Nr. 57: Dream of the horse now inside me:

I see my old horse in a field, with a fence between him and me. We cannot get together. I am very sad and sit down on the ground. I ask him what I can do. He says that I must let go and relax. How do I have to do that? But then I try and suddenly, he just comes to me, embraces me and enters into me through my nose. He is now inside me, he belongs to me.

This comforting dream gives a wonderful image of what happens when a psychic content, until now projected onto a beloved person or animal, comes back into the psyche. It is now there as an inner agency, an energy that sustains the ego. The horse's advice to let go means in fact taking back the projection, which often remains unchanged after the death of the beloved, but prevents the real union, as the dream says. The horse entering through the nose means by way of the air or breath where, according to archaic belief, the soul enters and leaves the body. The white horse has now become an invisible 'good' spirit. Such spirits, who are known to manifest themselves through visions or shamanistic séances, are often perceived as something coming from the outside of the individual psyche. This dream, though, makes it quite clear that the horse spirit is a part of the dreamer's psyche.

M.-L. von Franz explains: «The possibility of integrating projected contents, instead of casting them out into extra-psychic space, does not arise until symbols of the self begin to appear. From this center, impulses proceed to a contemplative, thoughtful recollection of the personality. The contents now seen to have been projected are at the same time recognized as belonging to one's own psychic wholeness. Consequently the psychic energy belonging to these contents now flows toward one's own inner center, strengthening it and heightening its intensity.»[151] The black horse as a symbol of the self has, so to speak, prepared the ground for this development (fig. 43–45).

The dreamer felt from then on something akin to an increased healing power, which was confirmed by some surprisingly successful healing processes with her animal patients. Her old white horse remained with her. He had become her shamanistic helper animal and soul guide, who seemed to help her with her healing work.[152]

This is the last one of this dream series, making the reconnection to the first one. The white horse now becomes a winged horse:

Nr. 58: Dream of the inn with all the horses free:

My horse stands in a field without any fence. He lifts his head and neighs as he always did when I came to the stable. Then he turns and runs off at full gallop towards the wood. I am very disappointed about this. But in a second he reappears from the wood, flying, to take me along. He has real wings. I jump on his back and I enjoy his strength and each movement and above all his radiant love. We land on a beach in the warm evening sun. He asks me to start a shamanistic journey into the little crab hole in the sand. And off he goes at a gallop, but he leaves his wings with me. I take these wings of lovely white feathers and go to a little crab hole. I use the feathers to decorate the hole. The rest of them I bundle together and hang them on the palm tree above. Then I dive into the hole. First I have to remove quite a bit of scrub, but then I move on quite fast. I am expecting to meet my sea eagle, my totem animal. Instead I suddenly find myself in the room where all the heads of the horses were on the wall. (in the first dream) There is quite a lot going on. My horse is there. He happily bolts and kicks against the walls. The black horse is there, too, to help. All the

151 M.-L. von Franz, *Projection and Re-Collection*, p. 169.

152 In the mythology and rituals of shamans, the horse played a major role. It belonged to their beliefs, to their technique of ecstasy because it brought about a break-through from one level to another, from one world into the other worlds. It helped with the trance and made the flight into forbidden realms possible. See M. Eliade, *Shamanism: Archaic Techniques of Ecstasy*, chapter 13.

Fig. 43-44: Astrolabium, designed by Erasmus Habermel around 1600 in Prague, to get an orientation in the night-sky. According to an ancient Islamic tradition, the origin of the Astrolabium, its different circular discs (giving different latitudes on earth) together with the disc that points to the stars, the skydisk so to speak, are held together by a world axis, with a horse functioning as its pin. In the center of the cosmos there is the horse, which holds the world together. The removal of the horse figure makes the Astrolabium fall apart. The horse as a symbol of the self.

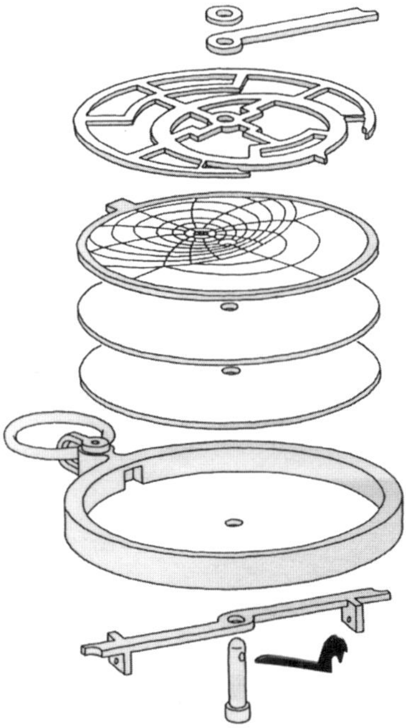

Fig. 45: The different parts of the astrolabium, that gives an orientation in the night-sky. The instrument was developed by Islamic astronomers.

horses come down from the wall. All of them dance and are happy. It is a great jumble and a wonderful atmosphere. I am in the middle of it all and I am stunned. The old lady sits on a bale of hay and seems to be amused. The horses leave the room and wait outside impatiently. The old lady says: 'Don't bother, there will always be horses coming here.' I leave the room and am very happy with all the horses around me.

The dreamer woke up with a great feeling of happiness, but later she felt lonely. On the personal level, the dream had been a reaction to a time of extraversion and at the same time feelings of emptiness and depression. It culminated in a vacation trip that was a complete failure from beginning to end. Life seemed to be on the point of standstill and old fantasies were resurrected of a complete change, of sunny beaches in warm countries, where there would be a better life. Now why does this dream occur just at that moment?

Her horse, her soul guide, flies away with her to a beach in a longed-for country which she knew in real life. Her horse is a winged horse now, a Pegasus, a creative possibility of intuition which can carry her to the land of her dreams. Amazingly enough, it is he who wants her to creep into the crab's hole, that is into total introversion. He also throws his wings off when leaving her back on the earth. He might have to do with the dreamer's high flying fantasies of a complete change of her outer life, as he takes her to that land of her longing, but it soon becomes clear that there is more to it. He is in fact a creative spirit in her life.

The beautiful white feathers, like the birds they come from, have to do with psychic entities of an intuitive and thinking character. Birds «stand for a nearly bodiless entity, an inhabitant of the air, of the wind sphere, which has always been associated with breath and therefore with the human psyche. Therefore, especially in the stories of North and South American Indians, where it is used very often, one meets the idea that gluing feathers to an object means that it is psychically real…. by attaching feathers to himself, the archaic man marks himself as a psychic and spiritual being.»[153] By arranging the white feathers around the crab hole and hanging onto the tree above, the dreamer reveals herself as being submissive to her spiritual destiny. The symbol of the tree with regard to the development of the personality is meaningful too. As an apple tree seed will always produce a apple tree and not a fir tree, the symbolic meaning of the tree is closely linked with individuation, with growing into what one is meant to be.[154] The whole ritual also seems to be like a protecting measure, because diving into the earth is a venture with uncertain outcome. But courageously the dreamer works through the scrub. There is no sea eagle, as she would expect, but surprisingly she finds herself in the realm of the great mother as in the first dream. But this time all is happiness, the horses being free and dancing around, the old lady content, the dreamer on her way with all the horses. And there is also her own horse and even the black horse.

153 M.-L. von Franz, *The Interpretation of Fairytales*, p. 67 f.

154 R. Abt, chapter "The Tree" in: R. Abt, I. Bosch, V. Mackrell, *Dream Child*, p. 123 f.

We can suppose that with this dream and its strong emotional impact, the unconscious compensated the extraverted feeling of emptiness and brought the dreamer back to her unconscious roots, where alone there is joy, life energy and meaning. Amazingly enough, it is her Pegasus intuition that brings her to the place of introversion. Consciousness easily forgets that the gift of being connected to the creative spirit of the unconscious and the gift of healing does not mean fun and sun, but imposes a serious task on somebody. And it is dangerous, because forgetting about it and being lost in extraversion might have much worse consequences than for someone who appears to live on a more superficial level unscathed. Keeping the contact to the unconscious is indispensable, and it is hard work, like working through the scrub of everyday demands and still remaining connected in active imagination and introversion to the deeper levels of the psyche. Feeling lonely in the outer world is the price to pay and cannot be avoided. The dreamer, as a consequence of her negative mother complex, had the tendency to run or rather to fly away from life's dull and confining aspect. But this problem cannot be covered up merely by changing the external life conditions. There is scrub everywhere. The everyday symbolism of her holiday trip spoke a clear language. Compensating the danger of flying off into unreal fantasies, the dream places all the weight onto the down-to-earth work and connection to the motherly unconscious, the dreams and active imaginations and her painting, which she had abandoned for some time. If ever she were to move to that faraway country, as she was fantasizing, she would have to keep the contact to the real source of her life, the unconscious. I myself considered the idea of moving to be nonsense, but as the dreamer was clinging to this plan, I had to accept it and also the possibility that the she could run into serious difficulties. Whether or not she came out of it unharmed or even having grown to higher consciousness, would then depend on her relation to her horses, her instincts, to the unconscious.

In an older dream, this woman was flying through the air, when suddenly her white horse appeared besides her. At first she was frightened, because she thought he might be dead, but the horse reassured her that he was alive and no angel. So they flew together for quite a while. With the last dream, he has actually brought her down onto or even into the earth. She can now allow her creative intuition to become a reality in her earthly life.

How necessary the horse's help is with creative work is shown in the following dream. When Marie-Louise v. Franz shrank from the huge undertaking of the fascinating creative work about Arabic alchemy, feeling unable to embark on it because of her severe illness, she had the following dream:

Nr. 59: Dream of the Arabian mare:

I dreamt that I saw a plump Arabian mare which was obviously pregnant. Then a voice suddenly said: «Get on and ride this mare». I hesitated and objected that I was old and sick. But the voice repeated its request. Finally I tried to get onto the mare and to my surprise I could do so and had a ride on this wonderful animal.[155]

This dream encouraged her to jump into the saddle and start this new creative work. And finally she succeeded, despite her severe physical handicap. However, she had to dictate it as she could no longer write by hand. Thus she was able to complete her last book – the pinnacle of her life's work – the commentary on the Arabic alchemical treatise called *Hall ar-Rumuz* (The explanation of the Symbols), written by Mohammed ibn Umail.[156]

In her essay on "Nike and the waters of the Styx", Marie-Louise v. Franz points out that the poisonous water of the Styx, the river in the Underworld encircling the realm of the dead, can only be held in a horse's hoof or the hoof or horn of a Skytian ass. All other materials, even gold, would immediately be destroyed by this water. She explains that the Styx not only has to do with death but also with the secret principle of order and truth, a kind of unconscious regulating principle of ultimate authority which is probably based on certain unconscious tendencies within the collective unconscious. The water of the Styx cannot be contained

155 I report the dream as M.-L. von Franz told it to me. It might appear in other places in a slightly different form.

156 M.-L. von Franz, *Psychological Commentary on Mohammad ibn Umail's Hall Ar-Rumuz*, Corpus Alchemicum Arabicum I A.

because it destroys all other vessels. Psychologically this refers to a creative problem.[157] The horse's hoof or the horn of the ass, carriers of life energy, enable dangerous unconscious contents to be addressed. This is the only way to draw and contain whatever wishes to be brought to light from the collective unconscious according to an unknown order. If this potential is not expressed in a creative way, it might cause serious irritation, depression or even a pre-psychotic state. With man, it is often the anima which is connected to the horse in this creative aspect, as we have seen in the dream of the horse filled with phosphorus, and as we will see in the next dream. The anima can assist with the production of new creative material.

C. G. Jung sculptured a primitive woman out of the outside wall of his tower in Bollingen. She is extending her hand to get the milk of a mare. He saw this image in a shadow play on the wall (fig. 45). Jung explains in a letter that this woman is his anima in the form of a many-thousand-year-old ancestor.[158] According to Jung's own interpretation, this image points to the age of *Aquarius*, which comes under the sign of *Pegasus*. In this future aeon, the feminine will apparently be assigned a special role; the milk seen coming into the hands of the anima would provide her with outstanding energy, writes Jung. A literal translation of the accompanying inscription reads: «The forward-leaping Pegasus – a votive jet of the water carrier». This is a reference to the meaning of the word Pegasus, which actually means "steed of the source". Pegasus is here depicted in his feminine aspect, which points to its unconscious nature. It has to do with the coming unconscious 'Zeitgeist', about which Jung was able to give some basic ideas.[159]

157 M.-L. von Franz, *Archetypal Dimensions of the Psyche*, p. 281.

158 C. G. Jung, *Letters* Vol. III. Letter from the 13. XII. 1960 to Dr. Ignaz Tauber, and: A. Jaffé, *Aus Leben und Werkstatt von C. G. Jung*, p.141.

159 A. Jaffe (ed.), *C. G. Jung, Bild und Wort*, p. 194.

Fig. 46: Pegasus and Anima, sculptured by C. G. Jung on the wall of his tower in Bollingen.

The last dream, dreamt by a 40-year-old man, seems to point right into these depths.

Nr. 60: Dream of the black horse called Circe:

I am in the ocean. It is night — the military is planning an operation, a mission. There is a battle going on and a journey under the sea is required. This was a long, involved dream. I only clearly recall the last part of the dream as I wake up: I am in the sea with a group of military men. There is a mission to take a boy who has been stranded in the war across the channel. It is night and all of us are in the dark sea. The whole group wants this assignment, although it is very dangerous and life-threatening. One man gets the job. He's amazingly positive as a figure, strong, confident, solid - a military hero. He is riding a horse (in the ocean), a swimming horse. The horse's name is 'Circe' He wants the assignment so much that he pushes and shoves the others out of his way.

Another man on land drops the boy off on land and the soldier riding 'Circe' picks the boy up and puts him on his horse and sets off to get the boy to the other side of the channel – a most dangerous assignment, very dangerous and wild and without any guarantee of getting the boy across alive; but this man has the most amazing 'can do' attitude, inspiring confidence in the face of death. Also his horse has this same attitude. He tells the boy, "When Circe (his horse) found out she might take you across the channel she didn't know whether to jump over all those other people (the other soldiers in the water who wanted the mission) or knock them down – she couldn't wait." Circe horse is loving it – can't wait to go – the man and horse exude that type of amazing confidence that CAN DO this. I feel this in the dream – I am this man, I am this boy, I am this horse, I am the water.

The beginning of the dream is an image that befits a critical situation in life: it is night, a battle is going on and a journey under the sea is called for. According to the dreamer's association, he felt as if he were in a war in his actual, difficult life situation. However, the task to be accomplished, the rescue mission, has to take place on the inner level. War is being waged not only in the outer life, but also in the unconscious.

The sign Nr. 7 of the *I Ching*, the Chinese *Book of Changes*, is called 'The Army'. M.-L.von Franz speaks at length about this sign of the I Ching in her article about "Nike and the Waters of the Styx". As there is a strong similarity with the initial situation of the dream, we shall look at it more closely. The sign «contains the image of water under the earth [...] Just as ground water is hidden under the earth, an army was latent in the peasant population (in China), which could be called up at a time of war and used as a potential for war. Delved into a bit deeper, this image would mean that the potential for unconscious tension is present beneath the field of consciousness (the earth), and that this might become dangerous if it cannot be drawn off. If this hexagram is to be interpreted for an individual situation, then, as Jung once indicated, it is related to the *danger of a pre-creative state*. Too much water gathered under the earth means irritability, destructive moods and depression that might even end up in pre-psychotic states. The individual lines of the sign speak about how to deal with the army, for instance by maintaining conscious discipline and routine as in the front line. Or about the leader of the army who commands from the midst of his troops. That would be the ego consciousness in the service of the king, that is, the self. Consciousness actively engages in the conflict instead of letting itself be pushed around.»[160]

This helps us to plunge into the beginning of the dream. Somewhere in the unconscious there is a battle going on, something dangerous in the unconscious psyche of the dreamer, a destructive clash of opposites. A night sea voyage is required, like the one of Jonas in the belly of the whale. We recall that on his flight from God, Jonas fell into the sea. God sent a whale to swallow him up and only after three days and three nights was the prophet, who prayed for the mercy of God in the belly of the whale, restored to life. [161] This biblical tale describes the passing through a time of complete darkness and depression. *«It is night and all of us are in the dark sea»*, says the dream. This is an uncanny situation with too much water, where one could drown. As this archetypal dream must also be seen as mirroring a collective problem, the phrase *«all of us in the dark sea»* can be understood as referring to the darkness of our time and the dangerous accumulation of destructive energies in the collective unconscious. Yet to

Fig. 47: Odysseus and Circe. Greek vase painting.

160 M.-L. von Franz, *Archetypal Dimensions of the Psyche*, p. 278.

161 *The Bible*, Jon.2.

bring about a solution, to accomplish the mission of the salvation of the child, remains a task for the individual.

The next step in the dream is that the military is now obviously disciplined and focused on a definite mission. The chaotic initial situation is clearing up. Instead of the remote, unspecified conflict, the battle somewhere far away in the unconscious, there is now determination and capacity for coordinated action and there is an assignment. For the dreamer this might have been a time where things became clearer, and some intuition about the ultimate goal behind all the troubles of his life appeared at the fringe of consciousness. This has to do with this assignment to take a boy who has been stranded in the war across the channel. The dream says that the mission is dangerous, life-threatening and without any guarantee of getting the boy to the other side of the channel alive. Yet all the men want to accomplish this mission. So all the male energy is directed towards this goal, although only one man can perform the final task. This man is *«amazingly positive as a figure, strong, confident, solid – a military hero.»* So the archetypal image of the hero comes up, which is now obviously needed in consciousness. We will come back to the hero and the child, but let us first go into the symbolism of Circe and the black horse.

The black horse the hero is riding is called 'Circe'. Again we have a black horse, as in the last dream, where we associated it with eros and the goddess Isis/Aphrodite. Here it bears the name of Circe, the Greek goddess with a notorious reputation, as she was the one who cast a spell onto the friends of Odysseus on her island, turning them all into swine (fig. 46). Only with the help of the god Hermes with his golden rod, who gave him a magic herb, could Odysseus avoid this fate and prevent her from bewitching him. Instead of fighting her, he now began a loving relationship with the goddess and so persuaded her to restore his friends to human form. After they had all happily stayed on her island for a whole year, they finally wanted to return home. However, Circe made it clear to them that they first had to cross Ockeanos, the great stream encompassing the flat circle of the earth, in order to get down to Hades and the terrible Persephone, goddess of the Underworld. There they would have to find Teiresias, the blind old seer, the only one who had not been dissolved like the other shadows in the land of the dead, but had been able to keep his insight and wisdom. Only he would be able to reveal to them the way home. They were all terrified about this dangerous journey, but Odysseus, like a true hero, imbued them with confidence and courage and performed all the tasks that Circe had set him. Circe then helped the crew to sail home by sending them a favourable wind.

It is not just by chance that the dream brings in this old myth. Circe, daughter of the sun god Helios and Perse, a daughter of Ockeanos, living on an island in the sea, lives on the threshold between consciousness and the unconscious, between land and water. She is an anima who, like an island in the sea, appears in a man first as an erotic fantasy. As a powerful sorceress, she casts her spell on him and transforms him into a swine. The swine in its negative aspect is a symbol of voluptuousness and carnal lust. In fact, the dreamer himself associated this state of mind with the actual situation he had gone through after his divorce, «a being overwhelmed by sexual promiscuity, with many women around, like an addiction, the spellbinding fascination of sexuality».

The problem with our interpretation is that in the dream, Circe does not appear as a negative sorceress, but as a powerful and helpful black horse! The black horse with the name of a goddess is a sacred animal, at home both in the water and on land. It can carry and sustain the hero in his dangerous venture in the dark sea and it provides him with instinctual energy and vitality. While this military hero stands for a goal-oriented male consciousness that can keep to a direction and remain on course with strength and determination, she symbolizes an anima, an inner state of mind, an unconscious feminine side that «mediates the relationship to the deep-seated meaningful wholeness of his personality. If a man heeds this element of feeling, which is also involved in his relationships with women, rather than rejecting it as 'nonsense,' he can [...] cause it to be more favourably disposed toward him.»[162] In this case we might say that in taking seriously his unconscious feeling side, coming up in the form of erotic fantasies, without losing the reins and being overrun by it, a man motivates the goddess, as it were, so that she provides him with her power and carries him towards his goal. This is what happened to Odysseus, who prevented Circe from turning him into a swine and began a loving relationship with

162 M.-L.von Franz, *Archetypal Dimensions of the Psyche*, p. 275.

her. She then helped him on his way. As a grand-daughter of Ockeanos, she is also familiar with the Underworld. She therefore knows the way to the land of the dead, where there is lost wisdom to be found. Odysseus' journey into the Underworld is actually what Jung himself did when he plunged into the collective unconscious to bring up new meaning from ancient neglected wisdom. Like the wisdom of Teiresias, this seems to be the only thing that will not even dissolve in the netherworld, though it has to be brought up by living humans on their way time and again.

So the blackness of the swimming horse Circe also has to do with her nocturnal side, which knows the way into the unconscious. She is an unconscious instinct that provides the hero with all the power and vitality needed for his heroic deed. However, according to the dream, the Circe horse is so wild and unruly in her drive to save the child that she is even a threat to the surrounding people. «*When Circe found out she might take you (the boy) across the channel, she didn't know whether to jump over those other people [the other people who might have taken the mission, the other men in the ocean] or knock them down — she couldn't wait.*» So for cooperation she obviously needs a good rider who can handle an unruly wild horse. It needs the strong mind of the *hero in his most positive sense,* who is able to bring this instinctual energy into line, channelling it into the dangerous task. The hero is therefore a role model for a strong consciousness which is able to connect to the instinctual bases of the unconscious feminine, without being overrun by it. Whether or not consciousness will be able to deal with the anima-horse power is actually the crucial point. So the archetype of the hero is not out of date, as feminists would have us believe, because only a strong, courageous and motivated consciousness is able to deal with the instinctual powers of the unconscious. We always have to keep that in mind, for instance in analysis! If the ego is not blown up into inflation by the archetype of the hero, a balance between hero, horse, boy and ego consciousness can come into being, as the dream suggests. Then there might arise this *amazing confidence, that can-do-this-attitude* which we so often miss in external life and which only the connection to the unconscious source of energy can provide us with. As the dreamer says in his associations, he was deeply impacted and impressed by the attitude of willingness to fulfill the assignment, the energy, vitality and strength of both the horse and the rider, inspiring confidence and hope.

Now we have to amplify the child. In the experience of humans, the child imparts a state of beginning which can activate awe and amazement in us. For a little child, the world is full of wonders, full of future possibilities; everything is a new and original experience, and the child's reactions to it are spontaneous and genuine. The whole world seems to be created anew in the eyes of a little child. That makes the child symbol an image for an original, unconscious and instinctual state of beginning and at the same time for a potential future. The child symbol in a dream therefore often paves the way for a future development of the personality. The divine child, as it appears all over the world in mythology and religions, is often a culture bringer, that is a new awareness, a future consciousness.

On the other hand, a little child is helpless and weak and has to be protected from danger, like all baby animals. In its initial state, the archetypal child is threatened, orphaned, abandoned like Moses, Jesus and all the persecuted children in myths and fairytales. As a new content from the unconscious, it is weak, small, underestimated, but at the same time gifted with divine power. The child symbol thus contains the greatest possible opposites. This also makes it a mediator, a future possibility for uniting the disparate tendencies in the human personality. Jung says that it personifies the strongest drive of a human being, namely the drive of self-realization. This drive is a law of nature and therefore an impregnable force.[163] The child symbol therefore often appears as an anticipation of the self (fig. 47).

Like all archetypal symbols, the child archetype has also a negative side. It manifests itself on the personal level as, for instance, a state of immaturity, of childishness and unreasonable demands on life and one's fellow men. M.-L.von Franz has discussed the type of man with such features in her book about the *Puer Aeternus,* the eternal youth.[164] The identification with this figure is the problem of an alarmingly large number of both young and older men nowadays and also the animus of women. It is not difficult to recognize this type of man in our pleasure-seeking society, but also where it is not so obvious, these traits are widespread. Women can

163 C. G. Jung, "The Psychology of the Child Archetype" in: *The Archetypes and the Collective Unconscious* [Coll. Works 9/I], § 289.

164 M.-L. von Franz, *Puer Aeternus – A Psychological Study of the Adult Struggle with the Paradise of Childhood.*

Fig. 48: *Puer Aeternus.* Painting by Peter Birkhäuser, 1960. In the dream associated with the painting, a wonderful, divine boy entered the artist's garden and visited him «His horse was small but an extremely powerful wild creature, a bundle of energy. It reminded me of a wild boar.»[165] «The new spirit of the coming age of Aquarius, riding on a white beast (Pegasus). Half-horse, half-boar, wherever he stretches his hands, new life begins to bloom […]. He is the complete man of the future.» (M.-L. von Franz)[166]

165 E. Wertenschlag-Birkhäuser, *Windows on Eternity*, plate 18, p.85.

166 M.-L.von Franz, *Light from the Darkness*, p. 48.

often tell you something about it, because this problem particularly affects human relations. This means that in an adulterated way, the child archetype is lived out in order to avoid opposites, instead of courageously facing the battle of the opposites, as the dream suggests. Only by enduring the painful battle of the opposites between what one is and what one should or could become, can the unexpected and often underestimated new creative impulse in a life evolve. This is the new child, the beginning and also the end, the origin and the future. Taking it across the channel means taking it to a new land, giving it new ground, apprehending it on a new basis. Maybe this means a new consciousness beyond the turmoil of all the conflicts in everyday life, although without absconding from it, and a new acceptance of the superiority of this inner centre, which we call the self. That would signify a new religious attitude.

The *puer aeternus* is a symbol of the self. It is represented as a little, threatened, helpless child, but at the same time, it is only this child who can unite the opposites. «Help me and I will help you», says the stone, the central symbol of the self in alchemy. This needs great courage and confidence, for the black horse Circe is a dark and sinister power that can either be motivated to cooperate, or can throw off the rider into the abyss. In an individual this would mean dissolution and psychosis; in the collective it would be the outbreak of war. The dreamer's feeling *«I am this man, I am this boy, I am this horse, I am the water»* emphasizes the point that all this – as well as the collective aspects – belong to his own psyche. Moreover it is also an image of man as a union of consciousness and the unconscious as far as it is possible, with all the seemingly impossible tasks this might entail.

According to the dream, saving *the puer aeternus* in the war-situation of the collective unconscious is the most urgent task, but also the most impossible one for the individual from a statistical point of view. I take encouragement from the following quotation of Marie-Louise von Franz when she says that «this would mean that if enough individuals concentrated on the inner center, the self, then the possibility would arise that nature, through *synchronistic events,* might take the side of their military group. That sounds almost superstitious or absurd, but if we reflect that it probably corresponds to an evolutionary tendency of nature that human beings, in comparison to other higher mammals, have developed a significantly higher level of consciousness, it might then also be inferred that this evolutionary tendency continues its thrust in us and that those human groups and single individuals who are situated along the line of evolution have the best chance of survival in the course of world history.»[167]

To sum up: we can now connect the Circe-horse-anima to the "forward leaping Pegasus" in his feminine aspect, giving its milk to the anima, as Jung chiselled it into the wall of his tower. We might then understand this great archetypal dream as speaking about the goal of the future astrological age of *Aquarius,* which, according to astrological speculation, we are about to move into.[168] The goal would be to save the divine child, the self and the future of men with the help of the feminine 'horse energy' from the unconscious.

Finally I would like to mention an another topic connected to the horse symbol that must be psychologically true, as we find it in so many fairytales. It is the motif of the horse sacrifice. Sometimes, at the end of the hero's quest, the head of the helpful horse has to be cut off for the final redemption. Usually the horse itself asks for this dreadful task to be performed by the hero, who cannot understand why he should sacrifice his best helper in this way. But then the horse transforms and takes on human shape, usually a prince or a princess. «When a redeemed prince or god steps forth from a sacrificed animal in a fairytale, this symbolizes the sudden disclosure of the spiritual meaning that seems to lie behind the 'rightness' of the animal instinct. And at the same time it means that on the one hand people should follow their unconscious instinctive impulses, but that at a certain point in the curve of their lives they will demand that they sacrifice them. Instinct itself demands to be sacrificed, and in so doing reveals its spiritual aspect.»[169] One can say that through that sacrifice, the human form of the self, which is hidden behind the natural life energy of the horse, becomes visible. It appears as an animal, an instinct, but is in fact the *principium individuationis*, an unconscious drive towards individuation. It is probably even the strongest instinct in man.[170] To redeem the spiritual

167 M.-L. von Franz, *Archetypal Dimensions of the Psyche*, p. 272.

168 C. G. Jung, *Aion*, [Coll. Works 9/II], §149 (88).

169 M.-L. von Franz, *Archetypal Dimensions of the Psyche*, 90 f.

170 M.-L. von Franz, *Shadow and Evil in Fairytales*, p. 310.

aspect of the animal helper, to bring it into human form on the level of consciousness, is only possible by the sacrifice of that natural energy flow that carries us through outer life and which one usually takes for granted as long as everything goes well. This sacrifice has to do with an artificial state of complete introversion.[171] To know the moment for this sacrifice does not seem to be the responsibility of the ego. But as the motif of beheading our best friend and helper shows, it is a most difficult task that is asked of us.

Certainly old age brings up this problem in a special way when increasing physical weakness cannot follow the energy flow into extraversion any more and a painful deprivation of mobility must be accepted. Sometimes it is also a creative idea that wants to come up from the unconscious, forcing us to cut down all extraverted activity. Outer life then is sometimes like being under a spell! Things keep falling down, one bangs one's head on the door frame, the car breaks down, holiday trips go wrong, ongoing projects get bogged down etc. Something wants to transform, to come into consciousness in an understandable form. This process is disturbed by too much of the usual extraverted efficiency.

There might always be moments in life where a deeper insight into what carries us through life becomes necessary. And as we usually think that our health and life energy is only a matter of outer circumstances, accepting an inner force as a regulating centre of our whole life and personality means a real sacrifice of the ego.

Summarizing, we can say that wherever we meet the horse in dreams, it can express a *dynamic libido* aspect which aims at *individuation*. As a source of life energy, the symbol of the horse is also closely connected to the *mother*, the *body* and *sexuality*. The *panic* reaction from the unconscious has to be kept well in mind as an expression of a destructive side of the horse instinct. The *extrasensory perception* of the horse symbolically has to do with the instinctive semi-conscious *spontaneous creative side* bringing wisdom from the depths into consciousness. It mirrors the relationship between bodily instinct and intuition or inspiration.

171 M.-L. von Franz, *Shadow and Evil in Fairytales*, p. 258, and C. G. Jung, *Symbols of Transformation* [Coll. Works 5], § 658.

The symbolism of the horse is most complex and the mythological material is extensive. But I would now like to round up our overview by quoting Barbara Hannah when she said that all three animals, cat, dog and horse, represent helpful instinctual sides which – in some way or other – *aim at individuation.* This goal is common to them all, and their negative aspects are only constellated when we are not striving towards this goal ourselves. All three of them are considered to be *healing*, since the reconnection with these instincts has a healing effect on our life. As animals they are neither good nor bad. *Therefore the way they treat us depends on the way we treat them.* As they are domesticated animals, we bear the responsibility for them. We have to feed them and attend to their well-being. They are instincts we can and must take care of.[172]

Talking about these animals within the framework of our psychological consideration, their real and their symbolic characteristics merge. The cat is the most *independent and wild* of the three animals, but also the one which can most easily be treated cruelly and be neglected. It will always remain partly wild, but if we have the right attitude towards it and let it have its own way, it will return the favour by helping us. The dog has the *strongest emotional connection* with us. Thus it is an instinct which is quite familiar and we can and must have a good relationship with it. It also has the *strongest healing power* of the three. The horse is much bigger than we are; it can draw a carriage and we can learn to ride it. This big, powerful animal does all these things for us and yet how rarely it rebels against us despite its dangerous power! If this *instinctive energy* is constantly misused by rational, ambitious, extraverted consumption, there might come a time when it will no longer be with us and may be replaced by unaccountable lethargy. Then all the energy supporting us from the unconscious has gone and we must pay attention to the horse again. Taking the unconscious instinct into consideration needs a lot of patience, care, understanding and also the precise knowledge of how to deal with it. The horse can also give us the biggest help in *perceiving and supporting the coming unconscious 'Zeitgeist'*. We can only guess at the importance of the right relationship to this Pegasus-energy, not only for the individual but also for the coming age.

172 B. Hannah, *The Cat, Dog and Horse Lectures*, p.127 f. (my italics).

Fig. 49: Alter Real (Lusitano) stallion 'Urgeiro'.

Part IV

Appendix

1. Bibliography

ABT-Baechi, Regina: *Der Heilige und das Schwein*, Zürich 1983.

ABT, Regina, BOSCH, Irmgard, MACKRELL, Vivienne: *Dream Child*, Einsiedeln 2000.

ABT, Theodor: *Psychological Interpretation of Muḥammad ibn Umail's Kitāb Ḥall ar-rumūz* (Book of the Explanation of the Symbols), Corpus Alchemicum Arabicum I B (CALA I B), Zurich 2009.

- *Introduction to Picture Interpretation according to C. G. Jung*, Zurich 2005.

ABT, Theodor and HORNUNG, Erik: *Knowledge for the Afterlife – A Quest for Immortality*, Zurich 2003.

ARNOLD, Dorothea: *Falken, Katzen, Krokodile: Tiere im alten Aegypten.* Catalogue Museum Rietberg, Zürich 2010.

ASSMANN, Jan: *Ägyptische Hymnen und Gebete*, Zürich und München 1975.

BIRKHÄUSER, Sibylle: *Die Mutter im Märchen*, Egg 2003.

CHEVALIER, J. and GHEERBRANT, A.: *Dictionnaire des Symboles*, Paris, 1973.

COLLODI, C. and LAWSEN, L. A., *The Adventures of Pinoccio*, Oxford 1972.

COLUM, Padraic and CAMPBELL, Joseph: *The Complete Grimms's Fairytales*, New York 1972.

DE GUBERNATIS, Angelo: *Die Thiere in der indogermanischen Mythologie*, Leipzig 1874, reprint 1978.

DE LA GUÉRINIÈRE, F. R.: *Reitkunst*, Marburg 1817, reprint Hildesheim 1989.

DICKMAN ZARROW, Sheila: *Friendship and Healing – The Dreams of John Adams and Benjamin Rush*, Wilmette 2010.

ELIADE, Mircea: *Archaic Techniques of Ecstasy*, Princeton 2004.

GOETZ, Bruno: *Das Reich ohne Raum.* With commentaries by Marie Louise von Franz, Zürich 1962.

GERMOND, Philippe: *An Egyptian Bestiary*, London 2001.

HANNAH Barbara: *The Cat, Dog and Horse Lectures*, Wilmette 1992.
- *The Archetypal Symbolism of Animals*, Wilmette 2006.

HELSETH, Helle: *Some Animal Images in Fairytales and Dreams.* Diploma Thesis at the Research and Training Centre in Depth Psychology according to C. G. Jung and M.-L.von Franz, unpublished, Zürich 2010.
- "Die Vieldeutigkeit der Tiere im alten Ägypten", in: *Die Seele der Tiere,* Wolfenbütteler Forschungen 2001.

HORNUNG, Erik and BRYAN, Betsy M.: *The Quest for Immortality, Treasures of Ancient Egypt*, Washington 2002.

HOROWITZ, Alexandra: *Inside of a Dog,* New York 2010.

ISLER, Gotthilf: *Lumen Naturae*, Egg 2000.

INGOLDSBY, Pat: *The Peculiar Sensation of being Irish*, without place, year.

JAFFÉ, Aniela: *Aus Leben und Werkstatt von C.G. Jung*, Zürich 1968.
- (editor): *C. G. Jung. Bild und Wort*, Zürich 1977.

JUNG, Carl Gustav: *Symbols of Transformation*, Collected Works 5,
- Princeton 1967.
- *Psychological Types*, Collected Works 6, Princeton1976.
- *The Structure and Dynamics of the Psyche*, Collected Works 8, Princeton 1969.
- *The Archetypes and the Collective Unconscious*, Collected Works 9/1, Princeton 1959
- *Aion*, Collected Works 9/2, Princeton 1968.
- *Civilisation in Transition*, Collected works 10, Princeton 1969
- *On the Psychology of Western and Eastern Religions*. Collected Works 11, Princeton 1969.
- *Psychology and Alchemy*, Collected Works 12, Princeton 1968.
- *Alchemical Studies*, Collected Works 13, Princeton 1967.
- *Mysterium Coniunctionis*, Collected Works 14, Princeton 1974.
- *The Practice of Psychotherapy*. Collected Works 16, Princeton 1970.
- *Memories, Dreams, Reflections*. Recorded and edited by Aniela Jaffé, translated from German by Richard and Clara Winston, New York 1963.
- *Dream Analysis, Notes of the Seminar given in 1928-30,* London 1984.
- *Vision Seminars – Notes of the Seminar given in 1930-1934,* Princeton 1997.
- *Children's Dreams – Notes of the Seminar given 1936 – 1940,* Princeton 2008.
- *Letters*, Vol. I-III, ed. by A. Jaffé and G. Adler, Princeton 1980.

JUNG, Carl Gustav et al.: *Man and his Symbols.* London 1964.

MÜLLER, Josef: *Sagen aus Uri*, Vol. I, Basel 1969.

PINKOLA ESTES, Clarissa: *Women who run with the Wolves*, New York 1992.
REDFORD, Donald (ed.): *The Oxford Encyclopedia of Ancient Egypt* (3 Volumes), Cairo 2001.

SCHWEIZER, Regine: "Anima animalis. Der heilige Hund", *Jungiana* 8, Egg 1998.
SCHMID, Margrit Rosa: *Schwarz bin ich und schön*, Egg 2002.
SEIPEL, Wilfried: *Ägypten, Götter, Gräber und die Kunst, 4000 Jahre*
- *Jenseitsglaube*, Band I, Linz 1989.

VON DER LEYEN, Friedrich: *Deutsche Märchen aus dem Donauland*. Köln 1958.
VON FRANZ, Marie-Louise: "On Individuantion" in: *Man und his Symbols*, London 1979.
- *Introduction to Alchemy*, Toronto1980.
- *Puer Aeternus*, Santa Monica 1981.
- *The Way of the Dream*, Toronto 1988.
- *Individuation in Fairytales*, Boston and London 1990.
- *Light from the Darkness*, The Paintings of Peter Birkhäuser, Basle 1991.
- *Psyche and Matter*, Boston and London 1992.
- *The Feminine in Fairytales*, Boston and London 1993.
- *Shadow and Evil in Fairytales*, Boston 1995.
- *Projection and Re-Collection in Jungian Psychology*, Chicago 1995.
- *The Interpretation of Fairy Tales*, Boston and London 1996.
- *Archetypal Dimensions of the Psyche*, Boston and London 1997.
- *The Cat – A Tale of Feminine Redemption*, Toronto 1980.
- *On Dreams and Death*, Chicago 1998.
- *C.G. Jung – His Myth in our Time*, Toronto1998.
- *Psychological Commentary on the Book of the Explanation of the Symbols* (*Kitāb Ḥall ar-rumūz*) by Muḥammad ibn Umail, Corpus Alchemicum Arabicum I A (CALA I A), Zürich 2006.

VON STRÖM, Ake, BIEZAIS, Harald: *Germanische und baltische Religion*, Berlin 1975.

WERTENSCHLAG-BIRKHÄUSER, Eva. *Windows on Eternity*, Einsiedeln 2009.
WILHELM, Richard and BAYNES, Gary F.: *The I Ching or The Book of the Changes*, Princeton 1967.

2. List of Pictures

The Cat

Fig. 1: At the Studio Table. Painting by Peter Birkhäuser, in: Eva Wertenschlag-Birkhäuser. *Windows on Eternity,* Plate 23. Einsiedeln 2009. Photo © Birkhäuser Foundation, Basle.

Fig. 2: Cat. Bronze, The Egyptian Museum, Cairo (JE 29147), Photo © *The Quest for Immortality*, United Exhibits, Copenhague,

Fig. 3: Coffin of cat. Museum Egizio, Turin (Nr. 2369), in: W. Seipel, *Ägypten*, plate 488, Linz 1989, Photo © G. Lovera, Turin.

Fig. 4: Pharao hunting a lion. Painted lime stone, Metropolitan Museum of Art, New York (26.7.1453), in: D. Arnold, *Falken, Katzen, Krokodile. Tiere im alten Aegypten*, plate 11, Zürich 2010, Photo © S. Harkness.

Fig. 5: The Cat that Walked by Himself, in: *Just so Stories* by Rudyard Kipling, Hertfortshire 1993.

Fig. 6: Cat mummies. Egypt. Musée du Louvre, Paris, in: Ph. Germond, *An Egyptian Bestiary*, plate 183, London 2001, Photo © G. Dagliorti.

Fig. 7: Tomcat and Apophis. Tomb of Onuris-cha, Deir el Medine. In: Ph. Germond, plate 84, *An Egyptian Bestiary*, London 2001, Photo © J. P. Corteggiani.

Fig. 8: Bastet with her kittens. British Museum, London.

Fig. 9: Sekhmet. Pendant, Egyptian Museum, Cairo.

Fig. 10: The Cat. Painting by Peter Birkhäuser, in: Eva Wertenschlag-Birkhäuser, *Windows on Eternity,* Plate 10, Einsiedeln 2009. Photo © Birkhäuser Foundation, Basle.

Fig. 11: Pinocchio, in: Carlo Collodi, *Pinocchios Abenteuer*, Stuttgart 1986.

Fig. 12: The Witch's Cat. Source unknown.

Fig. 13: White Cat. Photo © Doris Abt.

Fig. 14: Tiger Cat. Photo © Sabine Abt.

Fig. 15: Cat with a mouse in its mouth. Winchester Cathedral, British Museum, London.

Fig. 16: Cat under the chair. Photo © Doris Abt.

The Dog

Fig. 17: Hunting dog of the Pharaoh. Ivory, Metropolitan Museum of Art, New York , in: D. Arnold, *Falken, Katzen, Krokodile. Tiere im alten Ägypten*, Zürich 2010, plate 100. Photo © Rogers Fund, 1940 (40.2.1).

Fig. 18: Rescue Dog at work. Photo © Mike O. Scherrer, Est Media.

Fig. 19: Friendship between Dog and Cat. Photo © Doris Abt.

Fig. 20: Anubis doing the embalming. Tomb of Sennedjem in Deir el Medine. in: W. Seipel, *Äegypten*, p. 134, Linz 1989, Photo © M. Büsing.

Fig. 21: Canopic chest of Queen Nedjmet. The Egyptian Museum, Cairo, in: E. Hornung et. al.,*The Quest for Immortality*, Photo © United Exhibits, Copenhague.

Fig. 22: The four Functions of Consciousness. From C. G. Jung, *Psychology and Alchemy* [Coll. Work 12], § 137.

Fig. 23: Mummy Tablet with Anubis. Musée du Louvre (E 5692), Paris, in: W. Seipel, *Äegypten*, Linz 1989. plate 512.

Fig. 24: Aztec dog. Museo Regional de Puebla, Conaculta Instituto Nacional de Antropología e Historia (10-203439), Mexico, Photo © Michel Zabe.

Fig. 25: Ascha with Kindergarden children. Photo © Doris Abt.

Fig. 26: Lazarus with licking dogs. Burgundy (France), ca. 1100.

Fig. 27: Dog in front of the offering table. Egyptian Museum Berlin (3317), in: W. Seipel, *Ägypten*, Linz 1989. plate 447.

Fig. 28: The dog with eyes in two different colours. Drawing of the dreamer.

Fig. 29: Stele with dog. Abydos. Musée du Louvre, Paris, in: P. Germond, *An Egyptian Bestiary*, plate 79, London 2001, Photo © Jacques Livet.

Fig. 30: Kai. Photo © Doris Abt.

Fig. 31: Greek goddess Hekate. British Museum, London.

The Horse

Fig. 32: Horse Head. Grottes de Chauvet, in: *The Dawn of the Human Spirit,* Copenhague 2000. Photo © United Exhibits, Copenhague.

Fig. 33: Horses with carts, from the tomb of Nebamun, British Museum, London. in: Ph. Germond, *An Egyptian Bestiary*, London 2001, plate 86. Photo © Jacques Livet.

Fig. 34: Statue of Louis XIV. Bronze, Musée du Louvre, Paris.

Fig. 35: Lusitano Stallion 'Dourado', Photo © Christiane Slawik.

Fig. 36: The nocturnal ascent of the Holy Prophet, in: Seyyed Hossein Nasr, *Islamic Science*, Kent 1976. Plate 11. Photo © Roland Michaud.

Fig. 37: Horse pulling a wheel, drawing of the dreamer.

Fig. 38: Horse pulling the sun disc, Nationalmuseet, Copenhague.

Fig. 39: La Dame à l'Unicorne, Tapistry, Musée National du Moyen-Age, Paris.

Fig. 40: Lusitano Stallion 'Dourado'. Photo © Christiane Slawik.

Fig. 41: Urartu horse bit. Museum of Anatolian Civilisations, Ankara.

Fig. 42: Black and white Horse. Photo © Claudia Baumgartner.

Fig. 43-44: Astrolabium designed by Erasmus Habermel. Facsimile by Martin Brunold, Abtwil in Switzerland. Photos © Doris Abt.

Fig. 45: Schema drawn by Martin Brunold, adapted by Th. Abt.

Fig. 46: Pegasus sculptured by C. G. Jung on the wall of his tower in Bollingen. Photo © Ulrich Hoerni, Stiftung der Werke von C. G. Jung, Zürich.

Fig. 47: Odysseus and Circe, painted vase found in the graves of Vulci (Italy), Museo Archeologico Nazionale di Vulci.

Fig. 48: Puer Aeternus by Peter Birkhäuser, in: Eva Wertenschlag-Birkhäuser, *Window on Eternity*, Plate 18. Photo © Birkhäuser Foundation, Basle.

Fig. 49: Alter Real (Lusitano) stallion 'Urgeiro'. Photo © Regina Abt.

Jacket:

Onuris-cha in front of four shakals (canis lupaster), 20th Dynasty, Deir el-Medina. Tomb of Onuris-cha (TT Nr. 359). The four shakals, one behind the other, convey all-embracing protection to the deceased. In: Ph. Germond, *An Egyptian Bestiary*, plate 86, London 2001, Photo © by Dominique Genet.

3. List of Dreams

The Cat

1. The cat with the knives 25
2. The bird in the hair 27
3. The cat Cleo and Wotan 29
4. The grey and white cat 30
5. Washing and three cats 31
6. The black cat and the knife 33
7. The cat and the hole in the wall 37
8. The cat and the distillation process 37
9. Pinocchio 40
10. The dictator 43
11. The wounded animal 44
12. The attacking black cat 50
13. Dream of the white dancing cat 51
14. The cat's condemnation 54
15. The cat as the Devil 57
16. The cat in the church 59
17. The cat's queen 64
18. The cat attacking another cat 66
19. The Bastet temple 67

The Dog

20. Ascha 77
21. Sissi 78
22. The dog turning like the finger of a clock 81
23. Deceased dog leaving over the bridge 85
24. Deceased dog coming back 91
25. Having to beg for the dog's help 99
26. The dog falling from the roof 100
27. Signpost in the shape of a cross 101

28. The pilgrimage 108
29. Dog stealing a cake 111
30. Attacking Doberman dogs 113
31. German shepherd dogs attacking a cat 115
32. Chichester cathedral and the Devil 117
33. The attacking wolf 119
34. John Adams 121
35. The frozen dog 124
36. The dog growing out of another dog 125
37. The baby puppy 131
38. The dog with diamond-shaped patterns instead of eyes 132
39. The bishop, God is a dog 135
40. The priest, the church and the vine grapes 138
41. The dog with gold eyes 141

The Horse

42. The starving horse 153
43. The attacking stallion 154
44. The horses and the ice water 155
45. The train and the coach 157
46. The white and the brown horse 159
47. The nine black horses 161
48. Drawing a horse and a carriage 163
49. The test on a horse 165
50. The horse, the cow and the unicorn 168
51. The cows turning into young horses 172
52. The horse/cow warning from a criminal 174
53. The phosphorous horse 177
54. The country inn and the horses on the wall 178
55. The country inn and the black horse 179
56. Working inside the horse 189
57. The horse now inside me 192
58. The inn with all the horses free 193
59. The Arabian mare 198
60. The black horse called Circe 200

4. Index

– A –

abolish 138
Adams, John 120–4
Adonis 69
Africa 124, 126
–, African 128
aggression 30, 32, 45, 53, 117, 122, 157, 159, 162
–aggressive 13, 51, 66, 75, 87, 112, 115
–, aggressiveness 111, 114, 116, 118
afterlife*; see Book of the Afterlife*
Aion 58
Aithon 154
alchemical
– work 59, 144
– text(s) 31, 75
alchemist(s); *see also sages* 32, 97, 101, 134, 140–1, 162, 170
alchemy 31, 41, 59, 80, 86, 88, 169–70, 183, 198, 208
–, alchemical text 31, 75, 79
–, dog in 80
alcohol 37, 38, 139
alien/ alienate 10, 38
Alsation dog 115
ambiguity 17, 21, 126
ambivalence 34
–, ambivalent 66, 98, 116
Amduat 88*; see also Book of the Dead*
American 120, 123, 128, 196
amplification(s) 14, 17, 33, 88, 96, 128–9, 134
– amplify 135, 206
amulets 23, 42
analysis 13–4, 36–7, 46, 81, 100, 113, 123, 164, 172, 184, 205
– analyse 26, 53, 129, 167
ancestor 10, 199
angel 59–60, 197
anger 30
anima 32, 36, 38, 49, 56, 63, 155–6, 161–2, 172, 177, 199–200, 204–5, 209
– of man 36
–, cat 37, 46, 54, 63–6, 70
animal(s); *see also insects; see name of animals: bat, bear, bees, birds, boar, buzzard, cat, cock, cow, dog, donkey, dragon, falcon, fish, flies, fox, goose, horse, ibis, insects, jackal, lice, lions, lynx, mice, midges, monkey, mouse, pavian, sheep, snakes, stork, tiger, unicorn, vermin, wolf, worms* 9–13, 25, 31, 41, 76–7, 96, 98–9, 106, 114, 120, 132, 141, 153, 159, 161, 172–3, 176, 178, 182, 184, 192, 198, 206
– as inspiration 12, 65
– (in) dream(s) 7, 12–3, 123, 131
– and behavior 11
– and man/ human being(s) 17, 20, 75, 80
– attacks 50, 66
– drives 135
– emotion 46
– in Ancient Egypt 7, 17
– in myths/ legends 13
– instinct(s) 8–9, 12, 75, 122–4, 171, 209
– kingdom 12
– -like 58, 68
– nature 124
– patient(s) 182–3, 193
– -people gods 11
– realm/ world 13, 19, 66, 124, 134, 183, 188
– soul 79, 140
– stories/ tales 11
– world 19, 66, 124, 134, 183, 188
–, attitude towards 89, 91
–, divine/ godly 17, 154
–, domesticated 13, 211
–, eye of the 133, 190
–, gods/ numina as , 11, 17, 139
–, grey 119
–, head(s) of 17, 44
–, helper/ helpful 40, 193, 210
–, image of 49
–, mistress of the 126, 180
–, mystical 169
–, nocturnal 80
–, numinous 19
–, pet 9–10, 21, 71
–, protect 20, 136
–, relate to/ relationship with 17, 19, 76, 89, 97
–, sacred 204
–, sacrifice 83

–, suffering 9
–, threatening 19
–, three 97, 170, 211
–, two 41
–, underestimated … instincts 123
–, union with 190
–, useful 23
–, wild 13, 71, 75, 80, 118, 150
–, wounded 44–5
animus 27, 30, 32, 77, 114–5, 119, 157, 161, 164, 167, 169, 176, 206
– attack 116
Anthony, Saint 34, 57–8, 136
anthropos 136
Anti–Christ 58
Antiquity 20
Anubis 17, 19, 83–4, 88, 98
Aphrodite 186, 203
Apollo 116, 138
–, Apollonian cult 138
Apophis 23, 26
Apuleius 186
Aquarius 199, 207, 209
Arabian
– Arab mystic 93
– Arabic 140, 198
– horse 179
– mare 154, 156, 198–9
archaic 10–12, 102, 164, 192, 196
archetypal 18, 116, 131–2, 138, 169, 170–1, 203
– background 14
– child 206
– contents 38
– dream(s) 7, 89, 120, 202, 209
– figures 180
– foundation 151
– images/ motif 89, 190
– level 14, 33, 63, 79
– material 13, 14
– meaning 190
– mother 114, 126–7
– power 65
– quality/ qualities 34
– structure 164
– symbols/ symbolism 85, 116, 125, 206
– world 65, 181, 183
archetype(s) 69, 118–20, 140, 149, 151, 162, 164, 171, 181, 186–7, 190, 205–6, 208
art 25, 60, 139, 144
– of riding 150
–, artist 12, 159, 207
Ascha 77, 107
Asclepios 106, 129
aspect; *see also cat aspect*
–, divine 132, 141
–, femine/ of femine 63, 70, 164, 199, 209
–, joyful 32, 63
–, daemonic cat 54
ass, The Golden Ass 186
associations 13, 55, 60, 88, 199, 205
Athanasius 118
attack(s) 30, 43, 45–6, 49, 81, 115, 117, 119, 127
–, animal 50, 66
–, animus 116
Attis 69
attitude 26, 37, 39, 42–3, 54, 56–7, 60–1, 85, 88, 98–9, 116, 119, 123, 138, 140, 156–7, 168–9, 201, 205, 208, 211
– of consciousness 69, 99, 112
– of devotion 144, 184, 191
– of eros 25
– towards animals/ instincts 89, 91, 130
– towards the unconscious/ inner world 33, 40–1, 96–7, 192
–, cat-like 43
–, Christian 58, 70, 100–1, 118
–, old/ new/ wrong 36, 113, 128, 180
–, rational/ scientific/ materialistic 62–3, 69
–, religious 11, 184, 208
attribute(s) 17, 136, 154, 170, 175, 186
authority 76, 136, 198
–, inner 12
autonomous/ autonomy 46, 82, 92, 99, 119, 151, 166

– B –

Ba 17, 20
background 9, 11, 14, 29, 58–9, 68, 105, 118, 124, 149, 187
–, mental/ of psyche 9, 11
– of symbol 14
balance 43, 46, 56–7, 66, 70, 99, 109–10, 159, 165–7, 187, 205
Balder 174
ball 166
bark 115–8

bat 14
Bastet; *see also Sekhmet* 20, 23, 27–8, 33–4, 36, 38–9, 51, 62, 67–9, 70
bear 32, 100, 118, 121, 167, 211
bedevilment 97, 186
bee 91–2
behavior 26, 61, 96, 157, 173
–, human quality of 11
belief 34, 56, 60, 192–3
–, popular 23, 45, 49, 83, 128
Benedictines 46–7
Bes 23, 178
bewitch 45
Beyond 18, 69, 83–4, 87–9, 112, 139, 144, 159, 173, 178
Biafra 80
Bible 79, 202
Bill of Rights 122–3
bird(s) 17, 19, 27, 37, 47, 173, 176, 196
–, black 159
Birkhäuser, Peter 12, 39, 207
birth 27, 38, 86, 114, 128–9, 132, 136, 164
bishop 135–6, 138–41, 144
black 25, 31, 53, 96, 166, 174
– and white 40, 42, 45, 64
– birds 159
– cat(s) 33, 40, 42, 45, 47–50
– dog(s) 113, 116, 119, 125, 128–30
– horse(s) 161–2, 179–80, 182–7, 193, 196, 200, 203–4, 208
– Madonna(s) 46, 186
– magic 49, 70, 114
blackness 31–2, 45, 186, 205
blind 14, 36, 40–2, 75, 81, 95–6, 111, 153, 176–7, 203
blood 29, 45, 54, 56, 92, 108, 119, 122–3, 134, 149
blue 59, 104, 13
boar 12
body 17, 27, 31, 60, 87, 114, 122, 124–5, 128, 135, 142, 149, 151, 153, 157–9, 182–3, 192, 210
– and psyche 92
– of dog 130
–, soul of 79
–, subtle 89
Bollingen 199–200
Book of the Dead 19; *see also Amduat*
Book for the Afterlife; *see also Amduat* 88
boy 40, 44, 63, 106, 200–1, 203, 205, 207–8
brain 9, 134, 144
– scientists 134
breeds 75
breast 50, 119
bridge 56, 85, 87–8
Bubastis 21, 23, 34
buzzard 188–90

– C –

cake 96–8, 111–2
cancer 50
cape 29–30
carriage 27, 48, 135, 157, 163, 211
– of the sun god 151
cat(s)10, 13, 16–9, 22, 24, 43–5, 55–6, 60–1, 68, 71, 78, 89, 96, 114, 116–9, 121, 144, 169, 178, 188, 211, 235
– amulets 42
– anima 37, 46, 54, 63–6, 70
– attacks 50, 66
– goddess 23, 30, 34, 39, 51, 67, 69
– headed 33
– instinct 26, 37–8, 45, 58, 61, 70
– -like 43, 51, 115
– shadow 46
– symbol 25, 29, 38, 47, 50, 65, 67, 70
–, black 33, 45, 47–50
–, black and white/ dark 40, 42, 49
–, blind 40–1
–, condemnation of a 54
–, creative side of 37–8, 65
–, daemonic ... aspects 54
–, dark (side of) 33, 47, 70
–, Egyptian 39
–, Ethiopian 70
–, feminine side of 47
–, grey 29–30
–, in dream(s)/ dream of 21, 25, 29, 32, 36–7, 54, 57, 59, 64, 66, 70, 115
–, joyful ... side/ aspect 32, 63
–, multicolored 27
–, nature of 21, 46, 49
–, three 31
–, tomcat 23, 25, 42, 70
–, two 27, 40, 42, 66
–, white 25, 30, 42, 45, 51–3
Catholic 29, 49, 17, 27, 31, 50, 60, 79, 87–9, 92, 114, 122, 124–5, 128, 130, 135–6, 142, 149, 151, 153, 157–9, 182–3, 192, 210

cave 29, 43, 141–2
cemetery 21
Cerberus 112, 130, 144
ceremonies 23, 106
chaos 19, 23
Chauvet 148–9
child 45, 78–9, 108, 127, 178, 203, 205
– archetype/ archetypal/ symbol 206, 208
–, as culture bringer 206
–, as state of beginning/ origin/ potential future 206
–, childbirth 93, 170
–, childish 40, 42
–, children 11, 27, 37–8, 40, 94, 100, 106–7, 121, 167–8, 173, 206
–, divine 206, 209
–, little 206
–, new(born) 131–2, 136, 161, 208
Christ; *see also Jesus* 55, 58, 141–2, 144, 170
–, Anti–Christ 58
–, dog is 142
Christian 17, 50, 53, 57–8, 61–3, 83, 120, 124, 136, 138–9, 142, 151, 157, 186
– attitude 58, 70, 100–1, 118
– church 29, 89, 153, 170
– creation myth 17
– culture 29–30, 46–48
– goodness 102, 104
– morality 117, 153–4
–, pre- 48, 49, 60, 151, 186
Christianity 58, 102, 138, 151, 183
church 29–30, 46, 48, 58–63, 89, 108, 110, 118, 124, 138, 153, 170, 174, 186, 188
Circe 200–5, 208–9
– horse 201, 205
civilization 23
claw(s) 21, 32, 45, 50, 188, 190
clean 31, 151, 179
cleaning/ cleansing 31, 88
clock, 81, 95
cock 96
collective 9, 52, 54, 82, 91, 110, 122, 127, 157, 169, 185
– consciousness 19, 120, 123, 180–1
– dream(s) 118, 120, 181
– life 13, 154
– problem 30, 55, 62, 64, 70, 119, 153, 181, 183, 202
– rule(s) 38, 48, 168
– situation 68–70, 120, 123
– unconscious 14, 38, 86, 89, 92–3, 120, 123, 164, 181, 183, 198–9, 202, 205, 208
Collodi, Carlo 40–1
communities 11 , 40–1
compensation 32, 58, 70, 99, 101, 140
complex 31, 36, 102, 182, 211
–, family complexes 33
–, inferiority 21, 50
–, mother 29, 100, 105, 125, 126, 127, 131, 162, 172, 191, 192, 197
–, negative mother 29, 100, 105, 125–7, 131, 191–2, 197
conception 27
condemnation of a cat 54
conflict 10, 56, 58, 66–7, 88, 101, 104, 122, 159, 202–3
consciousness 9–11, 14, 30, 34, 36–7, 45, 49, 54, 65–6, 68, 75, 82, 84, 93–5, 96, 101, 104, 108, 111, 117, 122, 131, 133–4, 139–40, 144, 152, 157, 162, 166–7, 169, 171, 173, 183–4, 190–1, 203–4, 206, 209–10
–, attitude of 69, 99, 112
–, Christian 57, 154
–, collective 19, 120, 123, 180–1
–, conscious 9–11, 13, 25, 32–4, 36, 42–43, 49, 51–3, 63–4, 70, 82–5, 89, 93–4, 96–7, 99–100, 108, 112, 122, 131–2, 1354, 156, 164, 166, 174, 176–7, 181, 184–5, 188, 191–2, 201, 210
–, conscious attitude 13, 42, 70, 85, 112
–, development/ evolution of 9,11, 58, 80, 112, 138, 150–1, 164, 181, 183
–, ego 81, 95, 129, 181, 201, 205
–, four founctions of 94–5, 163, 182
–, gold of 13
–, higher/ enlarged 98, 110, 132, 156, 170, 197
–, male 62, 204
–, pre-conscious 10, 133
–, unconscious and 10, 37, 80, 84, 104, 139, 204, 208
–, union of 69, 208
conservative 82–3, 144
constitution 122–3
cow 17, 168–70, 172, 174, 176
creative 36–38, 40, 42, 64–5, 69, 101, 104, 150, 161–4, 167–9, 173–4, 178, 196–9, 201, 208, 210

– energy 155, 159, 161–3
–, creativity 12, 29, 70, 102, 162, 168, 177
–, creation myth 17
–, creator 166, 171, 191
crisis 27, 162
cross 53, 87, 101–2, 104–5, 156, 174, 203, 205
crossroads 109, 110, 128, 179
cult, Apollonian 138
culture
–, bringer 206
–, Christian 29–30, 46–8
–, cultures 19, 45, 49, 130, 138, 164

– D –

daemonic cat aspects 54
dance/ dancing 23, 51–2, 62–3, 86, 110, 174, 176, 195–6
dangers 11, 19, 25, 29, 41, 65, 69, 101, 104, 116–7, 119–20, 123, 126–7, 139, 157, 159, 161, 173–4, 197, 201, 206
–, dangerous 13, 19, 26, 29–30, 33, 43, 52, 68, 70, 75, 81, 88–89, 100–1, 112–20, 123, 126, 138, 144, 151, 154, 158, 161, 174, 177–8, 188–9, 197, 199–205, 211
dark 12, 23, 25–7, 29, 32–3, 40, 42–3, 48–9, 50, 58, 78–80, 85–6, 88, 95, 97, 104–5, 114, 118, 138, 141, 151, 155, 170, 177, 200, 202, 204, 208
– darkness 14, 23, 25, 32, 42, 70, 85–6, 91, 101, 126–7, 129, 140, 142, 187, 202
– dog 124
– feminine/ side of feminine 30, 126
– horse 156
– mother 126–8, 182
– side 13, 30, 47, 62, 70, 116–7
daughter 97–8, 106, 115, 126, 176, 191, 204–5
dead 84–9, 92–3, 105–6, 112, 116, 129, 142, 149, 197–8, 203, 205
–, Book of the Dead 19
–, deceased 19, 42, 83–8, 91
death 17, 20, 44, 48, 49, 53, 69, 76, 85, 87–9, 92–3, 114, 119, 128, 136, 139, 153, 159, 182, 198, 201
– goddess/ god 112, 138, 144
– mother 127
– of dog 86, 129
–, after/ life after 18, 86, 130, 192
–, life and 45, 108
–, tree of 102
deity/ deities; *see also god/ goddess* 11, 34
Delphi 138
depression 25, 31, 33, 42, 53, 66, 86, 101, 104, 128, 159, 162, 195, 199, 201–2
desert 19, 34, 36, 58, 70
– sun 34, 36
destiny 25, 41, 66, 82, 104, 126, 131, 141, 181, 185, 187, 196
destruction 69–70, 88, 119, 122, 127–8, 144
development
– of consciousness 9, 11, 58, 80, 112, 138, 150–1, 164, 181, 183
–, processes(es) of 11
–, psychic 105, 131, 170, 185
devil(s)/ Devil 57–8, 63, 79, 96–7, 102, 117–8, 124, 151, 153–4, 162, 187
diamond(s) 132–5
Dickmann Zarrow, Sheila 120
dictator 42
Dionysos 69, 136, 138–9, 186
–, Dionysian 138–9, 140–1, 144
disc; *see sun disc*
disconnect 112
dismemberment 127–8
disposition, 94, 112, 190
dissolution 31, 208
distill 31, 37
divine 11–3, 65, 83, 102, 132, 138, 140, 141–2, 166, 177, 206–7, 209
– animal(s) 17, 154
divorce 125, 156, 204
doctor(s); *see also vet* 26, 78, 177
dog(s) 9–10, 12–13, 17–9, 21, 42, 44, 73, 88, 102, 104, 109–11, 121, 124, 126–7, 132–3, 137, 139, 143, 178, 188, 211, 235
– and Eros/ dog eros 77–8, 111, 142, 144
– as essence of relatedness 12, 63, 68–70, 75–6, 83, 103, 119–20, 129, 186–7, 190
– as feeling function 94–5
– as god/ Yama 83
– as guardian of soul 142
– as guide/ guiding 83–5, 108, 135–6, 140, 142
– as instinctive/ sexual greed 54, 111–2
– as symbol 76, 82, 111–2, 128, 135, 141, 144

– in alchemy 80
– in Ancient Egypt 129
– in (Greek) mythology 83, 129
– instinct 76, 80–3, 99–101, 105, 112–4, 116–7, 131, 139–40, 144
– is Christ 142, 144
– -tale 105
–, Alsatian 115
–, archetype of 118
–, black 116, 119, 125, 128–30
–, bringer of fire 144
–, Ceberus 112, 130, 144
–, dangerous 87, 114–5
–, dead/ death of 86, 89, 91–2
–, Doberman 113
–, dream of the dog 78, 81, 100, 111, 117, 125, 132, 141
–, faithful 107–8
–, feeling function of 96
–, god/ Yama as 136
–, healing 107
–, Hecate/ Hel 115
–, helpful 99
–, mythological 111
–, new 129, 132
–, old 62, 77, 129–30, 132
–, recreation/ revival of 92–4
–, shepherd 106, 114–6
–, two 113, 125, 129
–, types of 75
–, wild 75, 119
–, wolf; *see also wolf* 114
domestication 21, 149
–, domesticate 13, 21, 75, 211
donkey 153
door 29–30, 61–2, 88, 112, 134, 179, 188–9, 210
Dorneus 134
dragon 169
dream(s)
– girl 164
– interpretation 7, 149
–, animal(s) (in) 7, 9–14, 123, 131
–, archetypal 7, 89, 120, 202, 209
–, big 117
–, compensatory 91
–, death 86
–, understand/ meaning of 13, 14, 141
drive 67, 82, 141, 152, 163, 178, 182, 205–6, 209
–, animal drives 135
–, drivenness 36
–, instinctual drive 13, 66, 135
drug 139
dunghill(s) 140–1
dwarf 23
dynamism 151, 169–70

– E –

eagle 188, 190, 193, 196
ears 21, 84–5, 121
ecstasy 60, 69, 139, 193
egg 17
Egypt
–, Ancient 16, 17–20, 23–6, 28, 34, 42, 54, 90, 113, 129–130, 137, 150
–, Ancient Egyptian religion 17
–, Ancient Egyptian texts 19
–, Egyptian cat 39
Einsiedeln 46
emotion 25, 38, 46, 56–7, 75, 81, 96–7, 119, 144, 184
–, emotional 11, 89, 93, 96, 125, 134, 149–50, 166, 170, 197, 211
emotionality 30, 69, 151, 153
–, instinctual emotionality 122
emotions 36, 55, 70, 75, 88, 92, 105, 116, 118, 157
– and affect 138
– connected with dream/ archetype 76
–, emotional level 93
–, unconscious 45
enantiodromia 124
enemy/ enemies 19, 26, 58, 68, 79
energy
–, creative 155, 159, 161–3
–, life 13, 45, 80, 101, 119, 159, 197, 199, 209–10
envy 23, 32, 105
Epidaurus 106
equilibrium 92
–, mental 10
eros 27, 36, 50, 62–3, 68–9, 75–6, 78–9, 97, 103, 112, 141, 183, 186–7, 190–1, 203
– and dog/ dog eros 77–8, 142, 144
– (and) relationship 93, 105–6, 130, 140, 168
– -nature 79
– problem 67
–, attitude of 25

–, feminine Eros 169
–, instinctual 127
erotic 62, 183
– aspect/ promiscuity 111
– eroticism 52
– fantasy 156, 204
essence 56, 75, 103, 134, 170
Ethiopian cat 70
European 19, 34, 150, 154
Evangelists 67
evil; *see also devil* 23, 30, 33, 42, 49, 69, 79, 81, 87–9, 96, 108, 118–9, 126, 128, 151, 162, 174, 176–7, 180, 186–7
–, collective 120
–, deal with/ handle 105, 116–7
–, forces of 19
–, good and 56–8, 64, 88, 97, 104, 112
–, problem of 19, 117
excrement 101–2, 104–5
execution 49, 54–5
experience 12, 14, 23, 36, 38, 47, 53, 57, 60–1, 63, 69, 76, 79, 81, 85, 91–2, 94, 96, 124, 129, 139, 141, 144, 151, 156, 166, 169–70, 173, 185, 187, 206
extraction 38, 65
extrasensory perception 173, 210
extraversion 44, 195, 197, 210
eye(s) 21, 23, 42, 53, 81–2, 95, 100–1, 119, 121, 124–5, 128–9, 132–5, 141, 149, 172, 185–6, 189–92, 206

– F –

fairytale(s)*; see also tales* 13–4, 19, 30–1, 45, 54, 56, 63–5, 69–70, 82, 96–7, 105, 107, 110–1, 126–8, 170, 180–1, 184–6, 206, 209
faith 10
faithful; *see also dog* 21, 75, 103, 107–8, 136
Falada 181
falcon 17
family 33, 36, 53, 59, 66, 102, 170, 178
– complexes 33
fantasy/ fantasies 27, 49–50, 53, 58, 64, 139, 161, 169, 182, 189, 191, 195–7
–, destructive 25
–, erotic 156, 204
father 41–2, 63, 100, 106, 115, 118, 121, 176
feather(s) 193, 196
feeling(s) 21, 38, 43–4, 50–1, 55–7, 59–60, 64, 66, 77, 82, 88–9, 97, 99, 119, 127, 135–6, 139, 144, 153, 162–3, 165, 169, 172–3, 184–5, 189, 191, 198–9, 208
– function 25, 94
– of emptiness 197
– of happiness 79, 195
– of inferiority 25
– of love 180, 186–7
– relation 84–5
–, collective feeling attitude 54
–, instinctual 37, 85, 96, 176
–, unconscious 96, 204
female*; see also feminine* 21, 25–7, 33–4, 36, 38, 49–51, 66, 70, 79, 115–6, 136
– nature 30
feminine 46, 63–4, 67, 70, 79, 104, 113–4, 117–9, 138, 168, 170, 186, 199, 209
– creativity 102
– Eros 169
– in Christian culture 30, 47–8
– instinct 53, 66
– personality 32, 107, 116
– principle 68–9, 191
– self 25, 104, 164, 187
– soul 33, 62
– trinity 97
– unconscious 33, 54, 172, 204–5
–, dark 30, 126
–, image of 29, 48, 60–2, 127
–, independent 25, 48, 51, 62, 115–6
–, rejected 29, 33
–, shadow of 32, 49–50
fertility 27, 29, 34, 36–7, 114, 128, 136
fiery 36, 53, 70, 81, 87–8, 119, 144, 174
fight 19, 25, 51, 57, 112, 115–6, 127
fire 36–37, 45, 75, 81, 85, 87, 93, 111–2, 144, 154, 174–5, 186
–, first production of 80
–, hell/ purgatory 88
–, lake of 88
fish 17, 59, 169, 176
fledgling 17
flies 91–2, 156, 196
food 19, 22, 75, 112–3, 172–3, 180
foresight 23
forest 92
four 21, 38, 43, 67–8, 82, 94–5, 102, 135, 157, 163, 182–3

fox 40–2, 121
Frances of Assisi, Saint 153
Franz, Marie-Louise von 7–8, 11, 14, 30, 45, 65, 67–9, 75, 86–87, 89, 103, 105, 109–10, 113–4, 116, 127, 133, 139–41, 156, 158, 174, 176–7, 181, 187, 192, 198, 201, 206–8
freeze 126–7
French Revolution 122
Freud
–, Sigmund 62, 141, 153
–, Freudian 33
Freya (as Germanic goddess) 27, 48
function(s); *see also intuition*
–, four ...s of consciousness 94–5, 163, 182
–, feeling 94–5
–, sensation 40
–, thinking 43, 94
fur 29, 31, 46, 64
future 37, 77, 118, 127, 131, 162, 167, 174, 199, 206–9

– G –

Garm 87
German shepherd 77, 106, 114–6
Germanic 149, 154, 159
– god 27, 30, 48, 119, 162, 174
– goddess 27, 48
gnosis 58
god(s) 20, 79, 93, 104, 135–6, 140–1, 153, 175, 202
–, animal(–people) 11
–, dog as 135–6, 140
–, Germanic 27, 30, 48, 119, 162, 174
–, image of 20, 186
–, will of 19
goddess(es) 19, 22, 60, 123
– of love 27, 34, 48, 68
– of moon 37, 114, 128
–, cat 23, 30, 34, 39, 51, 67, 69
–, Germanic 27, 48
–, mother 27, 29, 36, 48–9, 65, 69, 102, 126, 186–7
–, nature 29, 126, 128, 186
Goetz, Bruno 68
gold 13, 41, 97–8, 101, 141–2, 198
–, golden 41–2, 104, 111, 142, 203
good
– and evil 56–8, 64, 88, 97, 104, 112
– god 104
– with the good 97
–, goodness as Christian attitude/ behavior 54, 62, 100–1, 104, 117, 157, 168, 185
goose/ The Goose Girl 181
grandmother 59–61
grape leaves 135–6
greed/ greediness 32, 36, 97, 105, 111–2, 116, 119, 136, 144
–, dog as instinctive/ sexual 54, 111, 120
Greek 27, 48, 106, 112, 129, 178, 202–3
grey 29–30, 44–5, 119
guide 37, 75, 82–3, 100–1, 110, 130, 132, 138, 144, 149
–, dog as guide/ guiding dog 83–5, 108, 135–6, 140, 142
–, soul 56, 83, 95, 105, 193, 196
Guinefort, Saint 107

– H –

Hades 88, 136, 203
hair 27, 49, 50–1, 87, 149, 176
Hall ar–Rumuz 84, 198
Hannah, Barbara 7, 40, 70, 76, 86, 117–8, 158, 167–9, 211
Hathor 17, 27, 34, 168
hatred 81, 105
head(s) 27, 37, 45, 50, 54, 75, 81–2, 84, 95, 100, 113–4, 125, 128, 156, 168, 178, 183, 189, 193, 210
– and body 122
– cut off 44, 181
– of animal(s) 17, 44
– of dog/ Anubis' 83
– of horse(s) 180, 209
healing 29, 33, 42, 44–7, 69, 70, 77, 107–8, 117, 129, 138, 170, 174, 186, 189, 191, 193, 197
– effect 35, 51, 105–6, 211
– impulse 13–4, 144
– side 34
–, healer 50, 128, 144, 178, 187, 190
health 11, 23, 99, 170, 210
heart 25, 29, 50, 91–2, 118–20
Hecate 48, 114–5, 117, 127–8
Hel (Germanic goddess of underworld) 48, 87, 127
hell 56, 58, 144, 154
– fire 88

helper 25–6, 75, 80, 130, 149, 209–10
–, shamanistic ... animal 193
helpful
– animal 40, 184
– horse 99, 161, 204
Hermes 83, 203
hero 56, 63, 65, 105, 126, 176, 180–81, 185–6, 200, 203–5, 209
Herodot 23
Hindu mythology 136
homeopathy 117
hoof 174, 198–9
Hornung, Erik 7, 17, 20
Horowitz, Alexandra 75
horse(s) 10, 42, 44, 89, 100, 118, 145, 148, 150, 153–4, 158, 160, 165, 167–8, 172, 175, 191, 198–9, 207–8
– as dynamism/ dynamic libido 151, 169–70
– as inspiration 38, 138–9, 178, 210
– as intuition 38, 85, 94, 127, 163, 178, 190, 196–7, 203, 210
– as sexual aspect of instinct 210
– as soul guide 196
– coming out of the sea 151
– entering through nose 192
– -god 151
– heads 180
– (in) dream 13–4 149, 155, 161, 168, 174, 192, 210
– instinct 166, 173–4, 176–7, 181, 210
– power/ energy of 163, 173, 205, 209
– sacrifice 209
– symbol 14, 83, 149, 151, 156, 161, 164, 177–8, 182, 193, 194, 209–11
– woman 156
– worship 149
–, Arabian 179
–, black 161–2, 179–80, 182–7, 193, 196, 200, 203–4, 208
–, brown 159
–, Circe 201, 205
–, flying/ winged 178, 193, 196–7
–, ghost horse 161
–, helpful 99, 161, 177, 204, 209
–, panicking 157, 163
–, phosphorous 177
–, pulling 163–4
–, riding 149, 150, 159, 164, 169, 200
–, swimming 200, 205
–, white 159, 176, 182, 185, 188, 192–3, 197
–, wild 149, 205
human
– body 17, 60, 183
– form/ –shaped 46, 203, 209–10
–, instinct in 8, 83, 209
– nature 30, 65, 123–4, 135, 138–9
–, modern 10
– psyche 34, 171, 186, 196
– relatedness 120, 190
– relations 70, 208
– soul 20
–, humanized 117
–, superhuman 13, 17
hunt (n, vb) 11, 20, 34, 49, 67, 75, 80, 116, 120, 180,
–, wild hunt(er) 70, 116
–, with-hunt 48
hunters 11, 22, 70, 156, 170, 180
husband 27, 44, 82, 111, 125, 127, 129, 155–6

– I –

I Ching 77, 201
ibis 17
Ibn Umail; *see also Senior* 75, 84, 93, 133, 198
identity 43, 83, 122
ideology 123
illness 34, 42, 45, 49, 50, 53, 191, 198
image
imagination, active 161, 188, 197
independence 21, 40, 62, 67, 70, 115
–, independent 10, 21, 25, 27, 38, 43, 48, 50, 66, 70, 115–6, 211
individuality 50, 164
individual(s) 11, 48, 51, 60, 62, 65, 69, 119–20, 122–4, 131, 140, 151, 176, 192, 203, 208, 211
–, individual instinct 70
–, individual nature 110
–, individual personality 164, 174
individuation 8, 37, 41, 59, 83–4, 94, 110, 134, 158–9, 164, 168, 172, 184–5, 187, 192, 196, 209–11
inertia 127
inferior 40, 94–5
– function 25, 40, 94–5
– inferiority 21, 25, 50
inflation 65, 112, 124, 176–8, 189–90, 205

–, inflated 190
infrared 171–2
inherited disposition 190
initiation 128
innate 91
insects 92
insight 12, 23, 57–8, 62, 91, 99–100, 105, 123–4, 129, 134, 176, 190, 203, 210
inspiration 12, 38, 65, 138–9, 178, 210
instinct(s) 9–11, 13, 39, 42, 65, 86, 91, 97–8, 106, 120, 136, 150, 153, 157, 197, 211
– and consciousness 75
–, animal 8–9, 12, 75, 122–4, 171, 209
–, basis of our 135
–, cat 26, 37–8, 45, 58, 61, 70
–, dog 76, 80–3, 99–101, 105, 112–4, 116–7, 131, 139–40, 144
–, instinctive greed 111–2
–, mass 120
–, modes of 91
–, spiritual aspect of 171
–, underestimated animal 123
instinctual 37, 42, 48, 58, 82, 89, 96, 101, 114, 118, 120, 128, 130, 134, 153, 161–2, 169, 172, 174, 176, 183, 186–8, 204, 206
– basis 62, 117, 123, 126
– drive 13, 135
– dynamism 151
– emotionality 122
– eros 127
– libido 151, 154
– life energy/ life instinct 13, 191
– nature 10, 191
– power 80, 122, 151, 205
– reaction 46, 58, 112
– side 10, 140, 211
interpretation(s) 7, 13–4, 30–1, 81, 93, 105, 131, 141, 170, 191, 199, 204
–, dream 7, 149
intimate 22
intuition 38, 85, 94, 127, 163, 190, 196–7, 203, 210
–, horse as creative 178, 197
–, Pegasus 197
iris 191
Isis 129, 186, 203

– J –

jackal 17, 83
Jacob 110
jealousy 105, 136
Jesus; *see also Christ* 55–6, 206
jewel 134
Jonas 202
joy 23, 36, 39, 45, 60, 70, 80, 91–2, 116, 138, 158, 197
–, joyful 23, 29, 32, 34, 52–3, 62, 66
Jung, Carl Gustav 7, 10, 13–4, 29, 33, 48, 58–9, 77, 80, 82, 85, 87, 89, 93–5, 97, 99, 102, 104, 118, 120, 123–4, 126, 130, 134, 138–40, 158, 170–1, 190–1, 199–201, 205–6, 209

– K –

Kali 127
kill 19, 32, 44, 56, 84, 106, 108, 114, 127, 158
king 18, 54, 69, 105, 113, 127, 135, 176–7, 181, 202
–, kingdom 12, 19
kitchen 91–2, 101–2, 104
knife/ knives 23, 25–6, 33, 42
knowledge 10,13, 56, 60, 70, 105, 121–2, 177–8, 180, 191, 211
–, hidden 13
–, popular 49

– L –

ladder 110
Lampos 154
language 18, 80, 97, 141, 187, 197
– of the dream 13
–, archetypal/ symbolic 13
lavender 180, 186
Lazarus 109
laziness 40, 42, 70, 111
–, lazy 40, 70, 111, 141
leaves, grape 135–6
legend(s); *see also fairytales, myth, tales* 13–4, 30, 34, 48, 53, 57–8, 63, 80, 86, 93, 107, 114, 116, 151, 158, 161, 169–70, 174
–, Alpine/ mountain 49, 154

–, Christian 102
libido 80, 151–2, 154, 157–8, 161, 164, 168–9, 173, 185, 210
lice 17
life
– and death 45, 108
– energy 13, 45, 80, 101, 119, 159, 197, 199, 209–10
– impulse 45, 104
– principle 141
– quality 68
–, attitude towards 40–1, 192
–, biological/ physical/ earthly 169, 171, 197
–, collective 13, 154
–, conscious 32, 53, 96
–, essence of 56
–, everyday/ daily 17, 25, 54, 63, 66, 84, 101, 107, 141, 159, 188, 208
–, female/ ... of a woman 170
–, flow of 11
–, future 131, 167
–, goal of 110
–, instinctual/ ... instinct 13, 44, 126–7, 180, 191
–, joy of/ joyful aspect(s) of 36, 45, 60, 62, 80, 116
–, life–giving/ source of 93, 156, 190, 210
–, new 37, 45, 80, 84, 86, 127–8, 191, 207
–, outer/ real 23, 33, 50–1, 56, 66, 84, 109–11, 133, 144, 153–4, 170, 179, 188, 196, 201, 210
–, personal 13–4, 131, 182–3, 190
–, psychic 25, 86, 89, 93
–, quality of 23
–, religious 11, 62
–, spiritual 135
–, tree of 56, 102
–, water of 57, 65, 93
light 33, 36, 38, 42, 53, 57–9, 62, 70, 80–1, 85–9, 93, 111, 126–7, 129, 141, 144, 154, 156, 176–7, 179–80, 182, 186–8, 199, 206
– of nature; *see also lumen naturae* 133
lion(s) 19–20, 33–4, 36, 66, 80, 121, 188
Louis VI/ XIV 122, 152
love 11, 21, 44–5, 77, 79, 91, 121–2, 127, 132, 141, 155–6, 166, 168, 178, 180, 186–7, 193
– principle 191
– story 54, 172
–, goddess of 27, 34, 48, 68
lumen naturae; *see also light of nature* 177
lynx 118

– M –

magic 23, 48–9, 64–5, 70, 114, 176, 203
–, black 49, 70, 114
Mahabharata 135, 139–40, 144
mandala 164
mare 154, 156, 198–9
marriage 23, 111, 114, 125
Mars 116
Mary/ Virgin Mary 48, 186
masculine 47, 51, 64, 115, 118, 126, 168
mass 119, 123
–, instinct(s) 120
materia, prima 31, 97, 101, 105
matter (substance) 32, 38, 92, 134, 142
mediating 105
– quality 56, 169
mediator(s) 19, 37, 45, 56, 61–2, 183, 206
medieval 48, 54–6, 60, 108, 136, 138, 170, 177
Meinrad, Saint 46
mental/ mentally 10–11, 13
mercurius/ Mercurius 56, 68–9, 97, 162, 170
–, mercurial 42, 56, 58, 68, 162
mercury 45, 133
mice 23, 32, 40, 42
Middle Ages 48, 114
midges 17
midwives 46
milk 106, 168, 199, 209
mirror 13, 30, 85, 100, 119, 153–4, 165–6, 172
mistress 126, 180
money 96–8, 151, 182
moon 49, 138, 180, 186
–, goddess of 37, 114, 128
–, moonlight 27, 187
morality 30
–, Christian 117, 153–4
–, moral 76, 83, 112
mother 44, 53, 59, 61, 67, 78–9, 96–7, 100–1, 114–6, 124, 130, 136, 138, 154, 161, 168, 181–2, 188, 210
– complex 29, 100, 105, 125–7, 131, 162, 172, 191–2, 197

– Earth/ earth mother 53, 142, 156
– goddess(es) 27, 29, 36, 48–9, 65, 69, 102, 126, 186–7
– Nature/ of nature 100, 186
–, Great/ great mother 27, 34, 39, 69, 126–7, 180, 196
–, motherhood 29
–, negative 29, 100, 102, 105, 125–8, 131, 158, 178, 191–2, 197
mountain 49
mouse 17, 32, 47
mummies 21
music 23, 62, 65
mystic
–, Arab 93
–, mystical animal 169
mythology 14, 41, 56, 79, 83, 86–7, 114, 116, 119, 154, 156, 193, 206
– of Ancient Egypt 25
–, Greek 112, 129
–, Hindu 136
myth(s) 10, 13, 34, 80, 93–4, 110–1, 136, 149, 178, 204, 206
–, creation 17

– N –

naïve 119, 123
nature 13, 21, 50, 60, 66, 80, 91, 108, 110, 114, 127, 129, 136, 140, 151, 157, 161, 168–70, 174, 180, 185, 206, 208
– goddess 29, 68, 126, 128, 186
– of cat 46, 49
–, ambigous/ ambivalent 98, 116
–, animal 124
–, female/ feminine 30, 62
–, god of 139
–, helpful way of 85
–, human 30, 65, 123–4, 135, 138–9
–, inside/ inner nature 112, 139, 142
–, instinctual/ instinct and 9–10, 39, 191
–, laws/ rules/ values of 69, 79, 112
–, light of 133, 177
–, mother (of)/ Mother Nature 100, 186
–, opposition to 93
–, protection of 37
–, spirit and 10
–, unconscious/ ... of unconscious 56, 199
–, wild 23
–, wolf– 117
Nazis 114
neglection, neglect 10, 50, 153
nervous system 92
New Guinea 80
night
– world 27, 54, 182, 187
nightmare(s) 9, 158
–, nighmarish 13, 161
Nile 34, 80
nine 31, 131, 161–2
nobles 18
nose 30, 40–1, 83, 100, 144, 192
numina 17
–, numinous 19, 62, 154, 177
nurse(s) 156, 157, 168, 178

– O –

Odysseus 202–5
ocean 114, 151, 200, 205
Oceanos 205
Olympus 136
opinion 27, 33, 115, 191
opposites 19, 22, 45, 51–2, 155, 58, 63–4, 66, 69, 75, 89, 104, 112, 123–4, 135, 183, 188, 202, 206
–, conflict of 70
–, union of/ reconciling 42, 52, 54, 56, 122, 128, 208
oracle 77, 138, 173
orgiastic 23, 138
orientation 14, 102, 173
origin 11, 34, 65, 86, 93, 174, 184, 208
Osiris 17, 69, 130
overwhelm 204

– P –

pain 29, 44, 46, 50, 131, 157, 189
painter 12, 158
panic 36, 54, 112, 156–8, 161, 163, 210
Paracelsus 177, 186
paradise 19, 79, 169, 188–9
paradox 129, 141
patience 32, 77, 81, 106, 211
pattern 83, 134–5, 167
pavian 17
paw(s) 25, 30, 38, 43, 51, 54, 82, 174

Pegasus 174, 178, 196–7, 199–200, 207, 209, 211
perception 82–3
–, extrasensory 173, 210
persecution 48
Persephone 127, 203
personality 9–10, 46, 99–100, 104, 117, 135, 187, 192, 196, 204, 206, 210
–, cat 45
–, conscious 36, 42–3, 97
–, feminine 32, 107, 116
–, individual 164, 174
pet; *see also animal* 9–10, 21, 71
Peter, Saint 83
Pharaoh 19, 74, 88
phosphorous 177
physical 9
– aspect/ level/ reality/ side 36, 112, 134, 153
– existence/ needs/ life 142, 154, 169
– handicap/ weakness 198, 210
– intimacy 125
– symptoms 156–8
– well–being 23
–, psycho–physical reality 134
physicist(s) 134
pilgrimage 108–10
pillar 67–8
Pinkola–Este, Clarissa 116
Pinocchio 40–2
placate 11
Pluto 112
politics 64, 139, 176
Pope 136, 138
Poseidon 178
pregnancy 36, 78
–, pregnant 29, 34, 132
priests 30, 34, 59–2, 83–4, 135–6, 138, 140
prima materia; *see also matter* 31, 97, 101, 105
principium individuationis; *see also individuation* 209
processes(es) 10, 14, 27, 32–3, 47, 86, 88, 91, 106, 125, 129, 135, 164, 167, 171–2, 185, 187, 210
– alchemical/ of transformation 75, 93
– bodily/ somatic 92, 171
– distillation 37
– individuation 59, 94, 184
– inner 11, 89, 116, 131
– of develoment/ evolution 11, 94, 131, 181
– of realization/ becoming conscious 93, 131, 184
– of re-creation 93
– of washing 31
–, creative 199
–, healing 29, 45, 77, 190, 193
–, spiritual 38
–, unconscious/ in the unconscious 53
projection 23, 26, 31, 49, 69, 81, 118, 133, 142, 164, 192
Prometheus 80
promiscuity 111, 204
protection 19, 23, 34, 37, 44, 79–80, 124, 144, 156, 166
providence 20
psyche 18, 29, 35, 51, 70, 84, 87, 89, 91, 102, 106, 126, 135, 140–1, 154, 169, 171, 174, 184, 186, 191–2, 208
– and body/ matter 92, 134
–, archetypal level/ collective layer of 14, 33, 120
–, background of 9
–, centre of 104, 131
–, divine in 13
–, female/ feminine 53
–, fourfold structure of 94
–, instinctual 58, 183, 187–8
–, level of 13, 19, 33, 93, 96, 197
–, male 161
–, objective 83
–, psychically 11, 196
–, psychic development 105, 131, 170, 185
–, psychic situation 42, 69, 123
–, unconscious 10, 36, 45, 56, 120, 132, 144, 166, 202
psychology 19, 33, 42, 62, 69, 119, 158
–, depth 14
–, Freudian 33
–, Jungian/ of C.G. Jung 7, 14
–, psychological 9, 11, 18, 25, 46, 49, 68, 88, 89, 92, 106, 173, 177
psychosis 161, 208
puer aeternus 68–9, 206–8
puppy 131–5
purgatory; *see fire*
Puss in Boots 56

– Q –

queen 64, 127, 176, 181
quintessence 183

– R –

rage 30, 117
rainbow 80, 191–2
ram; *see also sheep* 17
rationalism 60, 62, 123
–, rational thinking; *see also science* 37
–, rationality 56
raving 36
Re 23, 26–7, 34, 42
reaction, instinctual 46, 58, 112
rebirth 60, 86
receptivity 118
reconnect 19, 82
recreation 92, 94
red 44–5, 59, 134–5
redemption 30, 46, 63–4, 181–2, 209
reflection 39, 125, 134, 164, 166, 191
Reich ohne Raum 6–9
reject 25, 29–30, 54, 60–1, 86, 140–1, 153, 204
rejuvenation 86
relatedness 12, 63, 68–70, 75–6, 83, 103, 119–20, 129, 186–7, 190
relationship(s) 27, 29, 36, 44, 51, 54–5, 57, 64, 66, 70, 75–6, 99, 105, 112, 115, 125, 132–3, 139, 150, 153–4, 156, 166, 203–4, 210–11
– to animal(s)/ instincts 13, 17, 19, 144
– to cats 50, 117
– to dogs 106
– to the unconscious 99, 167
– with husband 129
– with mother 126
–, Eros and 93, 130, 140, 168
–, problem of 67
relax/ relaxation 27, 70, 158, 192
religion(s) 11–2
– of Ancient Egypt 17
–, archaic 11
–, religious 11–2, 20, 55, 57, 61–2, 94, 138, 144, 157, 170
–, religious attitude 11, 184, 208
–, religious experience 61, 144, 170
–, religious problem 55
Renaissance 60–2
repression 13, 68
respect 13, 18, 34, 47, 65, 121, 123, 139–40, 144, 170, 184
responsibility 33, 40, 70, 82–3, 118, 210–1
resurrection 128, 130
Revolution, French 122
riding 48–9, 149–50, 159, 164, 166–9, 177, 179, 200–1, 203, 207
–, art of 150
rite(s) 40, 130
ritual(s) 11, 14, 83–4, 136, 138, 193, 196
river 17, 25, 62, 87, 156, 198
rose(s) 67–8, 180, 186–7
– pillar 67, 68
ruler 19, 136
– rule(s) 38, 58, 63–8, 121, 124, 127, 168
Rush, Benjamin 121–2

– S –

sacrifice 19, 63, 83, 99, 112, 144, 151
– animal 209
– of cat 55
– of dog 82, 128
– of ego/ self–sacrifice 140, 210
– of horse 209
saddle 165–7, 198
sages/ philosophers; *see also alchemists* 140, 177
Saint Anthony 34, 57–8, 136
Saint Frances of Assisi 153
Saint Guinefort 107
Saint Meinrad 46
Saint Peter 83
Santiago de Compostela 109–10
sarcophagi 18
scaffold 121–2
scarab 27, 170
science(s)
–, natural 60
–, scientific 55–7, 64, 123, 144
–, scientific rational thinking 37, 56
–, scientific world–view 55
–, scientist(s) 37, 88, 134
sea 14, 151, 188, 193, 196, 200–2, 204
seer 23, 176–7, 203
Sekhmet 33–6, 40, 70
self 23, 33, 41, 70, 79, 83, 96, 110, 121, 127, 141, 144, 153, 158, 167, 171, 190, 209
– as center 187, 208
– as inner guiding principle 142
– -awareness 112, 164
– -confident 32, 70

– esteem 21
– in matter 134
– -realization 206
– -recognition 133, 185
– -reflection 166
– -sacrifice 140
– symbol 131, 135, 166, 192–4, 208
–, dog as symbol of 135
–, experience of 170
–, feminine 25, 104, 164, 187
Senior; *see also Ibn Umail* 93
sensation 40, 94, 163
serpent 26
sexuality 27, 34, 62, 111, 153–4, 204, 210
–, sexual passion 81
shadow(s) 25–7, 49, 58, 70, 97–8, 104, 113, 140, 186, 199, 203
– and evil 174, 176
– of feminine/ female 32, 49–50
– problem 31, 105
– side(s) 31–2, 42, 81, 95, 101, 105, 144
–, cat 46
–, devilish 105
–, shadowy 25, 29–30, 144
–, witch 100
shaman 128, 178, 190
– rites 128
–, shamanistic 46, 188, 190, 192–3
sheep 75
Siberian shaman rites 128
signpost 101–2, 104–5
similia/ similibus 177
sin 63, 80, 136, 183
skeleton(s) 49
skin 29, 122, 125, 128–9, 182, 191–2
Sleipnir 178
snake 17, 19, 23, 42, 79–80, 108
–, snakes 42, 106
societies 80
–, society 11, 23, 29, 53, 120, 206
soul 10, 17–8, 20, 49–50, 53, 57, 63, 68–70, 83, 85, 107, 116, 120, 141, 152, 187–8, 192
– animal 79, 89, 140
– guide 56, 95, 105, 193, 196
– of dead/ deceased 84
– of dog 84
– water 93
–, feminine 33, 62
–, guardian of 142
–, image of god in 20
–, nature and soul 108
source 11
spirit(s) 27, 36–8, 49, 133, 149, 170–71, 192
– and nature 10
– of God 20, 140–41, 202
– of our time 68–9
– of renewal 69
– of unconscious; *see Mercurius* 45, 56, 58, 97–8, 162, 197
–, creative/ creativity of 69, 168, 196–7
–, Dyonisian 140
–, earth 138
–, evil 128, 162
–, extraction of 65
–, male 169
–, natural 139
–, new 69, 100, 140, 207
–, traditional 69
spiritual 136, 138, 196
– aspect of instinct 171, 209–10
– power 60, 62, 171
– quest 110
– renewal/ insights 69, 100
– traditions 170
– world/ realm 83–4, 104, 108, 142, 144,
–, new .... attitude 140
spirituality 47
split 10, 19, 48, 63, 68, 132
stallion 154–5, 175, 178, 212
stepmother 126–7
stone 133–4, 162, 170, 208
stories; *see tales*
stork 17
structures; *see also pattern* 11, 62, 82, 164
Styx 198, 201
suffer/ suffering 9, 21, 23, 25, 27, 29, 33, 36, 44, 50, 56, 76, 93, 98, 100, 102, 104–5, 130–31, 176, 185
suicide 49, 158
sun 38, 40, 56, 80, 159, 182, 193, 197
– disc 164–5
– god/ Sungod 23, 26–7, 34, 42, 88, 151, 204
–, desert 34, 36
suppression 48, 50, 157
–, suppress 10, 30, 54–5, 153
swim 14, 141, 200, 205
swine 203–4
symbol 12–4, 26–7, 41, 57, 68, 81, 93, 104–5, 110, 133–4, 159, 164, 169–70, 183, 187, 196, 204

– of self 131, 135, 166, 192–4, 208
–, archetypal 85, 116, 125, 206
–, cat 25, 29, 38, 47, 50, 65, 67, 70
–, child 206
–, dog 76, 82, 111–2, 128, 135, 142, 144
–, dream 83, 156, 164, 177–8, 182, 209–10
–, horse 14, 83, 149, 151, 156, 161, 164, 177–78, 182, 193, 195, 209–11
symbolism 45, 85–6, 94, 111, 125, 149, 168, 170, 178, 191, 197, 203, 211
symbolic 46, 59, 89, 92, 110, 128, 130, 151, 177, 180, 187, 211
–, language 13
–, meaning 13, 20, 102, 196
synchronicity/ synchronistic 77, 142, 191, 208

– T –

table 12, 59, 62, 65, 76, 78, 85–7, 113, 178
tail 21, 45–6, 76, 82, 84, 176
tale(s); *see also fairytale(s)* 10, 14, 30–1, 40, 45, 54, 56, 62–5, 69–70, 80, 82, 96, 98, 105, 110–11, 126–28, 156, 170, 176, 178, 180–1, 184–6, 202, 206, 209
–, folktales 14, 41, 63, 79, 176
–, stories 11, 34, 40, 42, 54, 79, 81, 108, 130, 135–6, 139, 144, 149, 153, 172, 185, 196
taxidermy 125, 129
teacher 25, 37, 106, 158–9, 165, 167
tempers 36, 46
temple 67, 106
text(s)
–, alchemical 31, 75
–, Ancient Egyptian texts 19
thief 79–80, 112, 162
thinking 33, 37, 43, 50, 65, 94–5, 111, 162–3, 166, 173, 196
three; *see also animal(s), cat(s)* 64, 96–7, 102, 112–4, 119, 125, 168, 170, 17, 178, 191, 202, 211
Thot 17, 34
thoughts 30, 49–51, 57, 77, 120, 167
–, dark/ depressive/ negative 25, 159
threat/ threaten 19, 25, 30, 45, 79– 81, 99, 102, 104–5, 108, 112–3, 115, 119–20, 126, 128–9, 131, 151, 162, 174, 200, 203, 205
threshold 87, 204
tiger 10, 51, 53, 115
time(s)
– of Paradise 19
– of the New Kingdom 17
– of transition 125
–, course of 34
–, medieval 48, 55, 108, 136
–, modern/ our 68–9, 108, 120, 202
–, Neolithic 169
–, old/ former times 80
–, pagan 154
–, Roman 98
–, three/ nine/ fifteen 31, 176
–, wheel of 164
tomcat; see cat
torturing 48
totality, preconscious 133
tower 199–200, 209
transformation 38, 51, 65, 70, 85, 87–8, 92–3, 96, 123, 127–8
transition 87, 89, 101, 125, 128, 165
tree 41, 58, 193, 196
– of death/ life 56, 102
tribe 80
trick 40–1, 144, 161
–, trickster 41–2, 111
trinity 97, 102
troubadours 48
Trundholm 165
twins 132
two(s); *see animal(s), cat(s), dog(s)*

– U –

ultraviolet 171
Umail, Ibn (Senior) 84, 93, 133, 140–1, 198
unconscious 9–10, 13–4, 19, 33, 36, 40–4, 46, 48–50, 56–7, 62–3, 65–6, 76, 82, 85, 88, 91, 94–6, 99, 110–2, 115, 127–8, 131–2, 138, 140, 142, 153, 157–9, 163, 166–7, 169, 176, 178, 180, 182, 184–5, 187–9, 201, 203, 206, 209, 211
– as nocturnal side 23, 27, 70, 205
–, collective 14, 38, 86, 89, 92–3, 120, 123, 164, 181, 183, 198–9, 202, 205, 208
–, consciousness and 10, 37, 80, 84, 104, 139, 204, 208
–, constellated in 81, 133

–, contact/ relationship to/ work with 58, 197
–, darkness of 32
–, energy/ powers of 80, 151, 162, 166, 205
–, express 64
–, fear of 139
–, knowledge of 191
–, maternal/ motherly 101, 126, 161, 191, 197
–, nature of 79, 98
–, overpowering 156
–, perils of 144
–, processes in 53
–, reaction from 177, 210
–, spirit of the 45, 56, 58, 97–8, 162, 197
–, transforming 83
–, view of 122
underestimated instinct/ unconscious/ psyche 106–7, 123, 169, 206, 208
underground 29–30
underworld 48, 88, 112, 114, 128, 136, 144, 151, 198, 203, 205
unicorn 168–72
universe 11
unus mundus 134

– V –

vampire 23
Venus 183, 186
vermin 70
vessel(s) 20, 37, 41, 140, 199
virgin 29, 53, 170
–, Virgin Mary 48, 186
voice 19, 44, 58, 107, 140, 149, 176, 198

– W –

war 30, 56, 66, 117, 119–201, 203, 208
wash/ washing 31–2
water 22, 25, 34, 57, 63–5, 79, 88, 91–3, 96, 100, 104, 155–6, 173–4, 188, 198–9, 201–2, 204, 208
wheel(s) 149, 163–4
white 25, 30–1, 42, 45, 50–3, 64, 126, 132, 135, 155–6, 159, 168, 170, 176, 180, 182, 185–6, 188, 192–3, 196–7, 207
–, whiten 32
wholeness 8, 12, 60, 68, 129, 134, 139, 187, 192–3, 204
wild 21–2, 34, 50–1, 63, 70–1, 91, 116, 119–20, 123, 149–51, 170, 172, 201, 205, 207, 211
– animals 13, 75, 80, 118
– nature 23
will
– of gods 19
–, free 21, 23
wind 20–30, 34, 36, 62, 100, 119, 155, 196, 204
wine 23, 34, 36, 136, 139
winged horse 178, 193, 196
witches 23, 46–51, 53–5, 63–4, 70, 81, 95, 98, 100, 114, 126–7, 154–6, 180, 182, 187
–, cats 49
–, hunts 48–9
wolf/ wolves 114–21, 144
–, dangerous 114, 118–9
–, nature of 117
work 12–3, 31–2, 38, 40, 57–8, 62–5, 76, 82, 96–7, 99, 123, 151, 154, 157–9, 166–7, 169, 178, 183, 189–3, 197–8
–, alchemical 59, 144
worms 17
worship 20, 34, 48, 108, 138, 149
Wotan 29–30, 116, 118–20, 162, 178
wounded
– animal 44–5
– cat 25, 30, 66
– feminine personality 107
– instinct 44

– Y –

Yama (god); *see also dog* 83, 136
Yudhisthira 135–6